T0328534

FROM THE MONGOLS TO
THE MING DYNASTY

FROM THE MONGOLS TO THE MING DYNASTY

HOW A BEGGING MONK BECAME EMPEROR OF CHINA, ZHU YUAN ZHANG

Hung Hing Ming

Algora Publishing
New York

Library of Congress Cataloging-in-Publication Data —

Names: Hung, Hing Ming, author.
Title: From the Mongols to the Ming Dynasty: How a Begging Monk Became Emperor
of China, Zhu Yuan Zhang / Hung Hing Ming.
    Description: New York: Algora Publishing, 2016. | Includes bibliographical
        references.
    Identifiers: LCCN 2016004842| ISBN 9781628941500 (soft cover: alk. paper) |
        ISBN 9781628941517 (hard cover: alk. paper)
    Subjects: LCSH: Ming Taizu, Emperor of China, 1328-1398. | China—Kings and
        rulers—Biography. | China—History—Ming dynasty, 1368-1644.
    Classification: LCC DS753.6.M5 H85 2016 | DDC 951/.026092—dc23 LC record
available at http://lccn.loc.gov/2016004842

Printed in the United States

TABLE OF CONTENTS

Table of Illustrations

INTRODUCTION

This book is about Zhu Yuan Zhang, Emperor Taizu of the Ming Dynasty (1368–1644), one of the greatest emperors in Chinese history. A dirt-poor peasant, he was struggling to survive under the abusive rule of the foreign Mongolian rulers of the Yuan Dynasty (1271–1368).

In 1344 when he was seventeen years old, a great famine struck Fengyang area (now Fengyang, Anhui Province), Zhu Yuan Zhang's home, and there were acute epidemics. His father, mother, elder brother and younger brother died. He was so poor that he did not have a small plot of land to bury his father. He could not find anything to eat, so he became a monk in a temple. Soon there was no more food in the temple, either. He had to go out to beg for food as a monk, a wandering mendicant.

Under the corrupt rule of the Yuan Dynasty, the Chinese people lived in great suffering. Uprisings broke out everywhere. Zhu Yuan Zhang joined the rebel forces under Guo Zi Xing in Haozhou (in Anhui Province).

Zhu Yuan Zhang was a man of great talent and bold vision. Very soon he established his own army. In 1356 he and his army crossed the Yangtze River and took Jinling (now Nanjing, Jiangsu Province). He had many good generals under his command such as Xu Da, Chang Yu Chun, Deng Yu and Hu Da Hai. Zhu Yuan Zhang's aim was to save the people from suffering. He prohibited his troops from looting and burning houses and killing civilians. This led many capable men such as Liu Ji, Li Shan Chang and Song Lian to join him.

At that time local warlords occupied different parts of China. Chen You Liang occupied the vast areas of Hubei Province, Jiangxi Province, Hunan Province and Guangdong Province. He established the State of Han. Zhang Shi Cheng occupied the areas of the northern part and southern part of Jiangsu Province and the western part of Zhejiang Province. He established the State of Wu. Fang Guo Zhen occupied the eastern part of Zhejiang Province. Chen You Ding occupied Fujian Province.

Zhu Yuan Zhang took Liu Ji's advice to knock out Chen You Ling, the strongest enemy, first. From 1361 to 1363, Zhu Yuan Zhang's army and Chen You Liang's army fought many battles. At last in the battle of Poyang Hu Lake (in Jiangxi Province) Chen You Liang was killed. The State of Han was conquered. In 1367 Zhu Yuan Zhang's army took Suzhou (in Jiangsu Province), the capital of Zhang Shi Cheng's State of Wu, and captured Zhang Shi Cheng. In 1367 Fang Guo Zhen surrendered. The eastern part of Zhejiang Province was pacified. In 1368 Chen You Ding was captured. Fujian Province was pacified.

On 4 January 1368, Zhu Yuan Zhang ascended the throne of the Ming Dynasty in Yingtian (now Nanjing, Jiangsu Province). In August 1368, the army of the Ming Dynasty took Dadu (now Beijing), the capital of the Yuan Dynasty. Emperor Toyan Temür of the Yuan Dynasty ran away to the north. The Yuan Dynasty fell. Very soon the whole of China was pacified.

Emperor Zhu Yuan Zhang adopted many measures which were beneficial to the people. He reduced or canceled the land tax in war-stricken areas. He practiced thrift. He prohibited officials from corruption. Under his rule, China entered into a period of peace and prosperity. Emperor Kangxi (1654–1722) of the Qing Dynasty (1636–1912) praised him highly, saying, "The Ming Dynasty under the reign of Emperor Zhu Yuan Zhang was more prosperous than the Tang Dynasty and the Song Dynasty."

The material for this book is taken from the following works:

History of the Yuan Dynasty (Chinese: 元史) by Song Lian (宋濂: 1310–1361) of the Ming Dynasty (1368–1644)

Continuation of A Comprehensive Mirror for the Aid of Government (Chinese: 續資治通鑒 or xuzizhitongjian) by Bi Yuan (畢沅: 1730–1797) of the Qing Dynasty (1636–1912)

History of the Song Dynasty (Chinese: 宋史 or songshi) by Tortox (˙ ˙ : 1314–1355) of the Yuan Dynasty (1276–1368)

History of the Ming Dynasty (Chinese: 明史 or mingshi) by Zhang Ting Yu (張廷玉: 1672–1755) of the Qing Dynasty (1636–1912)

Ming Dynasty Historical Chronicle (Chinese: 明史紀事本末 or mingshijishibenmo) by Gu Ying Tai (谷應泰: 1620–1690) of the Qing Dynasty (1636–1912)

A Comprehensive Mirror of the Ming Dynasty (Chinese: 明通鑒 or mingtongjian) by Xia Xie (夏燮: 1800–1875) of the Qing Dynasty (1636–1912)

1. Portrait of Zhu Yuan Zhang, Emperor Taizu of the Ming Dynasty

CHAPTER ONE: UNDER THE RULE OF THE MONGOLIANS

1. THE MONGOL EMPIRE

(1) Genghis Khan

A boy was born into the family of the head of a Mongolian tribe in the upper reach of Orhon River (now in Kentei, Mongolia) on 31 of May, 1162. His father named him Temujin. When his father died, Temujin succeeded his father as the head of the Mongolian tribe. He unified all of Mongolia by allying with the other tribes in Mongolia — or by conquering them.

Temujin held a grand meeting at the banks of the upper reaches of Orhon River in 1206. During the meeting he declared the establishment of the Mongol Empire and declared that he was its Emperor. All the kings and the ministers attending the meeting suggested that his title be Genghis Khan (in the Mongolian language, Genghis means "Sea" and Khan means "Lord," so this title suggests a lord as great and powerful as the sea). The capital of the Mongol Empire was Karakorum (and Karakorum is still there, in Mongolia).

At that time the main part of China was divided into three parts: the area from the Yellow River north to the southern border of Mongolia was ruled by the Jin Dynasty. The capital of the Jin Dynasty was at Zhongdu (now Beijing). In the area from the Yellow River south to the South China Sea was the Southern Song Dynasty. Their capital was Lin'an (now Hangzhou, Zhejiang Province). The northwest part of China (in what is now Gansu Province, Ningxia Hui Autonomous Region, the northern part of Shaanxi Province, and the western part of the Inner Mongolia Autonomous Region) was under the Western Xia Dynasty, who had their capital in Zhongxing (now Yinchuan, Ningxia Hui Autonomous Region). Temujin launched a series of campaigns against these neighbors, and the rest is history.

As early as in 1205 Temujin had led an army to invade the Western Xia Dynasty. In 1207 Temujin, who by then had become Genghis Khan, again was at the command of a great army attacking the Western Xia Dynasty, and he took their northern parts. In 1209 Genghis Khan led a great army in attacking Zhongxing. Li An Quan, the ruler of the Western Xia Dynasty, asked for peace by giving his daughter to Genghis Khan.

In February 1211 Genghis Khan personally led a great army marching south to attack the Jin Dynasty. The Mongolian army and the Jin army fought in the area in what is now the northwest part of Hebei Province and took several counties around Fengli County (now Zhangbei, Hebei Province). In September 1211 the Mongolian army took Dexing Prefecture (an area around Zhulu, Hebei Province). The Mongolians entered Juyongguan Pass (to the north of Changping, Beijing) of the Great Wall and marched towards Zhongdu (now Beijing), the capital of the Jin Dynasty. Genghis Khan sent armies to march south to take the vast areas of what are now in Hebei Province, Shandong Province and Shanxi Province.

The areas around Zhongdu, the capital of the Jin Dynasty, were not attacked. The message was clear enough already. Wanyan Xun, the Emperor of the Jin Dynasty, prudently sent an envoy with a load of tribute to see Genghis Khan and sue for peace. Genghis Khan accepted the tribute and the suggestion, and he had his army retreat out of Juyongguan Pass. In May 1214, the Emperor of the Jin Dynasty moved his capital to Bian (now Kaifeng, Henan Province).

Apparently the message was not that clear to the Ruler of the Western Regions. (The Western Regions included the areas of what are now the western part of the Xinjiang Uygur Autonomous Region of China, Kazakhstan, Uzbekistan, Turkmenistan, and Afghanistan). Genghis Khan sent some envoys to him in June 1219, and he had them put to death. In retaliation, Genghis Khan personally took charge of a great army to wage war against the countries in the Western Regions.

The Mongolian army took the city of Otrar (about 150 km SW of today's Chimkent, Kazakhstan). In March 1220, Genghis Khan was in what is now Uzbekistan. He conquered the city of Bukhara and two months later he captured Samarkand, the most important city of the Western Regions. In autumn 1221 Genghis Khan took the city of Balkh (now in Afghanistan). Then Genghis Khan sent his sons Jochi, Chagatai and Ögedei to attack Urgench (now in Uzbekistan), the capital of the Western Regions.

Shah Ala-ad-Din, the Ruler of the Western Regions, simply fled. Genghis Khan sent generals after him, with an army, but they could not catch him. The Mongolian army went on to capture many other cities in the Western Regions. By 1223, all of the Western Regions were conquered, and Genghis Khan appointed a general as the governor there. Genghis Khan himself took the lead of the main force heading to Eastern India in the summer of 1224, and then he returned to Mongolia.

While Genghis Khan was carrying out the western expedition, he appointed Mugali as the chief-commander to lead the war against the Jin Dynasty. As early as August 1217 Mugali had already commanded an army marching from Xijing (now Datong, Shanxi Province) into the Hedong area (now Shanxi Province). Mugali took many cities in Shanxi Province in 1218, and the next autumn Mugali led a campaign against the city of Zhending (now Zhengding, Hebei Province) and took it. Then he sent troops to take the prefectures situated to the north of the Yellow River. In October 1219, Mugali commanded an army in an attack on the area to the west of the Yellow River. The Mongolian army took Suide (now in Shaanxi Province), and then they took Bao'an (now Zhidan, Shaanxi Province). The Mongolian army also attacked the city of Yan'an (now in Shaanxi Province) but could not take it. In spring 1220 the Mongolians under Mugali marched south and took Qianzhou (now Qianxian, Shaanxi Province), Jingzhou (now Jingyang, Shaanxi Province) and Binzhou (now Binxian, Shaanxi Province).

Li Xian, the Ruler of the Western Xia Dynasty, was not entirely intimidated: In January 1226, he allowed Chigehexiangkun, an enemy of Genghis Khan, to stay in the lands of the Western Xia Dynasty and he refused to send his son to Mongolia as a peace hostage. Genghis

Khan personally took command of a great army and carried out an expedition against the Western Xia Dynasty.

In February the Mongolian army took Heisui City (the old site of this city is in Ejin Qi, Inner Mongolia Autonomous Region, China). That summer, the Mongolian army took Ganzhou (now Zhangye, Gansu Province) and Suzhou (now Dunhuang, Gansu Province). In spring 1227 Genghis Khan sent troops to attack Zhongxing (originally called Xingqing, now Yinchuan, Ningxia Hui Autonomous Region), the capital of the Western Xia Dynasty. Genghis Khan himself commanded the army crossing the Yellow River to attack Jishishan (now Linxia, Gansu Province). In February the Mongolian army took the city of Lintao (now Lintao, Gansu Province). In June Li Xian, the Ruler of the Western Xia Dynasty, now a bit more humble, surrendered. The Western Xia Dynasty was conquered.

However, Genghis Khan did not have long to savor this victory. By July he fell ill, and on 12 July Genghis Khan died at the age of sixty-six. His body was carried back to Mongolia and was buried in a place called Qiniangu Valley (a place that has never been identified).

(2) Ögedei Khan and Güyük Khan

After Genghis Khan died, his third son Ögedei took the position of Protector. In August 1229 Ögedei ascended the throne of the Emperor of Mongol Empire and was called Ögedei Khan. In autumn 1231 Ögedei Khan personally took the command of a great army to attack the Jin Dynasty. His younger brother Tolei and his nephew Möngke went with him. The Mongolian army crossed the Yellow River and attacked Fengxiang (now in the west part of Shaanxi Province), and in February 1232 they captured the city. Then Ögedei Khan led the Mongolian army in an attack on Luoyang (now in Henan Province) and Hezhong (now Yongji, Shanxi Province) and took them all.

In January 1233, Ögedei Khan commanded the Mongolian army to march south from Hezhong (now Yongji, Shanxi Province) and they crossed the Yellow River from Baipo (a crossing point to the north of Luoyang, Henan Province). In mid January Ögedei Khan reached Zhengzhou (now in Henan Province). Tolei ordered the Mongolian army under him to fight the Jin army in the Sanfenshan Mountain, in the area of Junzhou (now Yuzhou, Henan Province). The Jin army was disastrously defeated, and the Mongolian army under Tolei conquered the region. Then the Mongolian army took the vast area of what is now the southern part of Henan Province. In March Ögedei Khan ordered his General Subutai to lay siege to the city of Bian, the southern capital of the Jin Dynasty. Wanyan Shou Xu, the Emperor of the Jin Dynasty, got the message and sent his younger brother Wayuan E Ke to Mongolia as a hostage. Then Ögedei Khan went back to the grasslands of Mongolia.

The Emperor of the Jin Dynasty left Bian in January 1234 and fled to Gui-de (now Shangqiu, Henan Province). After he set out for Gui-de, Cui Li, the marshal of the Jin army at the western front, killed Wanyan Lu Shen, the general appointed by the Emperor of the Jin Dynasty to defend the city of Bian. Cui Li then surrendered to the Mongolian army and handed over the city of Bian to them. In April Subutai at the head of the Mongolian army entered the city of Bian. In June the Emperor of the Jin Dynasty fled to Cai (now Runan, Henan Province), whereupon General Taca'er ordered the Mongolian army under him to lay siege to the city.

Who wants to stand up to the Mongolian horde? In January Emperor Wanyan Shou Xu of the Jin Dynasty passed the throne to his nephew Wanyan Cheng Lin, and then he committed suicide by hanging. In the same month the Mongolian army took the city of Cai by storm. Wanyan Cheng Lin was captured and killed. The whole Jin Dynasty was conquered by the Mongol Empire.

In November 1242 Ögedei Khan died at the age of fifty-six. Töregene, Ögedei Khan's empress, Güyük's mother, held the supreme power and controlled the court of the Mongol Empire for five years after the passing of Ögedei Khan. In July 1247, Ögedei Khan's eldest son Güyük succeeded to the throne of the Mongol Empire. Güyük Khan stayed on the throne for three years and died in March 1249 at the age of forty-three.

(3) Möngke Khan

After Güyük Khan died, there was no emperor of the Mongol Empire for several years. In June 1252, the kings and great generals of the Mongol Empire gathered together in a place by the side of Orhon River. Some of the kings and generals recommended that Möngke should become Emperor. Möngke was Tolei's son. When he was young, he was recognized as being very clever. Ögedei Khan took him as his adopted son. Möngke had followed Ögedei Khan in battle against the Jin Dynasty. So Möngke ascended the throne of the Mongol Empire and became Möngke Khan.

In June 1253, Möngke Khan ordered his younger brother Kublai to carry out an expedition against the State of Dali (now Yunnan Province). In July Kublai marched westward. In August Kublai and his army reached Lintao (now in Gansu Province). In October Kublai and his army crossed Dadu River (now in Sichuan Province). After marching for one thousand kilometers of the mountain road, the Mongolian army reached Jinsha River (now Jinsha River, Yunnan Province). In January 1254 Kublai had his army attack the city of Dali (now in Yunnan Province), the capital of the State of Dali, and they took it in less than a month. The State of Dali was conquered. Duan Xing Zhi, the King, was captured. Kublai appointed General Yinianghedai to defend the area of Dali, and he appointed Liu Shi Zhong as the Governor. Liu Shi Zhong, together with Duan Xing Zhi (the former King of the State of Dali), would govern the area of Dali. Then Kublai commanded the main force to go back to the Mongol Empire.

In February 1259 Möngke Khan appointed some ministers and generals to defend Karakorum, the Mongol capital, and he personally headed up an army to carry out an expedition against the Southern Song Dynasty. He decided to enter via the west part of Shu (now Sichuan Province). He ordered General Zhang Rou to command an army to go with Kublai to attack Ezhou (now Wuchang District, Wuhan, Hubei Province) and then march to Hangzhou (now Hangzhou, Zhejiang Province), the capital of the southern Song Dynasty.

Möngke Khan led the Mongolian army across the Yellow River in February while the river was frozen. In April Möngke Khan reached Liu Pan Shan Mountain (unlike certain cities, the mountain is still standing, between the southern border of Ningxia Huizu Autonomous Region and the northeast border of Gansu Province). In October Möngke Khan reached Lizhou (now Guangyuan, in the north part of Sichuan Province). Then Möngke Khan commanded the Mongolian army to cross Jialing River (now in Sichuan Province) and they reached Jianmen (in today's Sichuan Province). Möngke Khan reached the city of Hezhou (now Hechuan, Sichuan Province) in

February 1260, and Möngke Khan ordered his troops to attack the city fiercely.

The Song army fought very bravely and beat back the attacks of the Mongolian troops many times. In March there was a thunder storm which lasted for more than twenty days. The Mongolians were stuck at the foot of the city walls of the city of Hezhou, and in June Möngke Khan fell ill. On 27 July 1260 Möngke Khan died at the age of fifty-two. The officials and generals of the Mongol Empire had to withdraw back to the north with the Khan's body.

While Möngke Khan was attacking the area of Shu, his younger brother Kublai started his southern march. In November 1259 Kublai started from Kaiping (situated in Zhenglan Qi, Xilin Gol, Inner Mongolia Autonomous Region, China), the Upper Capital of the Mongol Empire. In February 1260 Kublai gathered the kings and generals under him in Xingzhou (now Xingtai, Hebei Province). In

May the Mongolian army under Kublai reached Puzhou (now Fanxian, Henan Province). In July they reached Runan (in what is today Henan Province). In August they reached Huangpi (now in Hubei Province). The Mongolian troops gathered ships along the Yangtze River and got ready to cross the Yangtze River.

Prince Muge sent an envoy from Hezhou; he reached Huangpi on 1 September and told Kublai the news that his brother Möngke Khan had died; and he asked Kublai to go back north to take the position of khan. But Kublai said, "Möngke Khan has ordered me to carry out the southern expedition. I will not go back without victory." On 4 September Kublai led the Mongolian army across the Yangtze River. On 8 September they reached the city of Ezhou (now Wuhan, Hubei Province) and laid siege to the city. Kublai commanded the Mongolian army to attack the city of Ezhou many times, but they could not take it.

The ministers of the Mongol Empire began plotting to put Ariq Böke on the throne in September 1260. Ariq Böke was Tolei's seventh son, Kublai's younger brother. Kublai's wife Nambui got word of this. She sent secret envoys racing to Kublai to ask him to come back immediately to take control of the situation. In order to explain why he was leaving Ezhou, Kublai declared that he would take the Mongolian army and march to Lin'an (now Hangzhou, Zhejiang Province), the capital of the Southern Song Dynasty. Jia Si Dao, the Chancellor of the court of the Southern Song Dynasty, who was sent by Emperor Zhao Yun of the Southern Song Dynasty to defend Ezhou, sent an envoy to Kublai to ask for peace. The Emperor of the Southern Song Dynasty promised to cede the area to the north of the Yangtze River to the Mongol Empire and send 200,000 bolts of silk to the Mongol Empire as tribute. That was a decision that saved a lot of lives. Then Kublai commanded the main force to go back north. On 13 December Kublai reached Yanjing (now Beijing).

(4) Kublai Khan

On 1 March 1261 Kublai reached Kaiping, the upper capital of the Mongol Empire. The kings and the ministers of the Mongol Empire came to meet him and made a formal appeal to him to ascend the throne of the Mongol Empire. He did so on 19 March and became Kublai Khan.

When Ariq Böke learned that Kublai had ascended the throne of the Mongol Empire, he declared himself Emperor of the Mongol Empire in Karakorum, the capital. That was a decision that would cost some lives. In July, Kublai Khan led an army against Ariq Böke. In November 1262, the Mongolian army under Kublai Khan and the Mongolian army under Ariq Böke fought in a place which is now in the south of Sukhbaatar, Mongolia. Ariq Böke's army was defeated and he fled to the north.

By July 1264, Ariq Böke understood that he could not raise an army to fight against Kublai Khan, so he went back and surrendered. Kublai Khan considered that Ariq Böke was a descendant of Genghis Khan, after all, and so he released him.

2. The Yuan Dynasty

(1) The Establishment of the Yuan Dynasty

In January 1267 Kublai Khan ordered that a new city be built in the area of Yan (now Beijing). It was named Zhongdu (meaning Middle Capital). In April, the new city was completed.

On 15 November 1271 Kublai Khan issued an imperial order to change the title of the reigning dynasty from "Mongol Empire" into "Yuan Dynasty." The word "Yuan" was taken from the following sentence: 大哉乾元 (read in Chinese as "da zai qian yuan"). "Qian Yuan" means the Heaven. The whole sentence means "How great is Heaven!" This sentence was taken from the Chinese classical book "Yi Jing" (易經 the Book of Changes). The capital of the Yuan Dynasty was set at the new city of Zhongdu, and in February 1272 Zhongdu was renamed Dadu (meaning Great Capital).

(2) The Destruction of the Southern Song Dynasty

As early as in May 1268 the Mongolian army had laid siege to the city of Xiangyang (in today's Hubei Province). Xiangyang was a strategically important city because it was situated by the north bank of Han Shui River. If it was controlled by the Mongolian army, they might sail down the Han Shui River to the Yangtze River. The Southern Song army defending Xiangyang fought very bravely and the Mongolian army could not take Xiangyang. In February 1273 the Mongolian army started one more fierce attack and at last took Xiangyang after five years' siege.

In January 1274 Emperor Kublai of the Yuan Dynasty decided to carry out a southern expedition to conquer the Southern Song Dynasty. He appointed General Bayan as the commander-in-chief to head up a force of 100,000 soldiers to carry out this plan. In February, eight hundred warships were built in Bianliang (now Kaifeng, Henan Province), and in June Emperor Kublai ordered the generals to start out.

In July, Emperor Zhao Ji of the Southern Song Dynasty died at the age of thirty-three. His son Zhao Xian inherited the throne at the age of four.

That same month, Bayan commanded the Yuan army to march south. In November they reached Xiangyang. Then Bayan divided his army into three groups to march along the Han Shui River. One group took warships to sail along the Han Shui River. The other two groups marched along the banks of the river. Bayan ordered some troops to march towards Yingzhou (now Zhongxiang, Jingmen, Hubei Province). Yingzhou was a city by the Han Shui River. Originally, Bayan intended to take Yingzhou, but when the Yuan army attacked the city of Yingzhou, the Southern Song army fought very stoutly and the Yuan army could not take the city. So Bayan changed his plan.

He gave up the attack of Yingzhou and commanded the army to go down southward along the Han Shui River. In October the Yuan army reached Shayang (now Shayang County, Jingmen, Hubei Province), along the river. The Yuan army attacked Shayang city and took it. In November the Yuan army reached Fuzhou (now Xiantao, Hubei Province). The governor of Fuzhou surrendered and presented the city to the Yuan army. In the same month the Yuan army reached Caidian (now in Huangpi, Wuhan, Hubei Province). In December Bayan commanded the Yuan army to launch a surprise attack and they took Shawukou (a place in the northeast of Hankou, Wuhan, Hubei Province).

Then more than 10,000 warships of the Yuan Dynasty entered the Yangtze River through Shawukou. Azhu, a general under Bayan, led the Yuan soldiers in the capture of more than a thousand ships of the Southern Song army, and he ordered the soldiers under him to build a floating bridge over the Yangtze River. Then he commanded his troops to cross the Yangtze River.

Later Bayan commanded the main force of the Yuan army to cross the Yangtze River via the floating bridge and they joined forces with the army under Azhu. Then Bayan commanded the Yuan army to attack Ezhou (now Wuchang, Wuhan, Hubei Province) and took it. Next, Bayan ordered General A'erhaya to command 40,000 soldiers to defend the city of Ezhou. He and Azhu commanded the main force to march east towards Lin'an (now Hangzhou, Zhejiang Province), the capital of the Southern Song Dynasty. On 1 January 1275 the Yuan army took the city of Huangzhou (now in Hubei Province). On 11 January the Yuan army attacked Qizhou (now Qichun, Hubei Province). The governor of Qizhou surrendered and handed over the city of Qizhou to the Yuan army.

On 2 February 1275 the Yuan army under Bayan reached Chizhou (now Guichi, Anhui Province — Qizhou may sound like Chizhou,

but they are quite distinct), which was situated by the south bank of the Yangtze River. After a fierce battle, the Yuan army took Chizhou. On 20 February the Yuan army attacked Raozhou (now Boyang, Jiangxi Province). An official in charge of Raozhou surrendered and handed the city over to the Yuan army. Success followed success. On 22 February the Yuan army attacked Linjiang (now Hexian, Anhui Province) and took it. On 24 February the Yuan army attacked Jiading (now Jiading, Shanghai) and took it. On 2 March Bayan commanded the Yuan army to enter Yingtian (now Nanjing, Jiangsu Province). In March the Yuan army took Zhenjiang (now Zhenjiang, Jiangsu Province). In June Emperor Kublai of the Yuan Dynasty ordered Bayan to command his army to march to Lin'an, the capital of the Southern Song Dynasty. On 20 November the Yuan army under Bayan took Changzhou (now Changzhou, Jiangsu Province). On 11 December they took Pingjiang (now Pingjiang District, Suzhou, Jiangsu Province). At that time Emperor Zhao Xian of the Southern Song Dynasty was just five years old. Power was in the hands of Grand Empress Dowager Xie, Zhao Xian's grandmother. She decided that in order to preserve the Southern Song Dynasty, the Emperor of the Southern Song Dynasty should declare himself a vassal to the Emperor of the Yuan Dynasty. On 9 January 1276 she sent an envoy to take a letter to Pingjiang to see Bayan. The letter asked Bayan to go to Chang'an Town (now in Haining, Zhejiang Province) to have peace talks with the officials of the Southern Song Dynasty and to accept the tribute sent by the Emperor. On 17 January, Bayan reached Ping'an Town, but the officials of the Southern Song Dynasty broke their promise and did not show up to negotiate the peace.

On 18 January Bayan commanded his army to march to the north of the city of Lin'an. Grand Empress Dowager Xie understood that resistance would be futile, and she sent an official to take the Imperial Seal of the Song Dynasty with an instrument of surrender to Bayan. Bayan accepted the Imperial Seal and the instrument of surrender. In February the Yuan army entered Lin'an. In March Emperor Zhao Xian of the Southern Song Dynasty, his mother Empress Dowager Quan, and some officials were escorted to Dadu, the capital of the Yuan Dynasty. In May they reached Dadu. Emperor Kublai of the Yuan Dynasty made Zhao Xian Duke of the State of Ying. But after Zhao Xian surrendered and Lin'an fell to the Yuan army, the war of resistance continued.

2. Hangzhou, the former capital of the Southern Song Dynasty

Zhao Shi, the King of Yi, was a brother of Zhao Xian, the former Emperor of the Song Dynasty. He had been sent to Fuzhou (now Fuzhou, Fujian Province) as the Governor of Fuzhou. On 1 May 1276 Chen Yi Zhong, a premier of the Southern Song Dynasty, and General Zhang Shi Jie made Zhao Shi Emperor of the Southern Song Dynasty in Fuzhou.

Emperor Zhao Shi appointed Chen Yi Zhong as the Left Premier, Zhang Shi Jie as the Deputy Head of the Chancellery, and Lu Xiu Fu as a member of the Chancellery. Wen Tian Xiang, a former premier of the Southern Song Dynasty, escaped from Zhenjiang (now Zhenjiang, Jiangsu Province) to Fuzhou. Emperor Zhao Shi appointed him as the Right Premier. In July Wen Tian Xiang was sent to carry out a military operation in the area of what is now Jiangxi Province. In November the Yuan army took Jianning (now Jian'ou, Fujian Province). Chen Yi Zhong and Zhang Shi Jie prepared a lot of seaworthy ships. Then Emperor Zhao Shi and all the officials went on board the ships and sailed southward to Quanzhou (now Quanzhou, Fujian Province). Then they sailed further south to Chaozhou (now Chaozhou, Guangdong Province).

In December Emperor Zhao Shi's ships reached the sea outside Huiyang (now Huiyang, Guangdong Province), and in February 1278 the ships reached Guangzhou (now in Guangdong Province). In March Emperor Zhao Shi reached Gangzhou (now Daxishan Mountain, Wuchuan, Guangdong Province), which stands by the sea.

In April Emperor Zhao Shi of the Southern Song Dynasty died at the age of eleven. Lu Xiu Fu and other officials made Zhao Bing, Emperor Zhao Shi's younger brother, Emperor of the Southern Song Dynasty at the age of eight. In June, Emperor Zhao Bing reached Yashan. Yashan was a mountain situated in the southern end of an island in the sea forty kilometers south to Xinhui County (now in Guangdong Province). Zhang Shi Jie ordered the soldiers to go into the forest on the island to cut woods to build some palaces for the emperor and houses for the officials and soldiers.

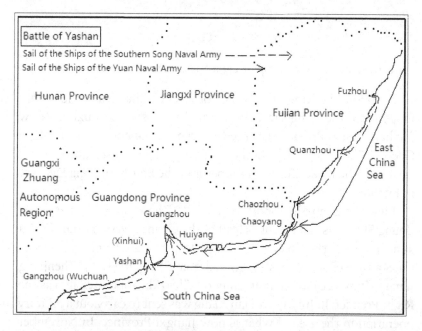

In June 1278 Emperor Kublai sent Zhang Hong Fan, a general of the Southern Song Dynasty who had surrendered to him, as the commander-in-chief to lead the naval forces to attack Yashan. In December the army under Zhang Hong Fan reached Chaoyang (in Guangdong Province). At that time, Wen Tian Xiang was commanding the Southern Song army in the area of Chaoyang. The Yuan army made a surprise attack and Wen Tian Xiang was captured.

Zhang Hong Fan kept Wen Tian Xiang with his navy. In January 1279, Zhang Hong Fan set sail for Yashan; there, he ordered his army to attack the warships under Zhang Shi Jie. The Southern Song army fought forcefully and it was hard to see any progress. Then Zhang Hong Fan forced Wen Tian Xiang to write a letter to Zhang Shi Jie to persuade him to surrender.

Wen Tian Xiang, once a premier and recently Right Minister, resolutely refused to do so, saying, "I will not betray my father and mother. How can I teach another person to betray his father and mother?" Zhang Hong Fan insisted that Wen Tian Xiang write the letter. Then Wen Tian Xiang wrote something which included the following words: "Since ancient times, nobody has ever been able to escape death. After I die, my true red heart will be left behind to shine on history." On 6 February, Zhang Hong Fan started a fierce attack on the warships of the Southern Song Dynasty. At that time Emperor Zhao Bing and Lu Xiu Fu were on a big ship which was linked up with other ships. Lu Xiu Fu saw that they had no way to escape. In order to avoid having the emperor captured and insulted, Lu Xiu Fu carried the young emperor on his back and jumped into the sea; they both were drowned to death. Zhang Shi Jie fought with all his might, but seeing that he could not save the Southern Song Dynasty, he too jumped into the sea and killed himself.

The captive minister, Wen Tian Xiang, was escorted to Dadu, the capital of the Yuan Dynasty. Zhang Hong Fan tried his best to persuade him to surrender, but Wen Tian Xiang resolutely refused. In December 1281 Wen Tian Xiang was executed. He died nobly and heroically.

(3) The Emperors of the Yuan Dynasty

Eventually Emperor Kublai, too, fell ill, on 1 January 1294. He died at the age of eighty on 22 January. He had been on the throne for thirty-five years.

In April 1294 his grandson Temür ascended the throne of the Yuan Dynasty, and he ruled for thirteen years. On 1 January 1307, Emperor Temür fell ill; he died on 10 January at the age of forty-two. Qayisang followed him on the throne of the Yuan Dynasty. Qayisang was Kublai's great grandson and Temür's nephew; he ruled for five years and died at the age of thirty-two in 1311. He was followed by Ayuur Balbad, Emperor Qayisang's younger brother, who ruled for ten years. Then Sidibala, Emperor Ayuur Balbad's son, ascended the throne. On 3 August 1323 Emperor Sidibala was assassinated in Nanpo, a place some fifteen kilometers south of Kaiping (situated in Zhenglan Qi, Xilin Gol, Inner Mongolia Autonomous Region, China), the Upper Capital. He was just twenty-one. He was on the throne for three years. The throne passed to four more relatives and then, on 8 June 1333, Toyan Temür, ascended the throne.

(4) The Birth of Zhu Yuan Zhang

3. Zhu Yuan Zhang leaves Huangjue Temple to beg for food

A man named Zhu Shi Zhen lived in Zhongli (now Fengyang, Anhui Province) of Haozhou Prefecture (now the area around Bengbu, Anhui Province). His wife was Lady Chen. They already had two sons. When Lady Chen was pregnant with a third child, she dreamed that a god put a bright pill of medicine in her palm. She took the medicine and she could smell its fragrance. On 18 September 1328 she gave birth to a baby boy. When this boy was born, the whole house was bright with red light. The neighbors saw the red light and thought that Zhu Shi Zhen's house was on fire. They all came with buckets of water to fight the fire, but when they got there, they found that the house was not on fire but was bathed in a red glow. This boy was named Zhu Yuan Zhang.

In 1344 there was a great famine in the area and acute epidemics broke out. Zhu Yuan Zhang's father, mother, the eldest brother and younger brother died. At that time, Zhu Yuan Zhang was seventeen years old. He was very poor and could not find a piece of land to bury his father. He had to rap his dead father in a mat made of reeds and bound the mat with a rope. He put the rope on his shoulder and carried the dead body of his father; he and his second elder brother were to go to the hill outside the village. But when they got to the foot of the hill, the rope broke and the mat with their father rolled up in it fell to the ground. Zhu Yuan Zhang's second elder brother went back home to get another rope while Zhu Yuan Zhang stayed by his father's side.

Suddenly there was a thunderstorm. Zhu Yuan Zhang ran to a temple in the village nearby to take shelter. The thunderstorm lasted for a whole night. When dawn came, he went back to the place where his father's corpse was. To his great surprise he found that his father had been buried and a grave mound had been built on it.

That piece of land belonged to Liu Ji Zu, who lived in the village. Liu Ji Zu heard about this and went to see the grave; he was greatly surprised. So he gave that piece of land to Zhu Yuan Zhang. Not long later the second elder brother also died. Zhu Yuan Zhang was all alone and had nobody to depend on. In September that year, he went to Huangjue Temple and became a monk. A month later there was no more food left for the monks, either. The monks had to go out of the temple to beg for food.

Thus Zhu Yuan Zhang became a mendicant monk. He went southwestward, begging for food all the way. He reached Hefei (now Hefei, Anhui Province). On the way he fell ill and fainted away. In his illness he could see two men in purple color clothes attending him. When he recovered, the two men in purple color clothes disappeared. Three years later Zhu Yuan Zhang went back to Huangjue Temple.

Chapter Two: Great Uprisings against the Mongolian Rule

1. The Uprisings

At that time the emperor of the Yuan Dynasty was Emperor Toyan Temür. Under his rule, the government of the Yuan Dynasty was corrupt. The Chinese people were suppressed and they lived in suffering. In May 1351 Liu Fu Tong, a man who lived in Yingzhou, first rose against the administration in Yingzhou (now Fuyang, Anhui Province) and took over the town.

In June, Fang Guo Zhen, a man in Huangyan (now in Zhejiang Province), who made a living by shipping salt, rose up in arms. He commanded the people under him to make raids on the Mongolian army by boat along the seashore.

In August, Li Er, Peng Da and Zhao Jun Yong of Xiaoxian (now in the north part of Anhui Province) rose up. They led the people to attack Xuzhou (in the north part of today's Jiangsu Province). In the same month Xu Shou Hui, a cloth merchant in Qizhou (now in the southeast part of Hubei Province), rose up in Qizhou. Chen You Liang, a man from Mianyang (now Xiantao, Hubei Province), came to join Xu Shou Hui. He became a secretary of Ni Wen Jun, a general under Xu Shou Hui. In September 1351 Xu Shou Hui took Qizhou (now Xishui, Hubei Province). In February 1352 Guo Zi Xing, a man of Dingyuan (now Dingyuan, Anhui Province), and his friend Sun De Ya held an uprising in Haozhou (now the area around Bengbu, Anhui Province) and took the city. Chelibuhua, the general commanding the Yuan army in that area, did not dare to advance and attack Haozhou. He just ordered the Yuan troops under him to capture innocent people and reported that they were the rebel soldiers so as to get a reward.

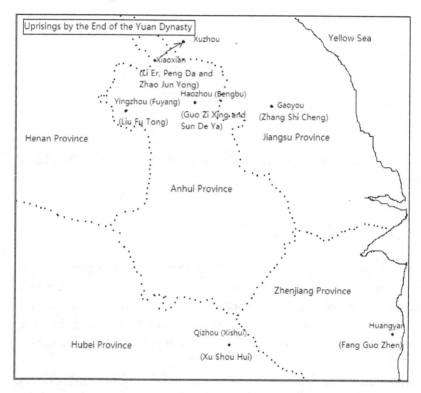

2. Zhu Yuan Zhang Joins in the Uprising Led by Guo Zi Xing

At that time our mendicant monk Zhu Yuan Zhang was twenty-four years old. He did not know what he should do in such troubled times, so he went to a Buddhist temple to make a divination. He was looking for guidance on seeking a hiding place. But the oracle's inscription he got back said that hiding was not a good solution.

He made another divination, asking about staying in the place where he was. But the oracle's response also said that was not a good solution. Then Zhu Yuan Zhang thought maybe it was Heaven's will that he should start an uprising, and he sought counsel on that. The oracle's response this time said that this was the best solution. So he made up his mind to start an uprising.

On 1 of the second March 1352 (1352 was an intercalary year which had two months of March), Zhu Yuan Zhang went into the city of Haozhou to see the rebel leader Guo Zi Xing. When he reached the gate of the house, the guards thought he as a spy. So they arrested him and brought him before Guo Zi Xing. When Guo Zi Xing saw Zhu Yuan Zhang, he was greatly surprised to see that the young man was strongly built and he marveled at the outstanding look of his face. When he talked with Zhu Yuan Zhang, he found that he was a man of great ability.

First, he appointed Zhu Yuan Zhang as the head of his bodyguards. Very soon Zhu Yuan Zhang showed himself to be trustworthy, indeed, and when there were battles Guo Zi Xing would consult with him. Then Guo Zi Xing sent him to lead soldiers in battle, and Zhu Yuan Zhang was always victorious.

Guo Zi Xing had an adopted daughter by the name of Ma. She was the daughter of Ma Gong, a good friend of Guo Zi Xing. Before Ma Gong died, he had entrusted his daughter to Guo Zi Xing; now the adoptive father married her to Zhu Yuan Zhang.

In September 1352 Tortox, the Premier of the Yuan Dynasty, attacked Xuzhou and took it. Li Er escaped, but he died soon after. Zhao Jun Yong and Peng Da led their defeated army in retreating to Haozhou. Sun De Ya thought that Zhao Jun Yong was a famous leader of the uprising, so he and other generals made him the head of the uprising army in Haozhou. But Guo Zi Xing did not like Zhao Jun Yong; rather, he was friendly with Peng Da. Sun De Ya said secretly pointed this out to Zhao Jun Yong, saying, "Guo Zi Xing is only friendly with Peng Da. He looks down upon you." These words made Zhao Jun Yong very angry. Then one day Zhao Jung Yong led some soldiers to Guo Zi Xing's house and arrested him and kept him in Sun De Ya's home as a prisoner, confined and humiliated with a wooden yoke over his neck. At that time Zhu Yuan Zhang was away, in a place north of the Huai River. When he heard that Zhao Jun Yong had arrested Guo Zi Xing, he immediately hurried back to Haozhou with Guo Zi Xing's two sons. They went straight to Peng Da and told him what had happened. Peng Da was very angry and immediately went with them to Sun De Ya's home and broke the yoke and saved Guo Zi Xing.

Since Xuzhou had been taken by the Yuan army, Tortox, the Premier of the Yuan Dynasty, commanded the main force to go back to Dadu. He ordered General Jialu to pursue the defeated uprising troops who had escaped to Haozhou. In winter General Jialu commanded the Yuan troops to lay siege to the city of Haozhou. Zhu Yuan Zhang persuaded Guo Zi Xing to forget his hatred for Sun De Ya and Zhao Jun Yong, and to work together with them to fight against the Yuan army.

In September 1351 Xu Shou Hui took Qishui (now Xishui, Hubei Province) and Huangzhou (now Huangzhou, Hubei Province). Then he proclaimed himself Emperor of the Tianwan Dynasty. He established his capital in Qishui. He made Ni Wen Jun Premier of the Tianwan Dynasty. In 1352 he sent troops to take all the prefectures and counties in what are now Hubei Province, Hunan Province, Guangdong Province and Jiangxi Province. Then he took Hangzhou (now Hangzhou, Zhejiang Province). But he could not keep control of these areas. Very soon he lost them all.

When Liu Fu Tong fomented his uprising, he honored Han Shan Tong as the leader of the uprising so as to encourage the people to join in — although Han Shan Tong was not a part of the rebel army. Han Shan Tong claimed to be a descendent of Emperor Huizong of the Song Dynasty (Emperor Zhao Ji, 1082–1135). The government of the Yuan Dynasty sent officials to arrest Han Shan Tong and kill him. Han Lin Er, Han Shan Tong's son, and his mother hid themselves in the mountain. In 1532 Liu Fu Tong took Zhugao (now in Xinyang, Henan Province), Luoshan (now in Xinyang, Henan Province), Shangcai (now in Zhumadian, Henan Province), and Queshan (now Queshan, Henan Province). Having taken theses places, Liu Fu Tong and his army took Yexian (now Yexian, Henan Province), Wuyang (now Wuyang, Henan Province), Ruzhou (now Ruzhou, Henan Province), Guangzhou (now Huangchuan, Henan Province) and Xizhou (now Xixian, Henan Province). His army developed into a force of more than 100,000 men. The Yuan army could not resist such a great army.

On 16 May 1353 General Jialu of the Yuan army died while laying siege to Haozhou. The Yuan army retreated and the siege of Haozhou was lifted. Many soldiers of the rebel army in Haozhou died during the siege. So Zhu Yuan Zhang went back to his home place and recruited seven hundred militiamen. He brought them to Haozhou. Guo Zi Xing was very glad and made Zhu Yuan Zhang a senior officer. Tang He and Xu Da, two officers in Guo Zi Xing's army, saw that Zhu Yuan Zhang was a man of great ability, so they committed themselves under the command of Zhu Yuan Zhang. At that time, the armies under Peng Da and Zhao Jun Yong were strong but the army under Guo Zi Xing was weak. Guo Zi Xing did not have the power to control them. Zhu Yuan Zhang was very worried about it. In winter of 1353 Peng Da and Zhao Jun Yong declared themselves kings, but Guo Zi Xing and Zhang De Ya remained marshals as before.

In this year Zhang Shi Cheng, a man of Baijuchang (now in Dafeng, Jiangsu Province) who made his living by transporting salt, rose up in rebellion. He commanded the uprising army to take Taizhou (now Taizhou, Jiangsu Province) and Gaoyou (now Gaoyou, Jiangsu Province). Then he established the State of Dazhou and proclaimed himself King of Cheng.

3. Zhu Yuan Zhang Establishes His Own Army

Zhu Yuan Zhang cherished a great ambition. He did not want to be always subordinate to others. In July 1354 Zhu Yuan Zhang handed over the seven hundred men under him to another officer, and he left Haozhou to go south with some troops commanded by twenty-four men.[1] Zhu Yuan Zhang commanded these twenty-four men to take Dingyuan (now Dingyuan, Anhui Province). In Zhangjiabao of Dingyuan, 3,000 militiamen were stationed in Lupai Camp. They had run short of food. Zhu Yuan Zhang wanted to persuade them to surrender. He selected Fei Ju and several men to go there with him on horseback. When they got close to the camp, Fei Ju saw that it was a large force, and he asked Zhu Yuan Zhang, "Shall we go back and get more men to come?" Zhu Yuan Zhang said, "It is not necessary to bring more men. It will only arouse their suspicion." And Zhu Yuan Zhang led the men to ride forward.

When they reached a stream, they all dismounted their horses and crossed to the camp of the militiamen. The commander-in-chief

---

1 Xu Da, Tang He, Wu Liang, Wu Zhen, Hua Yun, Chen De, Gu Shi, Fei Ju, Geng Zai Cheng, Geng Bing Wen, Tang Sheng Zong, Lu Zhong Heng, Hua Yun Long, Zheng Yu Chun, Guo Xing, Guo Ying, Hu Hai, Zhang Long, Chen Huan, Xie Cheng, Li Xin Cai, Zhang He, Zhou Quan and Zhou De Xing.

came out to meet Zhu Yuan Zhang. Zhu Yuan Zhang said, "Marshal Guo and you were friends before. Marshal Guo knows that you have run short of food and other enemies will come to attack you. Marshal Guo has sent me to talk with you. If you will join Marshal Guo's army, then you may go with me. If not, you should command your militiamen to move to another place to avoid the attack by your enemies." The commander-in-chief of the militiamen agreed to come over, but he asked Zhu Yuan Zhang to give him something as evidence of the promise he'd made. Zhu Yuan Zhang immediately unbuckled his sword and gave it to him. Then Zhu Yuan Zhang went back. He waited for three days, but the commander-in-chief of the militiamen did not come over. Zhu Yuan Zhang sent three hundred men to steal into the camp; they captured the commander-in-chief. Then all the 3,000 militiamen surrendered.

Miu Da Heng, a man of Dingyuan, had 20,000 militiamen under him. They were stationed in Hengjianshan Mountain, to the north of Dingyuan. The government of the Yuan Dynasty granted Miu Da Heng the title of Marshal of the militiamen and sent a man named Zhang Zhi Yuan to command these militiamen together with Miu Da Heng. Zhu Yuan Zhang ordered Hua Yun to command the 3,000 militiamen who had just surrendered to start a surprise attack by night on the militia camp in Hengjianshan Mountain. Zhang Zhi Yuan headed a force of militiamen to come out to fight, but they were defeated and he ran away. Then Zhu Yuan Zhang sent an envoy to persuade Miu Da Heng to surrender. Miu Da Heng agreed and came over with all his militiamen. By then, Zhu Yuan Zhang's army had grown into a great and strong army.

Feng Guo Yong, a man of Dingyuan, and his younger brother Feng Guo Sheng came with the men under them to join Zhu Yuan Zheng. Zhu Yuan Zhang was very glad to meet them; he was surprised to see that they were dressed as scholars. He asked, "You are wearing the clothes of scholars. I guess you must be Confucian scholars. Can you tell me what I should do to bring peace to the whole realm?" Feng Guo Yong answered, "Jinling is a forbidding strategic location. It is a good place for the capital of an emperor. I hope you will take Jinling first and found your dynasty there. After that you may send out your generals to conquer other places. In this way you may save the people from suffering. You may show your benevolence all around the realm.

You must not seek beauties and riches. Then you will be able to pacify the whole realm." At these words Zhu Yuan Zhang was very glad. Zhu Yuan Zhang kept the men in his command tent and always consulted them on top secret matters.

4. Zhu Yuan Zhang rises up in arms

Li Shan Chang, a man from Dingyuan, called on Zhu Yuan Zhang. Talking together, Zhu Yuan Zhang found that he was a man of wisdom. Zhu Yuan Zhang asked Li Shan Chang, "When do you think there will be quiet in the whole realm?" Li Shan Chang said, "In the Qin Dynasty rebellions broke out all over. Liu Bang was an ordinary man. He revolted against the Qin Dynasty. He was open-minded and magnanimous; he knew his subordinates well and he assigned the right person to accomplish the right task. He was merciful to innocent people. After five years fighting, he established the Han Dynasty and became the first Emperor. You were born in the area of Haozhou, which is not far from Pei where Liu Bang was born. There is a spiritual influence in that region from the beautiful mountains and rivers in the area of Haozhou. I suppose you have got this spiritual influence. If you follow the example of Liu Bang, you may bring peace to the whole realm very soon." Zhu Yuan Zhang highly praised Li Shan Chang for what he had said. He appointed Li Shan Chang as his secretary and often consulted him about strategic plans.

In July 1354 Zhu Yuan Zhang commanded his army to attack Chuzhou (now Chuzhou, Anhui Province). He sent Hua Yun as the vanguard ahead of the army. Hua Yun was a strong man with a very dark face. Suddenly several thousand enemy troops appeared. They were arrayed in battle formation. Hua Yun held up his spear and rode very quickly and fought through the enemy battle formation singlehandedly. The enemy soldiers saw the brave black-faced man and were all terrified. Whoever or whatever he was, they decided that this black-faced general was not someone they could stand against. The main force of Zhu Yuan Zhang's army came forward and started a fierce attack on the enemy battle formation. Then they took Chuzhou, and Zhu Yuan Zhang stationed his army in the city of Chuzhou.

In this month Zhu Wen Zheng and Li Wen Zhong came to join Zhu Yuan Zhang's army. Zhu Wen Zheng was the son of Zhu Yuan Zhang's elder brother's. Li Wen Zhong was the son of Zhu Yuan Zhang's elder sister, who had died. His father brought him to join Zhu Yuan Zhang. Li Wen Zhong was only twelve years old; seeing his uncle Zhu Yuan Zhang, he became playful and held onto the great man's clothes. Zhu Yuan Zhang said, "When a boy sees his mother's brother, he thinks that he has seen his mother."

Mu Ying, a ten-year-old boy, was another orphan who benefited from Zhu Yuan Zhang's magnanimity. His father died early, and his mother tried to get the boy away from the war zone but she, too, died. Zhu Yuan Zhang had pity on him and asked his wife Lady Ma to accept Mu Ying as their adopted son, and they took good care of him. Zhu Yuan Zhang granted Li Wen Zhong and Mu Ying the family name of Zhu. So Li Wen Zhong became Zhu Wen Zhong, and Mu Ying became Zhu Mu Ying.

At that time both Zhao Jun Yong and Peng Da had declared themselves kings, but they were always quarreling and fighting. In one fight, the soldiers under Zhao Jun Yong killed Peng Da. Then Zhao Jun Yong put Peng Da's troops under his own command. He planned to force Guo Zi Xing to lead an army to attack Sizhou (now Sixian, Anhui Province) and Xuyi (now Xuyi, Jiangsu Province). And he also had a plan to kill Guo Zi Xing. When Zhu Yuan Zhang got this information, he was very worried about Guo Zi Xing. He sent an envoy to see him and to convey Zhu Yuan Zhang's words to him: "When you were defeated in Xuzhou, you ran away to the south to

Haozhou. At that time if Marshal Guo had shut the gates of Haozhou and had not let you in, you would have been killed by the Yuan army. When you entered Haozhou, you put yourself in a higher position than Marshal Guo. And now you are going so far as to plan to kill him. It is immoral on your part to repay Marshal Guo's kindness with wickedness. Marshal Guo is easy to deal with. But his subordinates are now in Chuzhou. They have a great army. They are the ones you should be worried about." Having heard Zhu Yuan Zhang's words, Zhao Jun Yong realized that the consequence of killing Guo Zi Xing would be very grave. So he gave up the plan. Then Zhu Yuan Zhang bribed Zhao Jun Yong's subordinates, and Zhao Jun Yong let Guo Zi Xing go to Chuzhou with the army under him.

When Guo Zi Xing arrived in Chuzhou, he declared himself King of Chuyang. Zhu Yuan Zhang put all his troops, over 30,000 men in all, under the command of Guo Zi Xing. A month later Guo Zi Xing heard some slanderous words put forward against Zhu Yuan Zhang and he believed them. Guo Zi Xing took all military power from Zhu Yuan Zhang and wanted to transfer Li Shan Chang to work for him. Li Shan Chang wept and refused to leave Zhu Yuan Zhang. From then on Zhu Yuan Zhang had no right to command an army to fight. Guo Zi Xing and Zhu Yuan Zhang drifted apart.

But Zhu Yuan Zhang was all the more respectful to Guo Zi Xing. A general accused Zhu Yuan Zhang falsely in front of Guo Zi Xing. He said that Zhu Yuan Zhang did not do his best in battle, and Guo Zi Xing believed him. One day he sent this general and Zhu Yuan Zhang to go forth from the city of Chuzhou with some troops to attack their enemies. This general was wounded by an arrow when he had just got out, not far from the city, and had to go back. Zhu Yuan Zhang led the troops forward and fought very bravely. The enemy troops were defeated and ran away. Then Zhu Yuan Zhang brought back his victorious army. Guo Zi Xing felt ashamed to have believed the slander against Zhu Yuan Zhang.

At that time the generals presented treasures they had looted to Guo Zi Xing. But Zhu Yuan Zhang had prohibited the officers and soldiers under him from looting the people, and he had nothing to give Guo Zi Xing. Guo Zi Xing disliked him for that. Zhu Yuan Zhang's wife Lady Ma took everything she had and gave it to Guo

Zi Xing's wife Lady Zhang. Lady Zhang was very happy and Guo Zi Xing's attitude to Zhu Yuan Zhang gradually changed.

In October 1354 Tortox, the premier of the Yuan Dynasty, commanded an army in attacking Gaoyou. Zhang Shi Cheng commanded his army to go out of the city to fight the Yuan army under Tortox. Zhang Shi Cheng's army was defeated and retreated back into the city of Gaoyou. Tortox ordered the Yuan soldiers to lay siege to the city. Then he sent another army to lay siege to the city of Luhe (now Luhe, in the southwest part of Jiangsu Province) which had been occupied by an army under Zhao Jun Yong. The general defending Luhe sent an envoy to Chuzhou to ask Guo Zi Xing for help. Guo Zi Xing hated Zhao Jun Yong and would not send troops to rescue Luhe. Zhu Yuan Zhang went to see Guo Zi Xing and said to him, "Luhe and Chuzhou are as close as the lips and the teeth. If Luhe is taken by the Yuan army, Chuzhou will not be able to stand alone. Why should you ruin your great cause just for the grudges between you and Zhao Jun Yong?" Guo Zi Xing realized his mistakes and decided to rescue Luhe. Guo Zi Xing asked his generals, "Is any one of you willing to lead an army to rescue Luhe?" No one wanted to go because the Yuan army attacking Luhe was very strong. The generals said that they had prayed to their god and the god told them that it would not be proper to rescue Luhe. Zhu Yuan Zhang said, "You should make your decision by your heart, not by your prayer!"

Then Zhu Yuan Zhang and Geng Zai Cheng marched their troops east to Walianglei Stronghold, some five kilometers west of Luhe. The Yuan troops attacked this stronghold fiercely every day. By sunset the stronghold was seriously damaged and nearly fell. But Zhu Yuan Zhang commanded the soldiers to repair it. By the next morning they had totally repaired their defenses. But Zhu Yuan Zhang knew that it would be very difficult to rescue Luhe. He had to think of a way to retreat. He ordered his soldiers to retreat and gather all the food they could into the stronghold. Then he ordered some women to stand by the gate and hurl abuses on the enemy soldiers. The Yuan soldiers were surprised and did not dare to attack the stronghold because they did not know what tricks Zhu Yuan Zhang was playing. Then Zhu Yuan Zhang ordered his troops to go out of the stronghold and arrayed them in battle formation. All the people in the stronghold came out. Zhu Yuan Zhang ordered his troops to protect the people and all of them retreated back to Chuzhou safely. Not long later, the Yuan army came and started a fierce attack on the city of Chuzhou. Zhu Yuan Zhang laid an ambush by the side of a stream. He ordered Geng Zai Cheng to go out to fight. Geng Zai Cheng fought with the enemy; then he pretended to have been defeated and ran towards the stream. The Yuan troops ran after him and went across the stream and fell into the ambush. The soldiers in the city of Chuzhou came out with loud shouts that shook the sky. The Yuan troops were defeated and retreated.

Hu Da Hai, a man of Hongxian (now in Huai'an, Jiangsu Province), came to join Zhu Yuan Zhang's army. Hu Da Hai was a tall man with a face of iron color. When Zhu Yuan Zhang talked with him, he found that Hu Da Hai was a man of wisdom. So Zhu Yuan Zhang appointed him as the general to command the vanguards.

In January 1355 the army in Chuzhou had run short of food. Guo Zi Xing called all the generals under him to discuss where they should go. Zhu Yuan Zhang said, "It is really not the good way to stay in this isolated city. Now the only city we should consider going to is Hezhou. Although Hezhou is not a large city, it is strong. We should take this city by strategy. It would not be easy to take this city by force. In the past when we attacked the camp of the militiamen in Luzhou, we got more than 3,000 militiamen. We can select 3,000 of them and have them dress in green like the Yuan soldiers and have them do their hair like the Yuan soldiers. They should drive four camels loaded with goods as gifts for the Yuan soldiers defending the city of Hezhou. They should tell those soldiers that they are soldiers from Luzhou and they have escorted the envoy to Hezhou. They should tell the gate guards that the envoy will grant gifts to the soldiers defending Hezhou. Then the soldiers will open the city gate and let them into the city. Have 10,000 of our men put on red clothes. They should march after the soldiers dressed in green, and they should keep a distance of more than five kilometers. When the soldiers in green get close to the city, they should make a fire as a signal. When the soldiers in red see the fire, they should advance very quickly. In this way we will surely take the city of Hezhou."

Guo Zi Xing agreed with his plan. He ordered Zhang Tian You, who was Guo Zi Xing's wife's younger brother, to command the soldiers in green. Zhao Ji Zu disguised himself as the envoy. They started marching to Hezhou (now Hexian, Anhui Province) first. Geng Zai Cheng led the soldiers in red who started out later. When Zhang Tian You and his soldiers reached Douyangguan, near Hezhou, the people came out from the city to welcome them with meat and wine. It was already noon time. Zhang Tian You led his soldiers to another place for lunch. So Zhang Tian You did not light the signal fire at the appointed time.

Geng Zai Cheng was waiting for the signal fire and he thought that Zhang Tian You must have entered the city of Hezhou by then. He led his soldiers directly to the foot of the city wall. Yexiantemur, the Yuan general defending the city, ordered the guards to shut the gates. Then he ordered the Yuan soldiers to climb down the city wall by rope and fight. Geng Zai Cheng was wounded by an arrow. He had to sound a retreat. The Yuan soldiers ran after them to a place called Qianqiuba. In late afternoon, the Yuan soldiers withdrew back to Hezhou.

At that time Zhang Tian You and his men reached Hezhou and met with the Yuan troops. Zhang Tian You commanded his soldiers to fight the Yuan troops, and they won. They ran after the defeated Yuan soldiers to the west gate of the city. Tang He took the bridge over the moat and scaled the city wall using the same rope which had been used by the Yuan soldiers to climb out of the city. Tang He's soldiers followed his example and climbed up the city wall to capture Hezhou. Yexiantemür escaped at night. Geng Zai Cheng led his defeated soldiers back to Chuzhou and told Guo Zi Xing that Zhang Tian You's troops had all been killed. Not long later it was reported that the Yuan army had reached Chuzhou.

The general of the Yuan army sent an envoy into the city to demand that Guo Zi Xing surrender. Guo Zi Xing was shocked. He summoned Zhu Yuan Zhang to his house to discuss what they should do. At that time most of the troops had been sent out and they had only a few soldiers left to defend the city. Zhu Yuan Zhang ordered all of the soldiers defending the north gate, the east gate and the west gate to concentrate at the south gate. The soldiers were crowded in the street leading to the south gate. Then Zhu Yuan Zhang ordered the envoy of the Yuan army to crawl into the city to see Guo Zi Xing. The Yuan envoy was very rude and said some insulting words in front of Guo Zi Xing. The generals around were furious and wanted to kill him. But Zhu Yuan Zhang secretly told Guo Zi Xing, "If we kill the envoy, the generals of the Yuan army will think that we are afraid of them and killed the envoy who has witnessed the situation in the city. That will only speed up their attack on our city. It would be better to say something that will intimidate the envoy. Scare him and let him go. Our enemies will be afraid and dare not attack." Guo Zi Xing agreed and let the envoy go. The next day the Yuan army really withdrew.

Then Guo Zi Xing sent Zhu Yuan Zhang with some men to gather the defeated soldiers and then go forward to take Hezhou. Zhu Yuan Zhang took General Xu Da and Li Shan Chang and about fifty brave soldiers to march ahead. When they reached Hezhou, they knew that Zhang Tian You had already taken the city. Zhu Yuan Zhang entered the city and mollified the people.

Guo Zi Xing issued an order to appoint Zhu Yuan Zhang as the commander-in-chief of all the troops in Hezhou. At that time the generals were perverse and violent. They were killing and looting the people in Hezhou, and many generals took the wives and daughters of the people as their own. Zhu Yuan Zhang felt pity on the people. He summoned all the generals to his tent and said, "You have commanded soldiers to this city from Chuzhou. Many of you and your subordinates have taken the wives and daughters of the people by force. If there is no discipline in the army, how can we pacify the people in the city! All the women you have taken from the people must be returned to the people." The generals had to return the women and the people were very glad.

Zhu Yuan Zhang was the commander-in-chief of the army in Hezhou. But most of the generals were subordinates of Guo Zi Xing and they were not willing to be submitted to Zhu Yuan Zhang; only General Tang obeyed Zhu Yuan Zhang's orders. Li Shan Chang tried his best to mediate the relationship between Zhu Yuan Zhang and the other generals. Zhu Yuan Zhang issued an order to the generals to repair the city of Hezhou. Zhu Yuan Zhang and all the other generals shared the job. Zhu Yuan Zhang fixed a time limit of three days to complete the task. Zhu Yuan Zhang completed his task first, but all the generals did not complete their tasks within the appointed time limit. Zhu Yuan Zhang was very angry. He summoned them to his tent. He sat on a chair facing south. He spoke to the generals, saying,

"I have been appointed as commander-in-chief by Marshal Guo. It is not that I want to arrogate all the power to myself. Now none of you has completed your share of this task on time. What punishment shall I give you according to military Law?" All the generals were afraid and acknowledged that they had committed a crime, and they said that henceforth they would obey orders from Zhu Yuan Zhang.

In March 1355 Sun De Ya's army in Haozhou ran short of food. Sun De Ya commanded them to go to Hezhou for food. Guo Zi Xing really hated Sun De Ya. When he heard that Sun De Ya had sent his army to Hezhou for food, he was very angry. He immediately hurried there from Chuzhou. When Sun De Ya learned that Guo Zi Xing had come to Hezhou, he decided to go someplace else. He ordered the main part of his army to go first, saying he would leave later.

Zhu Yuan Zhang saw Sun De Ya's army heading off. He accompanied them for fifteen kilometers. Suddenly a soldier from Hezhou rushed up to report to Zhu Yuan Zhang that there had been a fight between Guo Zi Xing's army and Sun De Ya's, and that Sun De Ya had been captured by Guo Zi Xing. Zhu Yuan Zhang was very worried about Sun De Ya and wanted to ride back to Hezhou. But the soldiers under Sun De Ya who had gone first were very angry and they kidnapped Zhu Yuan Zhang and made him go on with them.

After traveling another kilometer, Sun De Ya's troops met with Sun De Ya's younger brother. The brother wanted to kill Zhu Yuan Zhang, but a general by the name of Zhang tried his best to stop him.

When Guo Zi Xing learned that Zhu Yuan Zhang had been kidnapped, he felt as much pain as if he had lost his arms. He sent Xu Da to go to Sun De Ya's army to negotiate with the kidnappers. The general named Zhang succeeded in persuading the soldiers to release Zhu Yuan Zhang, but the negotiator, Xu Da, was kept as a hostage. When Guo Zi Xing heard that Zhu Yuan Zhang had been released, he released Sun De Ya although he hated Sun De Ya very much. When Sun De Ya was released, the soldiers also let Xu Da go.

In this month Guo Zi Xing died. Zhu Yuan Zhang put Guo Zi Xing's army under him.

At that time Liu Fu Tong made Han Lin Er, Han Shan Tong's son, Emperor of the State of Song. The capital of the State of Song was Bozhou (now Bozhou, in the northwest part of Anhui Province). He sent an envoy to summon the generals in Chuzhou and Hezhou to

Bozhou, but only Zhang Tian You responded. When he came back, he brought letters of appointment issued by the premier of the State of Song. Guo Tian Xu, Guo Zi Xing's son, was appointed as the Great Marshal; Zhang Tian You was appointed as Right Deputy Marshal; Zhu Yuan Zhang was appointed as Left Deputy Marshal. Zhu Yuan Zhang said with a sigh, "How can I, as a true man, be controlled by others!" He refused to accept the appointment.

In this month Deng Yu, a man from Hongxian (in Huai'an, Jiangsu Province), came to join Zhu Yuan Zhang's army. He was sixteen years old. His father Deng Shun Xing had revolted and took Linhao (in the east of Fengyang, Anhui Province). In a battle against the Yuan army, Deng Shun Xing was killed. Deng Yu's elder brother had died of illness. So Deng Yu commanded his father's remaining troops to join Zhu Yuan Zhang's army in Hezhou. Zhu Yuan Zhang appointed him as a commander.

Chang Yu Chun, a man from Huaiyuan (now Huaiyuan, Anhui Province), was a strong and wise man. He was twenty-three years old. He had joined the rebel army led by Liu Ju. Chang Yu Chun found that Liu Ju let his men loot the people, and he found that Liu Ju was not fighting for a great goal. He intended to leave Liu Ju. He heard about Zhu Yuan Zhang in Hezhou, and he decided to go to Hezhou to have a look in April 1355. On his way he was overcome by a feeling of drowsiness. He lay down and fell into a deep sleep. In his sleep he dreamed of a god wearing armor and carrying a shield. The god shouted to him, "Wake up! Wake Up! Your true master has come!" It happened that Zhu Yuan Zhang and his followers were passing, on horseback. Chang Yu Chun immediately jumped up and begged Zhu Yuan Zhang to accept him as his subordinate and said that he was willing to serve as the vanguard of the army. Zhu Yuan Zhang said, "You have come to be my dependent because you are hungry. And you already have your own master. How can I take you from him?" Chang Yu Chun knelt down, touched his head to the ground and said with tears in his eyes, "Liu Ju is only a robber. He will not be able to accomplish anything. If I can serve a wise master, I would die for him." Zhu Yuan Zhang said, "Are you willing to go with me to cross the Yangtze River? It won't be too late to become my subordinate when we take Taiping."

4. ZHU YUAN ZHANG CROSSES THE YANGTZE RIVER AND TAKES JINLING

Zhu Yuan Zhang had stayed in Hezhou for a long time. In April 1355, he and his generals and officials planned to cross the Yangtze but they did not have ships suitable for crossing so wide a river. At that time Liao Yong An and Liao Yong Zhong, Yu Ting Yu and his sons, and others were at Chao Hu Lake (in Anhui Province); they had 10,000 men and over a 1,000 ships. They had their men anchor their ships by the lake shore to make camps on the water. Their camps were linked together to help them fend off possible attacks. Zuo Jun Bi, a general of the Yuan army, occupied Luzhou on the shores of that same Chao Hu Lake (now the area around Hefei, Anhui Province, including the area of what is now Chaohu). So the ships of Liao Yong An and the others were penned in by the Yuan army and could not leave the Lake.

Yu Ting Yu sent his son Yu Tong Hai as an envoy on 2 May 1355 to go by back roads to Hezhou to see Zhu Yuan Zhang and express their intention to submit to his authority. Zhu Yuan Zhang was very glad and said, "We were just planning to cross the Yangtze River and the naval troops in Chao Hu Lake have come in a timely way. Heaven has sent them to help us! We must not miss this chance." Then he personally took some troops to Chao Hu Lake. Liao Yong An, Liao Yong Zhong and Yu Ting Yu welcomed Zhu Yuan Zhang and his men.

Zhu Yuan Zhang and his men went on board the ships and they sailed out of Chao Hu Lake and reached the area of Tongchengzha (now Tongchengzha, Anhui Province). At that time Manzihaiya, a general of the Yuan Dynasty, arranged his troops in strategically important places of Tongchengzha and Marchang He River to stop Zhu Yuan Zhang's army from entering the Yangtze River. He himself commanded his naval forces, with big boats, to station themselves in Yuxikou (now Yuxikou, Anhui Province), the confluence where the Yuxi He River flows into the Yangtze River.

At this time Zhao Pu Sheng betrayed Zhu Yuan Zhang and turned to the Yuan Army. Liao Yong An asked Zhu Yuan Zhang's permission to let the navy be stationed in Huangdun (now Huangdun Village of Yuncao, Hanshan, Anhui Province) so he could have his soldiers attack the Yuan naval force under the command of Manzihaiya in Yuxikou. Zhu Yuan Zhang gave the permission.

Then Liao Yong An commanded his soldiers to take small boats to attack the Yuan army's big ships. That day it was raining hard. The small boats could move very quickly and flexibly. The ships of the Yuan army were big, both tall and heavy; they could not move quickly. So the soldiers under Liao Yong An defeated the Yuan navy. Zhu Yuan Zhang's ships entered the Yangtze River from Yuxikou and anchored by the north bank.

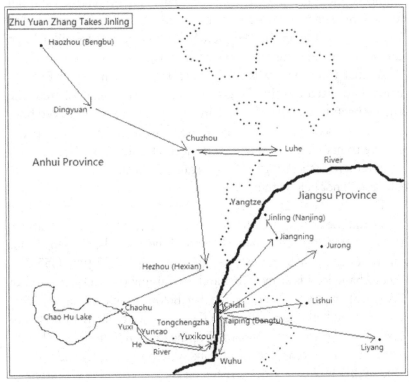

On 1 June 1355, Zhu Yuan Zhang commanded the generals and men to cross the Yangtze River. Liao Yong An went to see Zhu Yuan Zhang to ask him for instructions as to where they should go. Zhu Yuan Zhang said, "If we want to take Jinling, we must take Caishi first. Caishi is a big town. It must be strongly defended. Niuzhuji is facing the Yangtze River. It is not easily defended. If we attack Niuzhuji, we shall surely take it. Then from Niuzhuji we shall take Caishi." Then all the boats set sail and moved very quickly along the Yangtze River. Not long later, the troops under Zhu Yuan Zhang reached Niuzhuji (situated on the southern bank of the Yangtze River near Caishi).

The boat which carried Zhu Yuan Zhang came first. The boat was about ten meters away from the bank where Yuan soldiers had been arranged in battle formation. The soldiers under Zhu Yuan Zhang could not land immediately. At this time Chang Yu Chun, taking a fast little boat, arrived. Zhu Yuan Zhang ordered him to attack the enemy. Chang Yu Chun gave an answer and at the same time jumped from the boat to the bank, waving his spear, shouting loudly and killing Yuan soldiers. Under his fierce attack, the Yuan soldiers collapsed and ran away. Zhu Yuan Zhang's troops followed Chang Yu Chun and took Niuzhuji. Sped along by the momentum of the victory, Zhu Yuan Zhang commanded his army to march north and they took Caishi.

At that time there was a famine in Hezhou. Zhu Yuan Zhang's generals wanted to take the goods and food they had got from the enemy back to Hezhou. Zhu Yuan Zhang said to Xu Da, "We have luckily crossed the Yangtze River successfully. If we give up the chance to march forward and go back to Hezhou, it will be difficult for us to cross the Yangtze River again. Then the southeast part of China will not belong to us."

Then Zhu Yuan Zhang ordered the soldiers to cut all the mooring ropes and the boats were carried away to the east by the rapid flow of the Yangtze River. Zhu Yuan Zhang told the generals, "Taiping is not far from here. I shall go with you all to take it." On 2 June 1355 Zhu Yuan Zhang led his army on a march to Taiping (now Dangtu, Anhui Province) and took it on the same day. Before attacking Taiping, Zhu Yuan Zhang had ordered Li Shan Chang to write many bulletins to discipline the soldiers entering Taiping. When Zhu Yuan Zhang's army entered Taiping, these bulletins were posted all around the city. One soldier broke the rules written on the bulletins. He was arrested and executed in front of the people. From then on, all the troops in the city of Taiping exercised great discipline.

Tao An, a Confucian scholar, was at that time in Dangtu, his home place, to get away from the war. When Zhu Yuan Zhang entered Taiping, Tao An and Li Xi, an old Confucian scholar, came out of their homes and into the street to welcome Zhu Yuan Zhang with the people in Taiping. When Tao An saw Zhu Yuan Zhang, he said to Li Xi, "He looks like a dragon and has the graceful demeanor of a phoenix. He is an extraordinary man. From now on we have our true master." Zhu Yuan Zhang summoned Tao An to his office to discuss the important matters. Tao An took this chance to make some suggestions. To set the stage he first said, "Now the people resent the rule of the Yuan Dynasty. Heroes everywhere have risen up in arms. They attack cities and occupy lands. Each one is trying to prove he is the strongest. But they are only after wealth and treasure. They do not cherish the great goal of putting an end to the chaos caused by war, saving the people from suffering and pacifying the whole realm. Now you have commanded your generals and men to cross the Yangtze River. You have prohibited your subordinates from killing and looting the people. You have acted according to the instruction of Heaven and the sentiment of the people. In this way you will surely accomplish your goal."

Zhu Yuan Zhang asked Tao An, "I intend to take Jinling. What do you think of this idea?" Tao An said, "Jinling is a good place for the capital of an emperor. It is a place of strategically importance. It is protected by the natural barrier of the Yangtze River. If you make use of the geographical advantage of this place and send out troops in all directions to conquer the whole realm, your troops will be invincible. Heaven has provided Jinling to you!" Zhu Yuan Zhang was very glad at these words.

Zhu Yuan Zhang established the Office of the Marshal of the Taiping-Xingguo Wing. He himself took the position of the Marshal. He appointed Li Shan Chang as the Chief of Staff; and he appointed Wang Guang Ying and Tao An as senior officials to handle the affairs of the Office of the Marshal.

At that time Yuan troops were positioned all around the city of Taiping. Manzihaiya and Aluhui commanded the navy of the Yuan Dynasty to anchor their big warships by Caishi to stop the traffic between there and Taiping. In July 1355 Chen Ye Xian, the marshal of the militiamen of the Yuan Dynasty, and Kang Mao Cai, a general under Chen Ye Xian, commanded over 30,000 land troops and naval soldiers to attack the city of Taiping. Zhu Yuan Zhang personally commanded his troops to resist the attack by the Yuan army, and he sent Xu Da and Deng Yu to command some troops to make a denture to the back of the enemy and lay an ambush by Xiangcheng Bridge which was situated to the south of Taiping. When Chen Ye Xian attacked the city, he suddenly saw a big yellow cloud coming down over the top of the city and the mountain within the city. He was greatly scared and was defeated. When he was running away, he fell into the ambush and was captured.

When he was brought before Zhu Yuan Zhang, the latter untied the rope and set him free. Chen Ye Xian asked in great surprise, "Why don't you kill me?" Zhu Yuan Zhang replied, "The people of the whole realm are in rebellion. Heroic men have taken up arms everywhere. If one such hero wins, many people will readily follow him. If he is defeated, he will have to submit to the one who has defeated him. Since you call yourself a hero, you know very well why I have released you." Chen Ye Xian said, "Do you want me to order my troops to surrender? It is an easy thing to do." Then Chen Ye Xian wrote a letter to his troops and ordered them to surrender. The next day all Chen Ye Xian's troops came to the city of Taiping to surrender. When Manzihaiya and Aluhui saw that Chen Ye Xian had been defeated, they took their troops back to Yuxikou (now Yuxikou, Anhui Province).

In August Zhu Yuan Zhang sent Xu Da and other generals to command their troops in capturing Lishui (now Lishui, Jiangsu Province), Liyang (now Liyang, Jiangsu Province), Jurong (now Jurong, Jiangsu Province) and Wuhu (now Wuhu, Anhui Province). They successfully took all these cities. Then Zhu Yuan Zhang planned to attack Jinling.

Chen Ye Xian regretted that he had ordered his troops to surrender. When he heard that Zhu Yuan Zhang was going to attack Jinling, he secretly told his subordinates, "When you attack Jinling, don't fight very hard. When I get a chance to escape, I will join forces of the Yuan army." Zhu Yuan Zhang got word of this secret plan, and he summoned Chen Ye Xian to his office. He told him, "Different people have different aspirations. I will not force you to submit to me. You may go and join the Yuan Dynasty." Then Zhu Yuan Zhang let him go wherever he liked and let him decide which side he would be on.

Chen Ye Xian left. He gathered all the troops that had been under him. He stationed his troops in Banqiao (now Banqiao, Jiangsu Province) which was situated by the southern bank of the Yangtze River. He secretly united with General Fushou, the commander-in-chief of the Yuan army defending Jinling. Chen Ye Xian wrote a letter to Zhu Yuan Zhang which read, "The city of Jinling is protected by the Yangtze River from the north, northeast and northwest. There are high mountains in the southeast. The terrain of Jinling is perilous and it is disadvantageous to attack the city by land. In the past Wang Hun and Wang Rui of the Jin Dynasty were sent to attack Jinling. They spent several years building ships to cross the Yangtze River. Su Jun and Wang Dun of the Eastern Jin Dynasty took Jinling in their rebellions, but not by land. When the Emperor of the Sui Dynasty planned to take the areas east to the Yangtze River, he sent He Ruo Bi from Yangzhou, Han Qin Hu from Luzhou, and Yang Su from Anlu to sail to Jinling by boat. Now Jinling is protected by the Yangtze River by three sides. You have established the camps of your army which extend for fifteen kilometers. If you attack the city, you will worry that your enemy will attack from the back of your army. It is better for you to stay in Liyang. You may send an army to march east to attack Zhenjiang and occupy the critical places and cut your enemies' transport lines to Jinling. You may show your enemies that you are carrying out a protracted war. Then you may take Jinling without a battle." Reading this letter, Zhu Yuan Zhang understood that Chen Ye Xian was playing a trick to delay his attack.

So Zhu Yuan Zhang wrote a return letter which read, "People in the different dynasties who tried to take the area south to the Yangtze River had to gather a lot of ships because the Yangtze River, the widest natural barrier, prevented them from reaching the southern bank. Now my army has crossed the Yangtze River and has occupied the upper reaches of the river. I have got hold of the most critical part of the Yangtze River. I will not attack Jingling by warship. My army will march on land and will surely take Jinling. The situation today is greatly different from that of the different dynasties. Why you have suggested that I give up this sure-win strategy and presented such a protracted strategy?" Having read the return letter, Chen Ye Xian was still determined to go over to the side of the Yuan Dynasty.

In September 1355 Guo Tian Xu, Guo Zi Xing's son, and Zhang Tian You commanded the generals and men under them to attack Jinling. Chen Ye Xian had his troops go to Jinling and join forces with General Fushou of the Yuan army. A battle was fought by the side of Qinhuai River (south of the city of Jinling). Guo Tian Xu and Zhang Tian You were killed. The troops under Guo Tian Xu and Zhang Tian You ran back. Chen Ye Xian led his troops in hot pursuit. Chen Ye Xian chased the defeated enemy to Gexian Village (southeast of Nanjing).

Lu De Mao, the head of the militiamen in this village, planned to kill Chen Ye Xian. He sent fifty militiamen wearing green to welcome Chen Ye Xian at the entrance of the village. Chen Ye Xian did not know that they were planning to kill him, so he went into the village with fifteen soldiers. A militiaman in green stabbed him from his back with his spear and killed him. His son Chen Zhao Xian gathered the troops and stationed them in Fangshan (now in Jiangning, which is situated to the south of Nanjing, Jiangsu Province). Manzihaiya of the Yuan Dynasty sailed with his naval troops from Yuxikou to Caishi and anchored his ships by the southern bank of the Yangtze River. He intended to attack Taiping.

In December 1355 the Yuan army defeated Liu Fu Tong's army in Taikang (now in Henan Province). Then the Yuan army marched to Bozhou (now in the northwest part of Anhui Province), the capital of the State of Song. Liu Fu Tong, taking Han Lin Er, the Emperor of the State of Song, escaped to Anfeng (now Shouxian, Anhui Province).

On 1 February 1356 Zhang Shi Cheng sent his younger brother Zhang Shi De to attack Pingjiang (now Suzhou, Jiangsu Province). Zhang Shi De took the city; then he captured Huzhou (now in Zhejiang Province) and Changzhou (now in Jiangsu Province). Zhang Shi Cheng moved his capital from Gaoyou to Pingjiang. He destroyed the big Buddha statue in Chengtian Temple and used the temple as his palace.

All the family members of the generals and men of Zhu Yuan Zhang's army stayed in Hezhou. Since Manzihaiya had stationed his navy in Caishi, Zhu Yuan Zhang's ships could not cross the Yangtze River and all communication between the men of Zhu Yuan Zhang's army and their family members was cut off. On 25 February 1356 Zhu Yuan Zhang sent Chang Yu Chun to take some troops to the back of Manzihaiya's army so as to disperse the enemy forces. Zhu Yuan Zhang personally commanded an army to attack from the front. During the battle Zhu Yuan Zhang sent a detachment to march to the riverside where the Yuan army's big warships were anchored. The soldiers of this detachment set fire to the ships which were linked together, so all of them caught fire and were burned away. The Yuan army was disastrously defeated. Manzihaiya had a narrow escape. He fled to Pingjiang to seek shelter with Zhang Shi Cheng. From then on, the Yuan army had little power to prevent Zhu Yuan Zhang's soldiers from crossing the Yangtze River.

On 1 March 1356 Zhu Yuan Zhang commanded his troops to advance to Jinling both by land and by the river. His troops reached Jiangning (situated to the south of what is now Nanjing, Jiangsu Province) where Chen Zhao Xian's army camps were. Zhu Yuan Zhang's army attacked the camps and defeated the army under Chen Zhao Xian. All his soldiers, 36,000, surrendered. Chen Zhao Xian was captured.

Zhu Yuan Zhang set him free and made him an officer of the army. At that time the officers and men of Chen Zhao Xian's army who had surrendered were worried and afraid because they thought they would be punished. Zhu Yuan Zhang selected five hundred strong soldiers from among them and appointed them to be his body-guards. That night Zhu Yuan Zhang asked all his original body-guards to leave and ordered the new body-guards to go into his command tent to defend him. He let the new body-guards stand around his bed. Only Feng Guo Yong stood by his side. Zhu Yuan Zhang took off his armor and lay down on his bed and slept peacefully till dawn. From then on all the soldiers who had surrendered felt at ease.

On 10 March 1356, Zhu Yuan Zhang commanded his great army to attack the city of Jinling from all sides. Feng Guo Yong, commanding five hundred soldiers, charged and shattered the Yuan army's battle formation in Jiang Shan Mountain (now Zijin Shan (Purple Mountain), on the eastern side of Nanjing, Jiangsu Province) and entered through the outer wall of the city of Nanjing. Fushou, the commander-in-chief of the Yuan army defending Jinling, commanded the Yuan troops to come out of the city to meet Zhu Yuan Zhang's army. But the Yuan army was defeated.

Zhu Yuan Zhang's army broke into the city of Jinling. Fushou sat on the top of the city wall to command his soldiers in street battles. Someone tried to persuade him to escape. Fushou said, "I am an important official of the nation. If the city exists, I will exist. If the city falls, I will die. I will not go anywhere." He shot an arrow at the man who tried to persuade him to escape and killed him. A moment later Zhu Yuan Zhang's soldiers gathered around him and killed him too. The city of Jinling was taken. Kang Mao Cai led his troops to surrender to Zhu Yuan Zhang. Zhu Yuan Zhang won the city of Jinling and gained 50,000 people and soldiers.

When Zhu Yuan Zhang entered the city of Jinling, he summoned the original officials of the Yuan Dynasty and the elders of the city to his office and said to them, "The cruel rule and misgovernment of the Yuan Dynasty has led to the chaotic situation all over the realm. The people have been plunged into misery and suffering. I have commanded a great army to this city only to save the people from suffering. You may carry out your work as usual and should not have any apprehension. If any virtuous man wants to follow me so as to make great contributions to this process, I will assign him to a suitable position with due respect. I will do away all the improper laws and policies of the Yuan Dynasty." When the people heard these words, they were very happy. Zhu Yuan Zhang renamed Jinling as Yingtian. He established the Office of the Marshal of Tianxing-Yingtian Wing. He appointed Liao Yong An as the Marshal. Zhu Yuan Zhang highly praised Fushou's devotion. He ordered that the dead body of Fushou be buried with all due honor.

CHAPTER THREE: ZHU YUAN ZHANG BRINGS PEACE TO THE WHOLE REALM

1. ZHU YUAN ZHANG BRINGS PEACE TO SOUTHEAST CHINA

(1) Battles for the Cities in the Southern Jiangsu Province

Having taken Jinling, Zhu Yuan Zhang decided to aim next for Zhenjiang (now in Jiangsu Province). But he worried that the generals could not discipline their men and their men would kill and loot the people and cause widespread indignation. One day Zhu Yuan Zhang summoned all the generals to his office. He pretended to be very angry and listed all their mistakes in letting their subordinates go looting. Zhu Yuan Zhang declared that he would punish the generals according to law. Li Shan Chang tried his best to save the generals from being punished.

Not long later, Zhu Yuan Zhang appointed Xu Da as the Grand General to take command of the generals and go east along the Yangtze River to attack Zhenjiang. Before Xu Da and the generals left, Zhu Yuan Zhang warned them, saying, "Since I rose up in arms, I have never killed innocent people. You should always keep my instructions in mind and discipline the officers and men under you. When the city is taken, killing innocent people, burning the houses, and looting the people are strictly prohibited. Anyone who commits any of these crimes will be punished according to military law. Any of you who connive at committing such crimes will be punished." Xu Da and the generals all touched their heads to the ground and showed that they would obey Zhu Yuan Zhang's order.

On 16 March 1356 Xu Da commanded his army to attack the city of Zhenjiang. On 17 Xu Da took Zhenjiang. Yang Elezhe, the commander-in-chief of the Miao Nationality troops in the Yuan army defending Zhenjiang, escaped. Duan Wu and Dingding, two generals of the Yuan army defending Zhenjiang, were killed in battle. Xu Da entered the city of Zhenjiang through Renhe Gate (one of the three gates in the south wall of Zhenjiang). All the generals maintained strict discipline among their officers and men. The whole city was in great peace and order. Then Xu Da sent generals to attack Jintan (in Jiangsu Province) and Danyang (in what is now Jiangsu Province) and they took them all. Zhu Yuan Zhang appointed Xu Da and Tang He as the Marshals of the army defending Zhenjiang.

In June 1356 Zhu Yuan Zhang sent Deng Yu at the head of an army to attack Guangde (now in Anhui Province). Very soon Deng Yu took Guangde. Zhu Yuan Zhang then appointed him Marshal of the army defending Guangde.

On 1 July 1356 the generals proclaimed Zhu Yuan Zhang Duke of the State of Wu. The original Administration Office of the Yuan Dynasty in Jinling became the office for Zhu Yuan Zhang. At this time Han Lin Er, the Emperor of the State of Song, appointed Zhu Yuan Zhang as Manager of Governmental Affairs and the Right Premier. Zhu Yuan Zhang established the Executive Secretariat of the Area South of the Yangtze River. He made himself the Head of the Executive Secretariat. He appointed Li Shang Chang and Song Si Yan as the members of the Executive Secretariat. Not long later, Zhu Yuan Zhang established the Privy Council of the Area South to the Yangtze River. He entrusted Xu Da and Tang He with the affairs of the Privy Council. He established a Bodyguard Army and appointed Feng Guo Yong as its Commander-in-chief.

After Zhu Yuan Zhang had taken Jinling, he worried that Zhang Shi Cheng, who was at that time in Pingjiang (now Suzhou, Jiangsu Province), would stop his army from marching to the east. So he sent Yang Xian, a Confucian scholar, to Pingjiang to establish good relationship with Zhang Shi Cheng. When Yang Xian reached Pingjiang, he presented a letter Zhu Yuan Zhang had written to Zhang Shi Cheng. The letter read, "In the Han Dynasty, Kui Xiao occupied the area around Tianshui and became the most powerful and dominant man in that area. Now you are the most powerful and dominant man in the area around Suzhou. Now your situation is somewhat similar to that of Kui Xiao. I am sincerely happy for you. To keep a friendly relationship with their neighbors and to defend their own territories — these were the virtues of the people in the past. I admire these virtues. From now on you and I shall send envoys to communicate our ideas so as to avoid clashes between your army and my army in the border areas when rumors proliferate." Zhang Shi Cheng read the letter but he did not like it at all — Zhu Yuan Zhang had compared him to Kui Xiao, who had been a powerful warlord but one who never accomplished anything of lasting significance. He changed sides frequently and was defeated in the end; he died miserably, of frustration. So Zhang Shi Cheng detained Yang Xian and did not give a reply.

A man named Chen Bao Er had organized the people in Benniu Town of Changzhou (in Jiangsu Province), his home place, into an army. All his soldiers wore yellow scarves on their heads. When Xu Da took Zhenjiang, Chen Bao Er led his men to surrender to Xu Da.

Not long later Zhang Shi Cheng forced Chen Bao Er to betray Xu Da and ordered him to command his navy to help Zhang Shi Cheng to attack Zhenjiang. In July 1356 Xu Da had his troops destroy the ships under Chen Bao Er in Longtan (in Jiangsu Province). Zhang Shi Cheng sent an army to attack Yixing (same province). Geng Jun Yong, the general defending Yixing, was killed in the battle. Then the city of Yixing fell into Zhang Shi Cheng's hands.

When Zhu Yuan Zhang heard that Zhang Shi Cheng had taken Yixing, he said to Xu Da, "Zhang Shi Cheng was originally a peddler. He is very sly. Now he has come to attack Zhenjiang. This shows that our relation with him has changed. We should send troops to attack cities near his capital. We should strike first to gain the initiative."

Then Xu Da commanded an army to attack Changzhou (now Changzhou, Jiangsu Province). The army under Xu Da attacked the city for a long time, but they could not take it. Xu Da sent an envoy back to Yingtian (that is Jingling, now Nanjing, Jiangsu Province) to ask Zhu Yuan Zhang to send more troops to reinforce his army. Zhu Yuan Zhang sent 30,000 men to Changzhou.

(2) Clashes with Zhang Shi Cheng

In September 1356 Xu Da, Tang He and the other generals commanded their troops to attack Changzhou. Zhang Shi Cheng sent a great army to rescue Changzhou. Xu Da said to the other generals, "Zhang Shi Cheng's troops are bearing down menacingly. They are irresistible. We should defeat them by strategy." Then Xu Da sent some troops to lay an ambush in a place eight kilometers to the south of the city of Changzhou. He sent out detachments to start a surprise attack on the coming enemy troops. When Zhang Shi Cheng's recuing troops arrived and were arranged in battle formations, Xu Da personally commanded his army to fight with the enemy. As soon as the battle began, Wang Jun Yong led the cavalrymen to ride directly at the enemy battle formation. The enemy battle formation collapsed and the soldiers turned back and ran away. But very soon they fell into the ambush and were disastrously defeated. The commanding generals of Zhang Shi Cheng's army were captured. Zhang Shi Cheng began to feel afraid.

On 2 October 1356 Zhang Shi Cheng sent Sun Jun Shou as his envoy bringing a letter to Yingtian to see Zhu Yuan Zhang to ask for peace. Zhang Shi Cheng promised to pay the following tribute every year: 550,000 bushels of grain, 25,000 grams of gold, and 150,000 grams of silver. Zhu Yuan Zhang gave a reply letter to Zhang Shi Cheng, ordering him to let Yang Xian go back to Yingtian and to increase the tribute of grain to 1,375,000 bushels. In the letter Zhu Yuan Zhang also said, "A man should be open and candid. I hate those people who would not tell their true intentions but like to say boastful words." When Zhang Shi Cheng got the letter, he did not give any reply.

In November Zhang Shi Cheng seduced 7,000 soldiers who had recently joined Xu Da's army into betraying him and asked them to attack Xu Da's army from within when Zhang Shi Cheng's army came to attack from without. Then Zhang Shi Cheng had his army surround Xu Da's army in Niutang (a town which is situated to the south outskirt of Changzhou). Xu Da commanded his army to engage the enemy. But suddenly seven thousand soldiers attacked Xu Da's army from within. The situation was very unfavorable to Xu Da. Chang Yu Chun, the Deputy Marshal of the army, commanding Liao Yong An and Hu Da Hai, came to rescue Xu Da from outside in a great hurry. Then Xu Da's army attack Zhang Shi Cheng's army from the front and Chang Yu Chun's army attacked Zhang Shi Cheng's army from their back. Zhang Shi Chang's army was disastrously defeated. They ran back to the city of Changzhou. The seven thousand soldiers who had betrayed Xu Da also ran into the city of Changzhou. Zhang Shi Cheng sent his general Lü Zhen to enter the city stealthily to command the defense of Changzhou. Xu Da again commanded his troops to lay siege to the city of Changzhou.

In December 1356 Xie Guo Xi, the Marshal of the Army of Long Spears, came to attack Guangde (now Guangde, Anhui Province) from Ningguo (now Ningguo, Anhui Province). Deng Yu, the Marshal of Zhu Yuan Zhang's army defending Guangde, defeated Xie Guo Xi's army and captured Wu Shi Rong, the Commander-in-chief of Xie Guo Xi's army, and more than a thousand soldiers. Then Deng Yu sent Fei Zi Xian, a general under Deng Yu, to command an army to attack Wukang (now Wukang Town, Deqing, Zhejiang Province) and Anji (now Anji, Zhejiang Province). Fei Zi Xian took these two cities.

This year Ni Wen Jun, the Premier of Xu Shou Hui, took Hanyang (now Hanyang, Wuhan City, Hubei Province). He made Hanyang the capital of the Tianwan Dynasty and invited Xu Shou Hui, the Emperor of the Tianwan Dynasty, to live in Hanyang. By this time Chen You Liang, who had joined Xu Shou Hui in 1351, had been promoted as a marshal of Xu Shou Hui's army.

On 1 February 1357 Zhu Yuan Zhang sent Geng Bing Wen to attack Changxing (in the northern part of Zhejiang Province). Geng Bing Wen was Geng Jun Yong's son. Geng Jun Yong was killed in a battle in Yixing in July 1356. After Geng Jun Yong died, Zhu Yuan Zhang let Geng Bing Wen succeed his father's position and command the army originally under his father. When Geng Bing Wen with his army reached Changxing, Zhang Shi Cheng sent his general Zhao Da Hu to command 3,000 troops to meet Geng Bing Wen's army. After a battle Zhao Da Hu's troops were defeated. Zhao Da Hu ran away to Huzhou (now Huzhou, Zhejiang Province). On 3 February 1357 Geng Bing Wen took Changxing. Li Fu An, the general defending Changxing, was captured. Geng Bing Wen's troops also captured more than three hundred warships. Changxing was a place of strategically importance. It was situated to the northwest of Tai Hu Lake (now Tai Hu Lake, in the southern part of Jiangsu Province) and controlled the water traffic leading to Tai Hu Lake. By land, it was connected with Guangde, Xuancheng (now Xuanzhou, Anhui Province) and Shexian (now Shexian, in the southern part of Anhui Province). It was the gate leading to Jiangsu and Zhejiang. When Zhu Yuan Zhang knew that Geng Bing Wen had taken Changxing, he was very glad. He renamed Changxing as Chang'an and established the Office of the Marshal of Yongxing Wing. He appointed Geng Bing Wen as the Marshal of this wing of the army defending Chang'an.

Xu Da's army had laid siege to the city of Changzhou for a long time. When Lü Zhen entered the city of Changzhou, the food supply in the city was sufficient. But since the seven thousand soldiers who had been seduced by Zhang Shi Cheng to betray Xu Da entered the city, food supply was not sufficient for so many men. Xu Da commanded his army to attack the city fiercely. Seeing that the city was going to fall Lü Zhen ran away at night. On 8 March 1357 Xu Da took Changzhou. Zhu Yuan Zhang established Changchun Privy Council in Changzhou. He appointed Xu Da as the Head of Changchun Privy Council, and Tang He as the Deputy Head of Changchun Privy Council to command their troops to defend Changzhou.

In April 1357 Xu Da and Chang Yu Chun commanded their troops to attack Ningguo (now Ningguo, Anhui Province). Xie Guo Xi, the Marshal of the Army of Long Spears, left Ningguo and ran away. Baibuha and Yang Zhong Ying, the generals of the Yuan army defending Ningguo, shut the gates of the city and defended the city resolutely. Although the city of Ningguo was small, its city walls were strong. The troops under Xu Da and Chang Yu Chun attacked the city for a long time but could not take it. Zhu Liang Zu, the marshal of the Yuan army defending Ningguo, came out of the city to fight. In the battle Chang Yu Chun was wounded by a stray arrow. He came back to have his wound dressed with a piece of cloth and continued to fight. When Zhu Yuan Zhang heard about this, he went to Ningguo on 23 April and personally commanded the attack of Ningguo. He ordered the soldiers to put shelters made of bamboo and wood on the three sides and top of the carts. Under the protection of these carts, the soldiers moved to the foot of the city wall and started a fierce attack. Baibuha and Yang Zhong Ying saw that the city would fall very soon. They opened the city gates and let Zhu Yuan Zhang's army into the city. Zhu Yuan Zhang's troops captured more than 100,000 enemy soldiers and two thousand horses. Zhu Liang Zu was captured.

Zhu Liang Zu had been the marshal of the militiamen appointed by the Yuan Dynasty. When Zhu Yuan Zhang took Taiping in June 1355, Zhu Liang Zu came to Taiping to surrender to him. Zhu Yuan Zhang left him in place as marshal of the militiamen, as before. But later Zhu Liang Zu betrayed Zhu Yuan Zhang and went away. He fought Zhu Yuan Zhang's army and caused many casualties. Now that Zhu Liang Zu was captured, he was brought before Zhu Yuan Zhang. Zhu Yuan Zhang asked him, "Now what will you do?" Zhu Liang Zu answered, "The quarrel between you and me has come to an end. If you let me live, I will do my best to serve you. If you decide to kill me, I will not beg you to spare me." Zhu Yuan Zhang was moved by his words and set him free. He ordered Zhu Liang Zu to perform a meritorious service to atone for his crimes.

On 5 May 1357 Zhu Yuan Zhang ordered Zhang Jian and He Wen Zheng to command an army to attack Taixing (in Jiangsu Province). Zhang Shi Cheng sent an army to rescue the city of Taixing. General Xu Da Xing and General Zhang Bin defeated the rescuing army of Zhang Shi Cheng. Then the army under Zhang Jian and He Wen Zheng took Taixing.

In May, Yu Tong Hai and Zhang De Sheng, who had been promoted by Zhu Yuan Zhang to the rank of the Members of the Privy Council, commanded the navy to attack Maji Shan in Tai Hu Lake (now Maji Shan in Tai Hu Lake in Jiangsu Province). They forced Niu Jin, a general of the army of Zhang Shi Cheng, to surrendered and took Maji Shan. Then they sailed eastward to Dongdongting Shan (now Dongdongting Shan in Tai Hu Lake, Jiangsu Province). When the ships just got to the shore of Dongdongting Shan, Lü Zhen, a general under Zhang Shi Cheng, arrived with a great army. The generals under Yu Tong Hai suggested that they should leave so as to avoid fighting with such a great army. Yu Tong Hai disagreed with their suggestion. He said, "The enemy troops are greatly outnumbered our troops. If we retreat, we shall show to our enemies that we are weak and can be defeated. It would be better for us to go forward to meet the enemy troops." Then Yu Tong Hai charged at the head of his officers and men. The arrows of the enemy troops rained down. One of the arrows hit the right eye of Yu Tong Hai, but Yu Tong Hai continued to fight. He ordered a soldier to put on his armors and stood on his ship to supervise the battle. The enemy troops thought that man was Yu

Tong Hai. They did not dare to go forward and then they retreated. From then on Yu Tong Hai was blind in one eye.

In June 1357, Zhu Yuan Zhang sent Zhao Ji Zu, a member of the Privy Council, Marshal Guo Tian Lu, and Commander Wu Liang to command their troops to take Jiangyin (now Jiangyin, Jiangsu Province). The army of Zhang Shi Cheng defended Qinwangshan Mountain which was ten kilometers southwest to the city of Jiangyin. On 15 June Wu Liang took the lead and commanded his troops to start a fierce attack on the army of Zhang Shi Cheng defending the mountain. Suddenly there was a thunderstorm. The troop of Zhang Shi Cheng were defeated and escaped in great disorder. The troops under Zhao Ji Zu took the mountain. On 16 June Zhao Ji Zu and the other generals commanded their troops to attack the west gate of the city wall of Jiangyin. On 17 June Zhao Ji Zu and the other generals took Jiangyin. Zhu Yuan Zhang promoted Wu Liang to the rank of a member of the Privy Council and appointed him as the commander-in-chief of the army defending Jiangyin. Jiangyin was only seventy kilometers to Suzhou (now Suzhou, Jiangsu Province) where Zhang Shi Cheng was. It was situated by the southern bank of the Yangtze River and could control the traffic on the Yangtze River. It was really a strategically important place. Not long later Zhu Yuan Zhang ordered Wu Zhen, Wu Liang's younger brother, to lead some troops to reinforce the defense of Jiangyin. He advised Wu Liang, "Jiangyin provides a protective screen for us. You must restrain the officers and men under you. You should not establish any relationship outside Jiangyin. Don't accept any criminals who have been convicted and run away to you. Don't seek for trifling advantages. You should not seek to prevail over others. Your task is just to defend the boundary and let the people live peacefully." Wu Liang followed Zhu Yuan Zhang's order carefully. He ordered his soldiers to repair the city and make preparation against the attack by Zhang Shi Cheng's army.

In July 1357 Xu Da attacked Yixing (now Yixing, Jiangsu Province) from Changzhou. He sent Zhao De Sheng to attack Changshu (now Changshu, Jiangsu Province). At that time, Zhang Shi De, Zhang Shi Cheng's younger brother, commanded an army to defend Changshu. Before Zhao De Sheng left, Xu Da told him, "Zhang Shi De is a crafty man and good at fighting. If he wins, we cannot withstand his fierce attack. We must defeat him by strategy." On 3 July 1357 Zhao De Sheng reached Changshu and arranged his army under the city wall.

Zhang Shi De came out of the city to meet Zhao De Sheng's army. But very soon he fell into an ambush. His horse slipped and he toppled from the horse and was captured. Zhang Shi De was good at fighting and a resourceful man. He was beloved and supported by the officers and men under him. It was he who had commanded his army to take the west part of what is now Zhejiang Province for Zhang Shi Cheng. After Zhang Shi De was captured, Zhang Shi Cheng was disheartened. On 4 July Zhao De Sheng took Changshu.

Zhu Yuan Zhang transferred Deng Yu to Xuanzhou (now Xuanzhou, Anhui Province) from Guangde (now Guangde, Anhui Province). In July Zhu Yuang Zhang ordered Deng Yu and Hu Da Hai to attack Huizhou (now Shexian, Anhui Province). The armies under Deng Yu and Hu Da Hai took Jixi (now Jixi, Anhui Province) and Xiuning (now Xiuning, Anhui Province). Then they marched eastward to attack Huizhou. Basibuha, the general of the Yuan army defending Huizhou, and Wu Na, a commander of the Yuan Army, tried their best to resist the attack. Very soon they were defeated. On 7 July the troops under Deng Yu and Hu Da Hai took Huizhou. Basibuha ran away. Wu Na retreated towards Sui'an (now Chun'an, Zhejiang province). Hu Da Hai caught up with him. Wu Na killed himself. Zhu Yuan Zhang changed Huizhou into Xing'an. He promoted Deng Yu to the rank of a member of the Privy Council and ordered him to command an army to defend Xing'an.

In August 1357 Zhang Shi De was brought to Yingtian (that is, Jinling, now Nanjing, Jiangsu Province). When he was brought before Zhu Yuan Zhang, he received him with due politeness. He prepared a grand banquet to welcome Zhang Shi De and hoped that he would surrender. But during the banquet, Zhang Shi De kept his mouth shut. He neither ate anything nor said anything. When Zhang Shi De's mother heard about this, she asked Zhang Shi Cheng to send 275,000 bushels of grain and 10,000 bolts of cloth every year as tribute to Zhu Yuan Zhang so as to encourage him to release Zhang Shi De.

But Zhu Yuan Zhang refused to release him. Zhang Shi De was kept in jail and could not do anything. He secretly sent a man to take a letter to Zhang Shi Cheng, asking him to surrender to the Yuan Dynasty. Then he refused to eat anything. Several days later he died of hunger.

By then, Zhang Shi Cheng had been defeated many times. The situation was very unfavorable to him. He had to ask Manzihaiya, who had run away to Pingjiang (now Suzhou, Jiangsu Province) to take shelter with Zhang Shi Cheng after his defeat in Caishi, to write a letter to Dashitemuer, in Hangzhou (in Zhejiang Province) to ask him, as Governor of the Jiangsu-Zhejiang Area of the Yuan Dynasty, to accept his surrender.

Dashitemuer knew that Zhang Shi Cheng was a treacherous and unpredictable man and would change sides frequently. So at first he refused to accept Zhang Shi Cheng's surrender. But Yang Elezhe, the marshal of the troops of the Miao Nationality of the Yuan army under Dashitemuer, tried many times to persuade Dashitemuer to accept Zhang Shi Cheng's surrender. Dashitemuer at last agreed, and he appointed Zhang Shi Cheng as Supreme Official in charge of military affairs in the areas that were under his jurisdiction. So Zhang Shi Cheng changed all the flags to the flags of the Yuan Dynasty; but all the cities, the armies and all the food supplies were still under Zhang Shi Cheng's control.

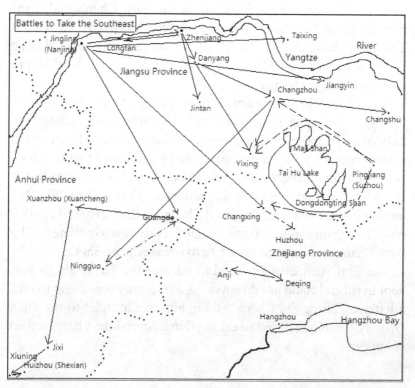

(3) Battles to Take the Cities in Zhejiang Province

Having taken Huizhou, Hu Da Hai commanded an army to attack Wuyuan (in the northwest part of Jiangxi Province). It happened that in August Marshal Yang Elezhe of the troops of the Miao Nationality of the Yuan army commanded 100,000 men to march from Hangzhou (in Zhejiang Province), trying to recover Huizhou. Deng Yu had only recently taken the city, and the defensive installations were not yet completed. Hu Da Hai had commanded part of the army to go and attack Wuyuan, so the force defending Huizhou was week. When the Yuan army arrived, Deng Yu inspired the soldiers to defend the city resolutely and he ordered the gate guards of the four gates of the city to open wide the gates. Marshal Yang Elezhe suspected that Deng Yu was playing some tricks. He hesitated and did not dare to issue the order to storm the city. Hu Da Hai got this information outside the city of Wuyuan. He immediately commanded his troops to hurry back to Huizhou day and night. When the troops under Hu Da Hai arrived, Deng Yu commanded the troops to attack the Yuan army from inside the city and Hu Da Hai commanded the troops to attack the Yuan army from outside the city. The Yuan army was attacked from the front and from the back and was disastrously defeated. Yang Elezhe ran away. The generals under him were killed or captured.

After the Yuan army attacking Huizhou had been defeated, Hu Da Hai commanded an army to take Wuyuan. On 1 September 1357 Wang Tong, a marshal of the Yuan army, had a quarrel with Temuerbuhua, the general of the Yuan army defending Wuyuan. Wang Tong came out of the city to surrender to Hu Da Hai. On 11 January 1358 Deng Yu led a great army to attack the city of Wuyuan. Temuerbuhua came out to fight but was killed in battle. 3,000 Yuan troops surrendered. Then Hu Da Hai took the city of Wuyuan.

In February 1358 Zhu Yuan Zhang appointed Kang Mao Cai, the marshal of the navy, as the Head of the Office of Agriculture. He said to Kang Mao Cai, "Now the war is going on heatedly. Military expenditures are needed urgently. The most important means to solve this problem is the development of agriculture. This is the reason why I have appointed you to this position. You and your subordinates should make an inspection to different places. You should carry out projects of repairing dikes so that the land in the high grounds can be irrigated and the land in low grounds will not be waterlogged.

The most important thing is to make sure that the water can flow properly. An official should consider the interest of the people and should not bring trouble to the people. If the officials build a lot of guesthouses so as to let the officials to stay, that will increase the burden of the people. This will bring great trouble to the people. This will be against my purpose of appointing you to this position." Kang Mao Cai did a good job on this position.

In February 1358 Li Wen Zhong commanded an army to march southward and defeated the troops of the Miao Nationality of the Yuan army in Changhua (now Changhua Town, Lin'an, Zhejiang Province) and then took Chun'an (in Zhejiang Province). On 18 March Deng Yu and Hu Da Hai came from Huizhou to Chun'an to join forces with the army under Li Wen Zhong. Then the troops under Li Wen Zhong, Deng Yu and Hu Da Hai marched to Jiande (in Zhejiang Province). Buha, the general of the Yuan army defending Jiande, ran away. The people of the city of Jiande opened the city gates to welcome the army into the city. Zhu Yuan Zhang appointed Li Wen Zhong as the Commander-in-chief of the armies defending Jiande. On 9 April Yang Elezhe, the marshal of the troops of the Miao Nationality of the Yuan army, commanded over thirty-thousand troops of the Miao Nationality to attack Jiande. They came from Hangzhou on land and by Fuchun Jiang River menacingly. Li Wen Zhong commanded the elite troops to meet the troops of the Miao Nationality marching on land and defeated the troops of the Miao Nationality. Li Wen Zhong ordered the soldiers under him to cut the heads from the dead bodies of the soldiers of the Miao Nationality and put them on a big raft. The big raft with the heads floated on the river. When the soldiers of the Miao Nationality coming on boats by the river saw the terrible sight, they were all scared and ran away. Not long later Yang Elezhe again commanded a great army of the Miao Nationality to attack Jiande. The troops under Li Wen Zhong and the troops under Deng Yu met the troops under Yang Elezhe and defeated them. In these two battles about 30,000 soldiers of the Miao Nationality surrendered. Yang Elezhe retreated to Wulongling Mountain (situated to the northeast of Jiande, Zhejiang Province) and stationed his army there. A month later Li Wen Zhong defeated Yang Elezhe, who raced back to Hangzhou.

The people of the Miao Nationality lived in the areas of what are now Hunan Province and Guangxi Zhuang Autonomous Region. By the end of the Yuan Dynasty, rebellions rose in the areas of the Yangtze River and Huai River. The Yuan armies were frequently defeated. Some officials of the court of the Yuan Dynasty suggested to the Emperor that the troops of the Miao Nationality could be used to suppress the rebellions. So the troops of the Miao Nationality were summoned to the area of what is now Zhejiang Province. The troops of the Miao Nationality defeated Zhang Shi Chang's army in the area of Jiaxing (in the northeast part of Zhejiang Province) and Hangzhou. But the soldiers of the Miao Nationality were cruel. They killed innocent people and sometimes when they took a place, they killed all the people there. The people suffered a lot. After Zhang Shi Cheng surrendered to the Yuan Dynasty, he hated Yang Elezhe and wanted to have him killed. Dashitemuer, the Governor of Jiangsu-Zhejiang Area of the Yuan Dynasty, also disliked him. So they secretly planned to get rid of Yang Elezhe. In August 1358 Zhang Shi Cheng was taking a great army to attack Hangzhou when Yang Elezhe came up the city wall to resist the attack. Ten days later Yang Elezhe was exhausted and he had run out of food. Yang Elezhe committed suicide by hanging himself to death. Zhang Shi Cheng took Hangzhou and Jiaxing. Dashitemuer was still the Governor of Zhejiang Province, but actually he had no power.

In September 1358 Yuan Cheng, Jiang Ying and Liu Zhen, the generals under Yang Elezhe, led their Miao soldiers to surrendered to Li Wen Zhong. They told Li Wen Zhang that Li Fu, one of their generals with 30,000 soldiers of the Miao Nationality, was in Tonglu (in Zhejiang Province) near Jiande and they said that Li Fu also wanted to surrender. After asking permission from Zhu Yuan Zhang, Li Wen Zhang personally went to Tonglu to accept Li Fu's surrender. Jiang Ying, Liu Zhen and Li Fu were put under Hu Da Hai's command.

In October 1358 Zhu Yuan Zhang sent Hu Da Hai to take an army to attack Lanxi (in Zhejiang Province). On 7 October Hu Da Hai captured Lanxi. He left some troops to defend the city and he himself took command of the main force attacking Wuzhou (now Jinhua, Zhejiang Province). When Hu Da Hai and his troops reached Wuzhou, they started a fierce attack. But the Yuan army defending it fought resolutely. Hu Da Hai attacked Wuzhou for a month but could not take the city.

When Xu Da attacked Yixing (now Yixing, Jiangsu Province) in July 1357, he could not take the city. Zhu Yuan Zhang sent an envoy to tell him, "Although Yixing is not a big city, it is a strong city. It cannot be taken quickly. I hear that the estuary of Tai Hu Lake is situated to the west of the city. It is an important route for the transportation of food supplies for Zhang Shi Cheng's army in Yixing. If you send troops to cut the supply route, the troops defending Yixing will run out of food. By that time you may attack Yixing and you are surely to win." And Xu Da sent Commander Ding De Xing to lead some troops to block the estuary of Tai Hu Lake.

On 9 October 1358 Xu Da successfully took Yixing. In this operation, Liao Yong An commanded the navy taking part in blocking the estuary. After Yixing had been taken, Liao Yong An ordered his forces to enter Tai Hu Lake, but they met Zhang Shi Cheng's army led by General Lü Zhen. Liao Yong An's ship ran aground and he was captured. Zhang Shi Cheng knew that Liao Yong An was a capable and brave man, good at naval battles. He wanted to persuade him to surrender, but Liao Yong An refused resolutely. Zhang Shi Cheng would not kill him and just detained him in Suzhou.

Zhu Yuan Zhang tried to exchange Liao Yong An for 3,000 of Zhang Shi Cheng's soldiers who had been captured. But Zhang Shi Cheng refused because he had asked Zhu Yuan Zhang to release his younger brother Zhang Shi De and Zhu Yuan Zhang had refused. Zhang Shi Cheng held Liao Yong An for eight years and at last he died in Suzhou. Later Zhu Yuan Zhang made him King of Chu posthumously.

On 30 November 1358 Zhu Yuan Zhang called Xu Da back to Yingtian from Yixing. He ordered him and Li Shan Chang to defend Yingtian. Zhu Yuan Zhang personally commanded Chang Yu Chun and Yang Jing, the commander of his Guard Army, to march south with 100,000 officers and men to take Wuzhou. The great army passed Ningguo (in Anhui Province) and Huizhou (now Shexian, Anhui Province). In Huizhou, Deng Yu recommended Zhu Sheng, an old Confucian scholar, to Zhu Yuan Zhang. Zhu Yuan Zhang summoned the scholar and had a talk with him. He asked, "What should I do to bring peace to the whole realm?" Zhu Sheng answered, "You should strengthen your military force and make good preparation for war;

you should develop agricultural production and accumulate a lot of food supplies; you should postpone proclaiming yourself a king." Zhu Yuan Zhang was grateful and accepted his suggestions readily. He placed Zhu Sheng in the position of a high level   advisor and often asked him for advice.

In December 1358 Zhu Yuan Zhang reached Lanxi (now Lanxi, Zhejiang Province). Wang Zong Xian, a man of Hezhou, was a Confucian scholar who lived in Yanzhou (now in the southwest part of Zhejiang Province) to evade war turmoil. Hu Da Hai recommended Wang Zong Xian to Zhu Yuan Zhang as a man of virtue and had profound knowledge. Zhu Yuan Zhang summoned Wang Zong Xian to Lanxi. When Wang Zong Xian arrived, Zhu Yuan Zhang was very glad. He sent Wang Zong Xian to Wuzhou to get information about the place. Wang Zong Xian went to the home of Wu Shi Jie, one of his acquaintances, which was about three kilometers away from the city of Wuzhou. Wu Shi Jie told Wang Zong Xian that there were disagreements among the generals of the army defending the city. Wang Zong Xian hurried back to Lanxi to report this important information to Zhu Yuan Zhang, who said happily, "When I take Wuzhou I will appoint you Governor."

At that time, Shimo Yi Sun, a senior official of the Court of the Yuan Dynasty, was the Commander-in-chief of the Yuan army defending Chuzhou (now Lishui, Zhejiang Province). His younger brother Shimo Hou Sun was one of the generals defending Wuzhou. His mother was staying in Wuzhou with his younger brother. When Shimo Yi Sun heard that Zhu Yuan Zhang had reached Lanxi and was ready to attack Wuzhou, he became very worried. He said with tears in his eyes, "The most important things for a man are loyalty and filial piety. He must be loyal to his emperor and filial to his mother. If he takes salary from his emperor but does not render services to his emperor, he is not loyal to his emperor. If his mother is in great danger but he does not go to save her, he is not filial. If a man is neither loyal to his emperor nor filial to his mother, how can he live in this world?" He made up his mind to go and do what he could to help Wuzhou. He discussed this matter with Hu Shen and Zhang Yi, two of his staff members. They decided to have several hundred chariots made, and Shimo Yi Sun ordered Hu Shen to take an army to Wuzhou by chariot. He himself took 10,000 officers and men by the route to Jinyun (now situated to the northeast of Lishui, Zhejiang Province) in coordination with the troops going by chariot.

In mid December 1358 the chariot troops of the Yuan army under Hu Shen reached Songxi (southeast of Jinhua, Zhejiang Province). Zhu Yuan Zhang said to his generals, "The troops defending Wuzhou are expecting the reinforcement troops sent by Shimo Yi Sun. This is the reason why they are so resolute. There are mountains in the area of Songxi. The roads through the mountains are narrow. It will be very difficult for the chariots to get through this area. If I send some elite troops to lay an ambush there, the chariots will be stopped. If the reinforcements are defeated, it will be easy for us to take Wuzhou."

The next day Zhu Yuan Zhang sent Hu De Shen, Hu Da Hai's adopted son, to the place southeast to the city of Wuzhou to lure the chariot troops astray. That morning Hu Shen saw a black stream of air rising in the northwest sky and a white stream of air rising in the southeast sky. Very soon the two air currents met and the black stream covered the white one. Hu Shen knew that it was a bad omen. But he was afraid that the troops would be scared. So he said to his troops, "Today we saw two streams of air fighting against each other. It is a good omen. If we go to battle, we will win!" The chariot troops moved forward with great difficulty. They suddenly met Hu De Shen's troops and fell into the ambush and were totally destroyed. Hu Shen escaped. No reinforcements were coming. Wuzhou was isolated.

Tiemuliesi, the commander defending Wuzhou, sent his generals to defend different parts of the city. But there were disagreements among them all. Ning An Qing, the deputy commanding general, sent Li Xiang, an officer under Ning An Qing, to steal out of the city wall by rope and basket. Li Xiang went to the camps of Zhu Yuan Zhang's army and saw the leader. He told Zhu Yuan Zhang that Ning An Qing wanted to surrender and that Ning An Qing would open the city gate to let his army into the city. Zhu Yuan Zhang accepted their surrender. On 20 December 1358 Zhu Yuan Zhang ordered his army to attack Wuzhou. Ning An Qing opened the city gate and let Zhu Yuan Zhang's army into the city. The generals defending Wuzhou were panic stricken. Very soon Tiemuliesi and Shimo Hou Sun were captured. After Zhu Yuan Zhang entered the city, he issued orders to prohibit his troops from looting, so the people of Wuzhou lived in peace. The day before Zhu Yuan Zhang attacked the city of Wuzhou, the people of Wuzhou had seen a five-colored cloud in the sky over the west of the city. They were very surprised. After Zhu Yuan Zhang had entered the city, people understood that it was the place where Zhu Yuan Zhang's army was camped.

Zhu Yuan Zhang changed the name of Wuzhou to Jinhua. He appointed Wang Zong Xian as Governor. Then he summoned the Confucian scholars in different prefectures to Jinhua. These Confucian scholars were: Xu Yuan, Hu Han, Wang Zhong Shan, Li Gong Chang, Jin Xin, Xu Zi, Tong Ji, Dai Liang, Wu Lü, Sun Lü, Zhang Qi Jing and Wu Shen, thirteen in all. Every day Zhu Yuan Zhang convoked them all in his office to have lunch. After lunch he asked two of them to give a talk on strategies for bringing peace to the realm and giving the people peace and security.

Zhu Yuan Zhang heard that Fan Zu Gan and Ye Yi were known for their profound knowledge and both of them were in Jinhua. Zhu Yuan Zhang summoned them too. Fan Zu Gan came to see Zhu Yuan Zhang with the book of "The Great Learning", one the great doctrines of the Confucius School. Zhu Yuan Zhang asked Fan Zu Gan to analyze the principles of the book, and Fan Zu Gan gave him a detailed explanation. Zhu Yuan Zhang highly praised him for his profound knowledge. Then he appointed Fan Zu Gan and Ye Yi as his advisors. Zhu Yuan Zhang ordered Wang Zong Xian, the Governor of Jinhua, to establish a school. He invited Ye Yi and Song Lian, a Confucian scholar with profound learning in Jinhua, to be lecturers on "Five Classics" (including "Classics of Change", "Classics of Poetry", "Classics of Rites", "Classics of History" and "Spring and Autumn Annals"). Since the war began, all the schools had been shut down. Now when the people heard the sound of the students reading books aloud, they were very happy.

Having taken Wuzhou, Zhu Yuan Zhang intended to take the other prefectures in the east part of Zhejiang Province. On 12 January 1359 he gathered all the generals and told them, "When we attack a city, we use fierce military force. But after we have taken a city, we must pacify the people with benevolence. When my armies entered Jinling, they did not do any harm to the people. So the city of Jinling was stabilized in a very short time. Now we have just taken Wuzhou. We must do our best to bring tranquility to the city so that the people will come back to their homes happily. When the people in the prefectures which have not yet been taken hear about this, they will be longing for our armies to come. When I get the news that you have taken a city or a prefecture and have not killed innocent people, I am extremely happy. It is a virtue for a commander not to kill people freely. It will be beneficial to the country and will also bring good fortune to your descendents."

In January 1359 Xu Yuan, a Confucian scholar in Leping (in Jiangxi Province), came to see Zhu Yuan Zhang. He told him, "Now the Yuan Dynasty is falling. The whole realm is in great chaos. Only the man with great talent and bold vision can control people of great talent. Only the man with great understanding can solicit people with great ability. You are now doing your best to pacify the realm and let the people live in tranquility. The only way to succeed is to solicit people with outstanding ability to come to your service." Zhu Yuan Zhang said, "Now the whole realm is in great chaos and the people suffering. I am now seeking people with great ability eagerly. I am now asking for their advices so as to pacify the whole realm." Xu Yuan said, "Then it will not be difficult for you to bring peace to the whole realm." Zhu Yuan Zhang appointed Xu Yuan as a senior advisor. Not long later Zhu Yuan Zhang appointed Xu Yuan as the Governor of Taiping (now Dangtu, Anhui Province) because Taiping was strategically important.

On 20 May 1359 Zhu Yuan Zhang was leaving Wuzhou to go back to Yingtian. He summoned Hu Da Hai to his office and said to him, "Wuzhou is a strategically important place in the east part of Zhejiang. I have appointed you as the Commander-in-chief of the army defending Wuzhou because you are a man of great ability. Boyanbuhua, the general of the Yuan army, is defending Quzhou. He is a man full of stratagems. Shimo Yi Sun is defending Chuzhou. He is a man of strategy. Shaoxing is occupied by Lü Zhen, a general under Zhang Shi Cheng. Quzhou, Chuzhou and Shaoxing are not far from Wuzhou. You should work in concert with Chang Yu Chun. When the chance comes, you should seize the opportunity to take these prefectures. Boyanbuhua, Shimo Yi Sun and Lü Zhen are powerful enemies. You should not take them lightly." Hu Da Hai took Zhu Yuan Zhang's advice readily. On that day Zhu Yuan Zhang left Wuzhou and he reached Yingtian on 1 June.

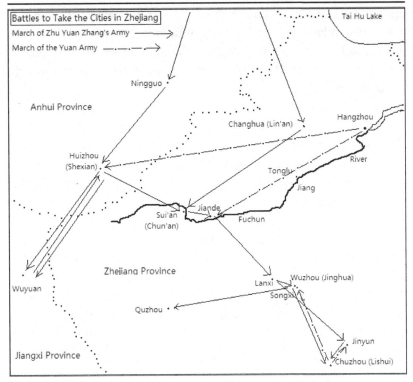

In September 1359 Chang Yu Chun commanded an army in attacking Quzhou. He ordered the soldiers to build wooden fences to surround the six gates of the city. He also ordered soldiers to build wooden towers on wheels, long wooden bridges, long wooden ladders as tall as the city wall, and hooks with long ropes. After these assault devices had been built, Chang Yu Chun ordered the soldiers to push them to the foot of the city wall. The soldiers were ready to climb up the wall using these devices. Chang Yu Chun also ordered the soldiers to dig a tunnel under the west gate. Then Chang Yu Chun ordered the soldiers to attack.

Boyanbuhua, the Yuan Commander-in-chief defending Quzhou, did his best to defend the city. He ordered his soldiers to take many bundles of dry reeds to the top of the city wall, spray them with oil and light them on fire. Then the soldiers threw the burning reeds down onto the wooden towers and bridges of the assault troops. All the equipment caught fire and burned away. The soldiers under Chang Yu Chun put long ladders to the city wall and climbed up. Some of the soldiers threw the hooks to the city top and climbed up using these ropes. Boyanbuhua ordered his soldiers to cut the long wooden ladders and the ropes with long-handled axes. He also ordered soldiers to dig deep ditches along the inner city wall at the west gate to prevent Chang Yu Chun's soldiers from entering through the underground tunnel.

Thus Chang Yu Chun's attack was not successful. He had to think of another way to take Quzhou. On 17 September 1359, Chang Yu Chun sent a detachment to launch a surprise attack on the barbican of the south gate of Quzhou and they seized it. His soldiers destroyed the cannons in that place. Then the main force began to attack the city fiercely. Zhang Bin, the deputy commander-in-chief of the Yuan army defending Quzhou understood that they could not resist such a fierce attack. He sent an envoy out of the city secretly to tell Chang Yu Chun that he would surrender, and that night he opened the west gate to let Chang Yu Chun's army into the city. Boyanbuhua did not know that the situation had changed and he continued to lead his officers and men in resisting the attack. Suddenly fire broke out. Chang Yu Chun had already sent his army into the city. The Yuan troops were defeated and ran away. Very soon Boyanbuhua was captured and Chang Yu Chun took the city of Quzhou. Zhu Yuan Zhang promoted Chang Yu Chun to the Privy Council. He appointed Wang Kai Commander-in-chief of the Quzhou defense army. Then Chang Yu Chun left Quzhou and went back to Wuzhou.

When Zhu Yuan Zhang reached Lanxi with a great force of men and was ready to attack in December 1358, Geng Zai Cheng was head of the vanguard troops. Zhu Yuan Zhang had him take his troops to Huanglongshan Mountain in Jinyun (now in Zhejiang Province) to prevent the enemy troops from reinforcing Wuzhou and, when the opportunity came, to take Chuzhou (now Lishui, Zhejiang Province).

Huanglongshan Mountain was a steep mountain with precipices on all four sides. Geng Zai Cheng had his soldiers build wooden fences along the top of the mountain so as to cut the path of anyone attempting to come through. When enemy troops came, Geng Zai Cheng defeated them all.

Shimo Yi Sun, the Commander-in-chief of the Yuan army defending Chuzhou, had Marshal Ye Shen station his army in Taohualing Mountain (between Lishui and Jinyun, Zhejiang Province); he had Lin Bin Zu, a staff officer, station his army in Gedu (now in the southern part of Lishui, Zhejiang Province); he had Commander Chen Shen Zhen station his army in Fanling Mountain (now in Wuyi, Zhejiang Province); he had Marshal Hu Shen defend Longquan (in Zhejiang Province). At that time the Yuan army officers and men were in very low spirits and did not have the resolution to fight.

In November 1359, Marshal Hu Shen of the Yuan army left his men in Longquan and went to Wuzhou to surrender to Hu Da Hai. He told Hu Da Hai that the Yuan troops defending Chuzhou were very weak and Chuzhou could be taken easily. Then Hu Da Hai sent his army to Fanling Mountain. Geng Zai Cheng took his troops, too, to Fanling from Huanglongshan Mountain to join forces with Hu Da Hai. Then they attacked the Yuan troops stationed in Fanling Mountain and defeated them. Geng Zai Cheng and Hu Da Hai commanded their troops to attack Yuan army camps in Taohualing Mountain and in Gedu. They defeated the Yuan army and took their camps. Then they had their troops to march to the foot the Chuzhou city wall. On 13 November Shimo Yi Sun commanded the Yuan army to go out of the city to fight. The Yuan army was defeated. Shimo Yi Sun fled. Geng Zai Cheng and Hu Da Hai took over. Zhu Yuan Zhang appointed Geng Zai Cheng as the commander-in-chief of the army defending Chuzhou. Soon after, Shimo Yi Sun collected the defeated Yuan soldiers and came back trying to recover Chuzhou. Geng Zai Cheng and his troops fought Shimo Yi Sun and Shimo Yi Sun was killed in battle.

(4) Liu Ji Comes to Assist Zhu Yuan Zhang

Hu Da Hai recommended Liu Ji, Song Lian, Zhang Yi and Ye Shen to Zhu Yuan Zhang. He told him that these four men were virtuous and capable men. In December 1359 Zhu Yuan Zhang sent an envoy to Wuzhou to invite them to Yingtian and in March 1360 they arrived. Zhu Yuan Zhang was very glad to see them. He offered them seats and said politely, "I have asked you to condescend to undertake a long journey here only for the benefit of the people."

Then he talked with them about the doctrines of Confucius School and the situation of that time and history. Liu Ji was a man of profound learning. Since he was young he had read books on astronomy, the art of war, and the theoretical basis of law. One day when he was making a tour of the West Lake (now in Hangzhou, Zhejiang Province) with some friends, a colored cloud rose in the northwestern sky. His friends said that was a cloud of celebration and they were ready to compose poems. But Liu Ji said, "This is an emperor's stream of air. In ten years an emperor will ascend the throne in Jinling. I will assist him."

At that time Hangzhou was still under the strict rule of the Yuan Dynasty. When his friends heard Liu Ji's words they were all very scared and thought that Liu Ji was a lunatic. Nobody knew how able a man Liu Ji was, only Zhao Tian Ze, a man from the Western Shu (now the western part of Sichuan Province), understood him. He compared him to Zhuge Liang, the most capable strategist in the period of "Three Kingdoms" (220–280).

A friend said to Liu Ji, "Now the whole realm is in great chaos. You are a man of great talent and ability. You may organize an army and take Wuzhou. You may pacify the areas of Zhejiang Province and Fujian Province. You will be able to take the areas south to the Yangtze River. You can be the king of these areas." Liu Ji said, "I hate Fang Guo Zhen and Zhang Shi Cheng very much. If I adopt your suggestion, then what is the difference between them and me? Heaven has appointed an emperor. You just wait and see." When Zhu Yuan Zhang took Wuzhou (now Jinhua, Zhejiang Province) and pacified the areas of Zhejiang Province, Liu Ji pointed at the sky and said to his friends, "Zhu Yuan Zhang has been granted the power by Heaven. This cannot be done just by human power." So when Zhu Yuan Zhang's envoy came to invite Liu Ji to Yingtian, he immediately accepted the invitation and went to Yingtian. When he saw Zhu Yuan Zhang, he presented "Eighteen Policies Adopted to Pacify the Whole Realm" to him. Zhu Yuan Zhang was very pleased to accept these eighteen policies and later he acted on them. The main points were: the man with great virtue would gain the power to rule over the whole realm; seize the opportunity to pacify the southeast part of China while Han Lin Er, Liu Fu Tong and the red scarf army were fighting the Mongolian Yuan army in Central China; avoid being the target of the Mongolian Yuan army; Yingtian should be the capital; first defeat Chen You Liang and defeat Zhang Shi Cheng later; reduce taxes and levies and the burden of the people so as to gain the support of the people, etc.

At that time Han Lin Er had proclaimed himself Emperor of the State of Song. He appointed Zhu Yuan Zhang as Left Deputy Marshal and Zhu Yuan Zhang accepted the appointment. So now he was regarded as a subordinate of Han Lin Er. On 1 January 1361 the head of the Department of Rites put a throne for Han Lin Er in a hall and asked Zhu Yuan Zhang and the officials to kneel down before the throne and chant congratulatory greetings to Han Lin Er.

Liu Ji was furious and said, "Han Lin Er is only a silly shepherd boy. Why should I pay respects to him?" He refused to kneel down and chant congratulatory greetings to the throne for Han Lin Er. Zhu Yuan Zhang summoned Liu Ji to his office and asked him why he had refused to pay respects to Han Lin Er. Liu Ji said, "Heaven has appointed you as the emperor." Zhu Yuan Zhang recognized that this was a man of foresight. Then he asked Liu Ji for plans to pacify the whole realm. Liu Ji said, "Zhang Shi Cheng is engaged in defending the areas he has already occupied, so there is no need to worry about him. Chen You Liang has put his master Xu Shou Hui under his control. He has occupied the areas along the upper reach of the Yangtze River. He is trying his best to conquer us. We must deal with him first. If Chen You Liang is defeated, Zhang Shi Cheng will be isolated and can be easily defeated. Then we can order our armies to march north to Central China and take that area. In this way your great cause of bringing peace to the whole realm will be completed. Then you may ascend the throne of an emperor." Hearing Liu Ji's words, Zhu Yuan Zhang was very pleased and said, "If you think of any good plans, just tell me."

2. Zhu Yuan Zhang Pacifies the State of Han

(1) Chen You Liang Proclaims Himself Emperor of Han

Xu Shou Hui, the Emperor of the Tianwan Dynasty, was in Hanyang (now Wuhan City, Hubei Province). He was under the control of Premier Ni Wen Jun. In September 1357 Ni Wen Jun tried to murder Xu Shou Hui but failed. Ni Wen Jun had to flee to Huangzhou (now in Hubei Province). At that time Chen You Liang, an enemy of Ni Wen Jun, commanded his troops to make a surprise attack on Ni Wen Jun and they killed him. Chen You Liang put Ni Wen Jun's army under his own command. In this way Chen You Liang became the most powerful man in the Tianwan Dynasty. He proclaimed himself premier of the Tianwan Dynasty. Xu Shou Hui could do nothing about him.

In October 1357 Chang Yu Chun, Liao Yong An and Wu Zhen commanded their troops to take Chizhou (now Guichi, Anhui Province) from Tongling (now Tongling, Anhui Province). Zhu Yuan Zhang ordered Li Wen Zhong to lead an army to march on land to Chizhou to support them by coordinated action. On 2 October 1357 when Li Wen Zhong's army was five kilometers away from the city of Chizhou, Chang Yu Chun, Liao Yong An and Wu Zhen arrived at the foot of the city wall of Chizhou by ship along the Yangtze River. Then all the troops by water and by land attacked Chizhou fiercely. The battle began in the morning and by noon the troops took the north gate of the city. They broke into the city by the north gate and captured Marshal Hong, the commander-in-chief of the army of the Tianwan Dynasty defending Chizhou. Marshal Hong was executed. They also captured Wei Shou and Xu Tian Hong, the deputy commanders-in-chief of the army of the Tianwan Dynasty defending Chizhou. In the evening Chen You Liang led a great army of more than one hundred warships in attacking Chizhou. Chang Yu Chun and the other generals commanded their troops to fight bravely and defeated Chen You Liang's army.

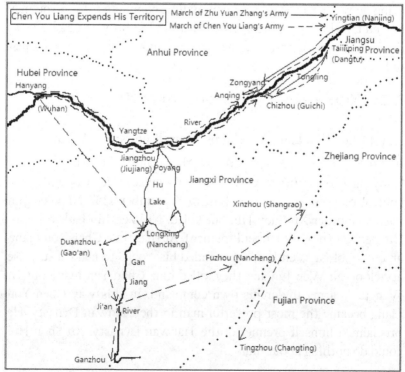

In January 1358 Chen You Liang commanded an army to attack Anqing (in Anhui Province) which was situated by the northern bank of the Yangtze River. Yu Jue, the Governor of the Huainan Province of the Yuan Dynasty, defended the city resolutely. He used Xiaogu Shan Mountain (now Xiaogu Shan Mountain, sixty-five kilometers southeast to Susong, Anhui Province), an island situated in the Yangtze River, as a natural protection for Anqing. He sent Hubayan, a marshal of the Yuan army, to command the naval troops to defend Xiaogu Shan Mountain. Chen You Liang's army came by warships from the upper reach of the Yangtze River. Hubayan commanded his naval troops to fight against Chen You Lian's army for four days and four nights, but at last he was defeated and ran back to Anqing. On 7 January 1358 Chen You Liang's army reached Anqing and started a fierce attack on the city. Chen You Liang sent Zhao Pu Sheng to attack the east gate, Zhu Kou to attack the south gate and he himself attacked the west gate. Chen You Liang's troops surrounded the city wall and attacked the city fiercely. At noon the city of Anqing fell. Fire rose everywhere in the city. Yu Jue knew that he could not save the city and he killed himself with his own sword.

Having taken Anqing, Chen You Liang sent Zhao Pu Sheng to take Zongyang (in Anhui Province). Zhao Pu Sheng was originally one of the leaders in Chao Hu Lake (in the same province). In May 1355 Zhao Pu Sheng and the other leaders such as Liao Yong An, Liao Yong Zhong, Yu Ting Yu and Yu Tong Hai in Chao Hu Lake submitted themselves to Zhu Yuan Zhang. But when Zhu Yuan Zhang was leading the boats across the Yangtze River, Zhao Pu Sheng betrayed him and ran off. He first joined the Yuan army. Then he went to join Xu Shou Hui and became a general under Chen You Liang. Zhao Pu Sheng was a fierce fighter. He used two broadswords in battle. On 1 April 1358 Chen You Liang sent Zhao Pu Sheng to attack Chizhou (now Guichi, Anhui Province) from Zongyang. Liu You Ren, the general defending Taiping (now Dangtu, Anhui Province) learned that Zhao Pu Sheng was attacking Chizhou, he commanded his troops to hurry to reinforce Chizhou, but he met the enemies near Chizhou and was killed in battle. Zhao Zhong, the general defending Chizhou, fought bravely but was killed in battle.

Then Zhao Pu Sheng took Chizhou. Having taken Chizhou, Zhao Pu Sheng assigned a general under him to defend Chizhou. In

May 1358 Chen You Liang took Longxing (now Nanchang, Jiangxi Province), Duanzhou (now Gao'an, Jiangxi Province), Ji'an (now in Jiangxi Province) and Fuzhou (now Nancheng, Jiangxi Province). In September 1358 Chen You Liang took Ganzhou (now in the southern part of Jiangxi Province), Xinzhou (now Shangrao, Jiangxi Province), Tingzhou (now Changting, Fujian Province) and Quzhou (now in Zhejiang Province). From then on the most part of Jiangxi Province was under Chen You Liang's control.

In March 1359 Chen You Liang sent Zhao Pu Sheng to attack Taiping (now Dangtu, Anhui Province). Hu Wei Xian, the Commander-in-chief of Zhu Yuan Zhang's army defending Taiping, sent General Cheng Yun and General Wang Bing to lead their troops against the troops under Zhao Pu Sheng and defeated them. They captured 27,500 bushels of grain. Zhao Pu Sheng dashed back to Zongyang. He established his camps by the banks of the Yangtze River to defend Zongyang. At that time Zhu Yuan Zhang concentrated his army to take the areas in Zhejiang Province. He was worried that Zhao Pu Sheng would attack Taiping and Yingtian when the defense of the areas in the lower reach of the Yangtze River was weak. In April 1359 he sent Xu Da and Yu Tong Hai with a naval force to sail up the Yangtze River to attack Zhao Pu Sheng in Zongyang. The army under Xu Da and Yu Tong Hai destroyed Zhao Pu Sheng's camps by the riverside. Zhao Pu Sheng gave up all his warships and fled to Anqing by land. Xu Da's army captured many big warships. On 11 April 1359 Xu Da and Yu Tong Hai recovered Chizhou. When Zhu Yuan Zhang got the news that Xu Da and Yu Tong Hai had taken Zongyang and recovered Chizhou, he was very glad. He promoted Xu Da to the rank of the Grand General and he appointed Yu Tong Hai as a member of the Privy Council.

In August 1359 Zhu Yuan Zhang sent Xu Da and Zhang De Sheng to command their troops to attack Anqing (now in Anhui Province). The troops under Xu Da and Zhang De Sheng took ships to sail up the Yangtze River. They landed in Wuwei (in Anhui Province). They reached Fushan (Fushan Mountain within Zongyang, Anhui Province) at night. They attacked the camps of Zhao Pu Sheng's army in Fushan. Commander Hu, the general under Zhao Pu Sheng, was defeated and ran away. Xu Da and Zhang De Sheng commanded their troops to pursue the defeated enemy to the area of Qianshan (now

Qianshan, Anhui Province). Guo Tai, a general under Chen You Liang commanded an army to meet the troops under Xu Da and Zhang De Sheng. Guo Tai's army was defeated and Guo Tai was killed. On 3 September 1359 Xu Da and Zhang De Sheng took Qianshan.

In September 1359 Zhu Yuan Zhang sent Yu Ting Yu to attack Anqing. Yu Ting Yu commanded his army to attack Anqing but could not take it. Yu Ting Yu was killed in battle while attacking the city of Anqing. The generals under Zhu Yuan Zhang were worried. Zhu Yuan Zhang said, "Zhao Pu Sheng is really a fierce fighter but he is not resourceful. Chen You Liang is arrogant and highhanded. He holds grudges against his subordinates who have better ability and have made great contributions to the realm. Let us plan to drive a wedge between Chen You Ling and Zhao Pu Sheng. Then it will be easy for us to take Anqing." Zhao Pu Sheng had a hanger-on. This hanger-on often provided tactics and strategies for Zhao Pu Sheng and enjoyed his trust. Zhu Yuan Zhang sent a man to make friends with this hanger-on. After that this man wrote a letter to this hanger-on but pretended to have mistakenly sent this letter to Zhao Pu Sheng. Having read the letter Zhao Pu Sheng suspected that this hanger-on had colluded with Zhu Yuan Zhang. This hanger-on felt that he was under suspicion and was very afraid. Then he deserted and turned himself over to Zhu Yuan Zhang. He told Zhu Yuan Zhang everything about Zhao Pu Sheng, including many of Zhao Pu Sheng's secrets. Then Zhu Yuan Zhang rewarded him richly and sent him to Jiangzhou (now Jiujiang, Jiangxi Province) to see Chen You Liang. The hanger-on told Chen You Liang all the secrets of Zhao Pu Sheng. Cheng You Liang was already very angry with Zhao Pu Sheng when Zhao Pu Sheng lost Qianshan. When he heard all his secrets, he was furious. He suspected that Zhao Pu Sheng was planning to betray him.

Chen You Liang sent an envoy to Zhao Pu Zheng in Anqing. Zhao Pu Zheng did not have the slightest idea that Chen You Liang already hated him very much. When he saw the envoy, he was immensely proud and told the envoy all the contributions he had made for Chen You Liang. This made Cheng You Liang angrier with Zhao Pu Sheng and he made up his mind to get rid of him. He sent an envoy to tell Zhao Pu Sheng that he would go to Anqing. On 5 September 1359 Chen You Liang arrived at Anqing from Jiangzhou by ship. Zhao Pu Sheng came out of the city to the riverside with a roasted goat to welcome Chen You Liang. But when Zhao Pu Sheng went up the ship, he was arrested and executed immediately. Chen You Liang put all the officers and men originally under Zhao Pu Shen under his own command.

When Chen You Liang took Longxing (now Nanchang, Jiangxi Province) in May 1358, Xu Shou Hui, the Emperor of the Tianwan Dynasty, wanted to move his capital from Hanyang to Longxing. In December 1359 he told Chen You Liang his intention to move the capital. Chen You Liang did not like this idea because if Xu Shou Hui came to Longxing (which was not far from Jiangzhou), he would be a threat to him. So Chen You Liang rejected Xu Shou Hui's plan. But Xu Shou Hui insisted on it. In December 1359, he ordered all the troops to start from Hanyang and sail down the Yangtze River to Jiangzhou. Chen You Liang ordered his soldiers to lay an ambush inside the city of Jiangzhou. He went out of the city gate to welcome Xu Shou Hui, and when Xu Shou Hui and all his followers had entered the city, Chen You Liang's soldiers shut the gate. Xu Shou Hui and his followers fell into the ambush inside the city. Xu Shou Hui was arrested and detained in Jiangzhou and the rest were all killed. Then Chen You Liang proclaimed himself King of the State of Han.

Since Zhao Pu Sheng had been killed by Chen You Liang, the defense of Zongyang was weak. In April 1360 Xu Da and Chang Yu Chun occupied the camps of Zongyang by the riverside. Chen You Liang took a great army to reinforce Zongyang and declared that he would march his army to Anqing. Chang Yu Chun expected that Chen You Liang would attack Chizhou. He discussed this matter with Xu Da and they made up a plan. They sent the best troops to hide themselves in the forest in Jiuhua Shan Mountain (now Jiuhua Shan Mountain, Anhui Province) which was situated south to Chizhou. They sent the old and weak soldiers to defend the city of Chizhou. On 1 May 1360 Chen You Liang commanding a great army came to Chizhou as expected. He commanded his troops to the foot of the city wall of Chizhou. Chen You Liang's troops attacked the city fiercely. The soldiers defending Chizhou stood on the top of the city wall. They waved flags and beat the drums loudly. At these signals all the troops hiding in the forest in Jiuhua Shan Mountain rushed out from the mountain to attack Chen You Liang's troops. At the same time the soldiers under Xu Da came on boats along the Yangtze River to cut the route of retreat of the troops of Chen You Liang. The soldiers in the city of Chizhou also rushed out to attack Chen You Liang's troops. Chen You Liang's troops were attacked from the front and from the back. They were disastrously defeated. More than 10,000 soldiers of Chen You Liang's army were killed and 3,000 were captured. Chang Yu Chun wanted to kill all of these 3,000 captives. He said to Xu Da, "These 3,000 captives were Chen You Liang's best soldiers. If we don't kill them, they will cause great trouble in the future. If we report this to the Duke of Wu, he will surely spare them." Xu Da disagreed and sent an envoy to Yingtian to report this matter to Zhu Yuan Zhang. Zhu Yuan Zhang said to the envoy, "Go back quickly and tell the generals to stop killing captives. The war has just begun. If we kill them, we shall drive our opponents to fight desperately. These 3,000 captives should be released. They can be used in the future." But Chang Yu Chun had already killed 2,700 captives. Only 300 remained. When Zhu Yuan Zheng heard about this, he was very unhappy and ordered Chang Yu Chun to release them.

In this month Chen You Liang took a great army by warship down the Yangtze River to attack Taiping (now Dangtu, Anhui Province). He took Xu Shou Hui with him. General Hua Yun, a member of the Privy Council and the Commander-in-chief of the army defending Taiping, arranged 3,000 men in battle formation outside the city gate to meet Chen You Liang's troops. Chen You Liang attacked the city for three days and three nights but could not take it. On 1 the second May (1360 was an intercalary year which had two months of May) Chen You Liang ordered his naval soldiers to anchor a huge warship southwest of the city of Taiping while the Yangtze River was at hide tide. The stern of the ship was as tall as the city wall. Chen You Liang's soldiers climbed up the stern and went to the top of the city wall. At that time the troops under Hua Yun had run out of food; they were starving and could not fight. So the city was taken and Hua Yun was captured. Chen You Liang's soldiers tied him up with a rope. Hua Yun shouted angrily at the soldiers who had tied him, "You scoundrels! You have tied me up. My master will punish you and cut you to pieces!" He jumped up with a loud shout and the rope broke. He took the broad sword of the soldier who was guarding him and killed six enemy soldiers with it. Then he shouted, "Chen You Liang is no match for my master. You should surrender now!"

The enemy soldiers were very angry and broke Hua Yun's head. Then they tied him to the mast of a ship and shot him with arrows. Hua Yun was stern and uncompromising. He did not stop condemning the enemy until he was killed by many arrows. He died at the age of thirty-nine. Wang Ding, a member of the Privy Council, and Xu Yuan, the Governor of Taiping appointed by Zhu Yuan Zhang, were also captured. They would not yield to the enemy and were killed.

While Hua Yun was fighting, his wife Lady Gao held her son who was three years old at her breast. She said to a maidservant by the name of Sun, with tears in her eyes, "The city is going to fall into enemy hands. And my husband will surely die for the city. If my husband dies, I will not go on living alone. But we must keep Hua Yun's descendent alive. After I die, you must take good care of this child." When Lady Gao learned that her husband had been captured, she jumped into the water and drowned herself. The maidservant buried Lady Gao, then she took the child and ran away. She came across Chen You Liang's troops and she and the child were brought to Jiujiang (now in Jiangxi Province). One night the maidservant stole out of the camp and ran to the home of a fisherman. She gave all her hair ornaments and earrings to the fisherman and begged him to let them stay in his home.

When Chen You Liang's troops were defeated, the maidservant left the fisherman's home with the child. While she was crossing the Yangtze River, the defeated troops of Chen You Liang took the boat and threw her and the child into the river. It happened that a log floated to them and they hung onto the log and floated to an island surrounded by reeds and lotus. The maidservant gathered lotus seeds to feed the child. They stayed in that place for seven days and seven nights. The child still survived. At midnight the maidservant heard a man talking to her. She woke up and saw an old man standing before her. The old man said that his name was Lei. The maidservant told the old man everything. The old man took them to walk out of that land through the river water. Soon thereafter, the old man brought them to the place where Zhu Yuan Zhang and his troops were. The maidservant, holding the child in her hands, knelt down before Zhu Yuan Zhang and choked with sobs. Zhu Yuan Zhang also shed tears. He put the child on his knees and said with emotion, "This is the son of a great general and he will become a great general too." Zhu Yuan Zhang granted the name of Hua Wei to the child. (Many years later,

Hua Wei really became a great general of the navy.) Then Zhu Yuan Zhang ordered that clothes be given to the old man, but the old man suddenly disappeared. Later Zhu Yuan Zhang made Hua Yun Marquis of Dongqiu Prefecture, Xu Yuan Marquis of Gaoyou Prefecture and Wang Ding Marquis of Taiyuan Prefecture posthumously.

When Chen You Liang attacked Taiping, he took Xu Shou Hui with him. After he had taken Taiping, he planned to kill Xu Shou Hui and proclaim himself emperor. On 3 the second May 1360, when Xu Shou Hui was sitting on a ship on the Yangtze River by Caishi, Chen You Liang sent a general to see him, pretending that he had some important things to report. When the general came before Xu Shou Hui, he struck Xu Shou Hui on the head and killed him. Then Chen You Liang proclaimed himself Emperor of the State of Han. He used Wutong Temple in Caishi as his palace. He appointed Zhou Pu Sheng as Grand Tutor, Zhang Bi Xian as Premier, and Zhang Ding Bian as Minister of War. All his ministers and officials stood by the bank of the Yangtze River and were ready to hold a celebration ceremony. They were to step forward row by row, kneel down in front of Chen You Liang and chant congratulatory greetings to him. But suddenly there was a great rainstorm so the celebration ceremony could not be held. After that Chen You Liang led all his ministers and officials back to Jiangzhou (now Jiujiang, Jiangxi Province).

(2) Chen You Liang Attacks Yingtian

After Chen You Liang had ascended the throne of the State of Han, he sent an envoy to Suzhou (now in Jiangsu Province) to ask Zhang Shi Cheng to act in coordination with him and attack Zhu Yuan Zhang. But Zhang Shi Cheng had been defeated many times by Zhu Yuan Zhang. So when Chen You Liang's envoy came, he hesitated and did not make any promises. But anyway, Chen You Liang decided to carry on the momentum of his victory in Taiping and attack Yingtian, the main city of Zhu Yuan Zhang. On the second of May 1360, Chen You Liang sent a great menacing army eastward on boats along the Yangtze River from Jiangzhou.

When the news came that Chen You Liang was going to attack Yingtian, all the people were shocked. Zhu Yuan Zhang summoned his generals and officials to discuss what to do. Some suggested that they should surrender; some suggested that they should give up the city of Yingtian and head for Zhongshan Mountain (now Zijin Shan Mountain, Nanjing, Jiangsu Province) in the eastern outskirts of Yingtian to defend themselves in the shelter of the mountain.

Liu Ji just sat there and kept his mouth shut with his angry eyes open wide. Zhu Yuan Zhang knew that he would have something to say. So he invited Liu Ji into an inner room and asked him for advice. Liu Ji said, "Those who suggested surrendering and those who suggested running away to Zhongshan Mountain should be killed!" Zhu Yuan Zhang asked, "What do you have in mind?" Liu Ji said, "Chen You Liang is now very proud of himself. When he comes deep into our territory, we may lure his army into an ambush and defeat them. It is easy to do. It is one of Heaven's rules that the one who strikes after his enemy has struck will win. We may wait at ease for the exhausted enemy. We shall surely defeat Chen You Liang. When you have defeated this most formidable enemy, your mighty reputation will spread all over the realm and your great cause of establishing a strong dynasty will be accomplished." At Liu Ji's words, Zhu Yuan Zhang became more resolute.

At this time some generals suggested that they should recover Taiping first so as to restrain Chen You Liang's advance. Zhu Yuan Zhang said, "This will not do. In the past our troops built new fortresses and dug deep ditches in Taiping to prevent attack by Chen You Liang. If Chen You Liang had attacked Taiping by land, he could not have taken the city. He attacked with huge warships and his soldiers climbed up the stern and then up to the top of the city wall. If we go to attack Taiping, we are not going to take the city in a short time. Chen You Liang is at the upper reaches of the river. He has ten times as many warships as we do. If our army is stuck at the foot of Taiping, we will not be able to advance to take the city or to retreat either. Then we will be in a very difficult situation."

Some officials suggested that Zhu Yuan Zhang should personally command a great army to go out of the city to meat Chen You Liang's army. Zhu Yuan Zhang said, "This is not a good idea either. When Chen You Liang hears that I have gone out of the city, he will send a detachment to fight me as a distraction. He himself will command his great navy of warships to sail down the Yangtze River to Yingtian. Chen You Liang's navy will reach Yingtian in half a day. In this case my foot soldiers and cavalrymen would have to cover a distance of over fifty kilometers to hurry back to rescue Yingtian. Everybody knows, it says in the book *On the Art of War* that a general should avoid hurrying to a battlefield from a long distance."

Zhu Yuan Zhang sent his envoy on a fast horse to Wuzhou to tell Hu Da Hai to take his troops and attack Xinzhou (now Shangrao, Jiangxi Province) so as to harass Chen You Liang's rear. He secretly summoned Kang Mao Cai, and he told him, "You were once a very good friend of Chen You Liang. I plan to lure him to change sides. Only you can accomplish this. Why don't you write him a letter and tell him that you are willing to surrender to him and be his planted agent inside my army. You can send some information about my army to deceive him and let his troops come by three routes — so as to reduce the force of his attack." Kang Mao Cai agreed.

At that time Li Shan Chang was standing by their side. He asked, "Just now we were worrying about Chen You Liang coming. Now, why are you planning to persuade him to come earlier?" Zhu Yuan Zhang said, "If we act late, Chen You Liang and Zhang Shi Cheng will cooperate with each other. That will do us greater harm. We will not be able to fend them both off, one from the west and the other from the east. If we defeat Chen You Liang first, Zhang Shi Cheng will think again." Li Shan Chang said, "That's right!"

Kang Mao Cai sent a servant as his envoy to go on a small boat up the Yangtze River to Jiangzhou to deliver the letter written by Kang Mao Cai to Chen You Liang. When Chen You Liang got the letter, he was very glad. He asked the envoy, "Where is Kang Mao Cai now?" The envoy answered, "He is now defending Jiangdong Bridge." Chen You Liang asked, "What kind of bridge is it?" The envoy answered, "It is a wooden bridge." Then Chen You Liang treated the envoy with wine and food. Chen You Liang sent the envoy back. Before the envoy left, Chen You Liang said to him, "Go back and tell Kang Mao Cai, when I reach Jiangdong Bridge, I will shout 'Old Kang' as a signal for Kang Mao Cai to act." The envoy went back to Yingtian and reported everything to Zhu Yuan Zhang. Zhu Yuan Zhang was very glad and said, "Chen You Liang has fallen into my trap." He ordered Li Shan Chang to lead the workmen to dismantle the wooden Jiangdong Bridge and rebuild it as a bridge of iron and stone structure. Jiangdong Bridge was a bridge over the Qin Huai River in the section outside Shuixi Gate (in Nanjing). Li Shan Chang led the workmen to work all through the night and completed the bridge the next morning. Zhu Yuan Zhang ordered Chang Yu Chun to command the 50,000 officers and men under him to hide by the side of Shihui Shan Mountain (now Mufu Shan Mountain, situated by the Yangtze River to the northwest of the city of Nanjing, Jiangsu Province). He ordered Xu Da to arrange his troops in battle formation outside the South Gate (now Zhonghua Gate of the city of Nanjing). He ordered Yang Jing to station his troops in Dasheng Gang (now Dasheng Guan, which is situated 15 kilometer to the southwest of the city of Nanjing). He ordered Zhang De Sheng and Zhu Hu to command the navy to sail to the Yangtze River outside Longjiangguan (now Xiaguan, Nanjing). Zhu Yuan Zhang personally led a great army in Lulong Shan Mountain (now Shizi Shan Mountain, situated by the Yangtze River to the Northwest of the city of Nanjing). He ordered the banner holders to hide the yellow banners on the left side of the mountain and the red banners on the right side of the mountain. He said to the banner holders and all the generals, "When the enemy comes, you hold up the red banners. Then, when you hold up the yellow banners, all our troops hiding in the mountain will come out to attack. All the soldiers should be combat ready."

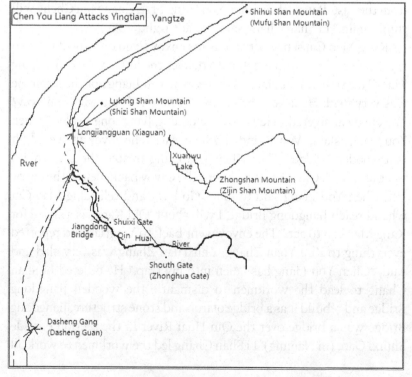

On 10 the second May 1360 Chen You Liang really commanded his great navy to sail eastward down the Yangtze River to Yingtian. He reached Dasheng Gang (now Dasheng Guan, Nanjing). Yang Jing commanded his troops to resist Chen You Liang's troops. The harbor of Dasheng Gang was narrow. It could only accommodate three warships. Then Chen You Liang ordered the naval troops to sail out of Dasheng Guang back to the Yangtze River. Then they sailed along the Yangtze River to the estuary of the Qin Huai River and sailed down the Qin Huai River to Jiangdong Bridge. Chen You Liang found that the bridge was not a wooden bridge but a bridge of iron and stone structure. He was greatly surprised. He shouted loudly, "Old Kang! Old Kang!" But there was no answer. Chen You Liang realized that he had been deceived by Kang Mao Cai. He ordered the ships to sail out of Qin Huai River to Longjiangguan (now in Xiaguan District, Nanjing). He sent 10,000 soldiers to land there and the soldiers erected logs to build a fence to protect their camps. At that time it was summer and it was very hot. Zhu Yuan Zhang's guards erected a big umbrella to shelter Zhu Yuan Zhang from the sun. Zhu Yuan Zhang was wearing purple armor, sitting under the umbrella to supervise his troops. When he saw that the soldiers were sweating under the sun, he ordered his guards to take off the umbrella. When the generals saw that Chen You Liang's troops had come, they wanted to start the battle immediately. Zhu Yuan Zhang said to them, "It is going to rain. Now let our soldiers to have their meal first. We shall attack our enemies when the heavy rain comes." But it was sunny and there were no clouds in the sky. The generals did not believe that a heavy rain would come.

Suddenly a strong wind rose from the northwest and it blew dark clouds over the sky. Very soon it rained heavily. At this moment the red banners were held up. Zhu Yuan Zhang ordered the troops to destroy the fence and the enemy camps. The troops marched forward bravely and destroyed the fence and the enemy camps. Chen You Liang commanded his troops to fight. When the two armies met in battle, the rain stopped. Zhu Yuan Zhang ordered his soldiers to beat the drums. The sound of the drums shook the sky. Then Zhu Yuan Zhang ordered the banner holders to hold up the yellow banners. At this signal, Chang Yu Chun commanded his soldiers hiding by the side of Shihui Shan Mountain to rush out to attack Chen You Liang's troops. Xu Da's men also reached Longjiangguan from the South Gate. The navy under Zhang De Sheng came down the Yangtze River by boat and landed by the shore of Longjiangguan. Chen You Liang's troops were attacked from all sides. They were utterly defeated and escaped in great disorder. Many of them ran to their ships. But the Yangtze River was at low tide and many of the warships became stranded. Many of Chen You Liang's soldiers were killed or were drowned in the Yangtze River. More than 7,000 were captured. Zhu Yuan Zhang's troops captured more than one hundred huge warships and several hundred smaller ones. Chen You Liang escaped by boat. The soldiers searched the warship which Chen You Liang had been on. They found the letter sent by Kang Mao Cai and handed it over to Zhu Yuan Zhang. Zhu Yuan Zhang laughed and said, "What a foolish man Chen You Liang is!" Then he ordered the generals to pursue him.

Zhang De Sheng commanded his navy to pursue Chen You Liang to Cihu (now in Anhui Province). His soldiers burned Chen You Liang's ships. Chen You Liang and his soldiers escaped to Caishi (now in Anhui Province) and there, they deployed in battle formation. Zhang De Sheng attacked but he was trapped and was killed.

Liao Yong Zhong commanded his troops to charge the enemy. Hua Yun Long rode his horse to attack the middle part of the enemy battle formation. General Wang Ming broke into the enemy battle formation. He was wounded by a spear on the face and blood spilled out from his face and dyed his battle garment red but he continued to fight. He fought through the enemy battle formation from the front to the back three times and killed many enemy soldiers. At last the enemy battle formation collapsed and the defeated soldiers ran for their lives in great disorder. Chen You Liang ran away back to Jiangzhou (now Jiujiang, Jiangxi Province).

Carrying on the momentum of the great victory in Yingtian, Xu Da and Chang Yu Chun commanded their troops to attack Taiping (now Dangtu, Anhui Province). The general of Chen You Liang's army defending Taiping got the news that Chen You Liang had been disastrously defeated in Yingtian and was disheartened and did not have the will to fight. Very soon Xu Da and Chang Yu Chun took the city of Taiping. Having taken Taiping, Chang Yu Chun ordered his soldiers to dismantle the southwest part of the city wall because this part of the city wall was just beside the Yangtze River and to rebuild the city wall a distance from the Yangtze River. He ordered the soldiers to build strongholds by the side of the Yangtze River. Chang Yu Chun did all these because when Chen You Liang attacked Taiping on 1 the second May 1360, he ordered his naval solders to anchor a huge warship southwest of the city of Taiping while the Yangtze River was at high tide. The stern of the ship was as tall as the city wall. Chen You Liang's soldiers climbed up the stern and went to the top of the city wall. It was from this part of the city wall that Chen You Liang took Taiping. When this project was completed, the city of Taiping became a strongly defended city and was not easily attacked from the Yangtze River.

In the second May 1360 Hu Da Hai commanded his troops to attack Xinzhou (now Shangrao, Jiangxi Province) from Wuzhou (now Jinhua, Zhejiang Province). On 23 the second May his troops reached Lingxi (now Lingxi Town of Shangrao City, Jiangxi Province). Several thousand foot soldiers and cavalrymen of Chen You Liang's army came out of the city of Xinzhou to meet Hu Da Hai's troops. Hu Da Hai's troops defeated the troops defending Xinzhou and took the city of Xinzhou. Zhu Yuang Zhang appointed Hu Da Hai's son Hu De Ji as the commander-in-chief of the army defending Xinzhou. Then Hu Da Hai went back to Wuzhou.

Yu Guang was a general under Xu Shou Hui, the Emperor of the Tianwan Dynasty. He was the Commanding General of the Army defending Fuliang (now Fuliang, in the northeast part of Jiangxi Province). When Chen You Liang murdered Xu Shou Hui and ascended the throne of the State of Han on 3 the second May 1360, Yu Guang was very angry with Chen You Liang. In July 1360 Yu Guang commanded his troops to attack Raozhou (now Boyang, Jiangxi Province) and defeated Xin Tong Zhi, the general under Chen You Liang defending Boyang. Xin Tong Zhi ran away and Yu Guang took Raozhou. Yu Guang surrendered to Deng Yu and presented the city of Boyang to him. Raozhou was a strategically important city because it was situated by the side of Poyang Hu Lake. Chen You Liang sent his navy to attack Boyang several times. Deng Yu and Yu Guang defended the city resolutely and defeated Chen You Liang's army.

Anqing (now Anqing, Anhui Province) was an important city in the upper reach of the Yangtze River. At first Zhao Pu Sheng defended this city for Chen You Liang. But in September 1359 Chen

You Liang killed Zhao Pu Sheng and appointed a general under him to defend Anqing. Zhang Zhi Xiong, a general under Zhao Pu Sheng, hated Chen You Liang but he was forced to go with Chen You Liang to attack Yingtian. In the battle in Longjiangguan, he did not have the will to fight for Chen You Liang. After Chen You Liang's defeat in Yingtian, Zhang Zhi Cheng surrendered to Zhu Yuan Zhang.

Zheng Zhi Xiong knew the defense of Anqing very well, and he presented the stratagem for taking Anqing to Zhu Yuan Zhang. Zhu Yuan Zhang accepted the plan. In June 1360 Zhu Yuan Zhang sent Zhao Bo Zhong, one of the leaders in Chao Hu Lake who had submitted themselves to Zhu Yuan Zhang in May 1355, to command an army to attack Anqing. Zhao Bo Zhong successfully took the city of Anqing. But not long later Chen You Liang sent Zhang Ding Bian to attack Anqing, and Zhang Ding Bian took the city. Zhao Bo Zhong escaped back to Yingtian. Zhu Yuan Zhang was very angry and ordered that Zhang Bo Zhong be arrested. Zhu Yuan Zhang said, "The commanding general was not able to defend the city resolutely. When the city fell the commanding general ran away. He should be killed!" Chang Yu Chun tried his best to save Zhang Bo Zhong. He said to Zhu Yuan Zhang, "Zhang Bo Zhong joined you long ago and made great contributions to your success when you commanded the army to cross the Yangtze River. I hope you will spare him this time." Zhu Yuan Zhang said, "If I don't punish him according to military law this time, I will not be able to warn those who would commit the same crime later." Then he granted a bow to Zhang Bo Zhong and let him strangle himself to death with the string of the bow.

Ou Pu Xiang, a general under Xu Shou Hui, the Emperor of Tianwan Dynasty, was the commanding general defending Yuanzhou (now Yichun, in the west Part of Jiangxi Province). When Chen You Liang murdered Xu Shou Hui on 2 May 1360, Ou Pu Xiang hated Chen You Liang. On 24 September 1360 Ou Pu Xiang surrendered to Zhu Yuan Zhang and handed over the city of Yuanzhou to the army of Zhu Yuan Zhang. Chen You Liang was very angry and sent his younger brother Chen You Ren to attack Ou Pu Xiang. Ou Pu Xiang defeated the army under Chen You Ren and captured Chen You Ren. Chen You Liang was shocked. He had to send an envoy to make peace with Ou Pu Xiang. Then Ou Pu Xiang released Chen You Ren and let him go back to Jiangzhou.

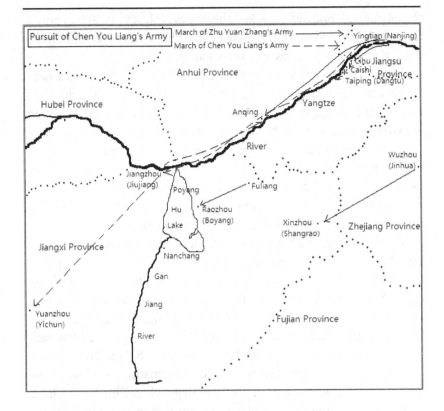

(3) Zhu Yuan Zhang Attacks Chen You Liang

In March 1361 Chen You Liang sent Li Ming Dao to lead an army to attack Xinzhou (now Shangrao, Jiangxi Province). The troops under Li Ming Dao took Caoping Town (22 kilometers east of Shangrao, Jiangxi Province) so as to prevent Zhu Yuan Zhang's army from reinforcing Xinzhou from Zhejiang Province. Hu De Ji, the commanding general defending Xinzhou, sent Xia De Run to recover Caoping Town. Xia De Run fought bravely but was killed in battle. Then the troops under Li Ming Dao took Yushan (in eastern Jiangxi Province). When Hu Da Hai heard that Chen You Liang had sent Li Ming Dao to attack Xinzhou, he sent Miu Mei, a general under him, to command some troops to reinforce Xinzhou. Miu Mei commanded his troops to fight against the troops under Li Ming Dao in Dongjinqao (in the east of Yushan, Jiangxi Province) and recovered Yushan. Miu Mei marched his troops near Xinzhou and cut the route of retreat of Li Ming Dao's troops. In June 1361 Li Ming Dao's troops lay siege to the city of Xinzhou and attacked the city fiercely. Hu De Ji had only a few solders defending the city. He ordered his soldiers to shut all the gates tight and defend the city tenaciously.

He sent an envoy to Wuzhou to ask his father Hu Da Hai for help. Hu Da Hai immediately took a great army and hurried to Xinzhou. On 24 July 1361, seeing that his father had arrived, Hu De Ji commanded his troops to go out of the city of Xinzhou to attack Li Min Dao's army. They attacked Li Ming Dao's troops from the front. Hu Da Hai's troops attacked from the back. Li Ming Dao's troops were disastrously defeated. Li Ming Dao and Wang Han Er, the Supervisor of the army, were captured. Hu Da Hai sent soldiers to escort them to Li Wen Zhong in Jiande (now Jiande, Zhejiang Province).

Wang Han Er had an elder brother whose name was Wang Pu. Wang Pu was a general under Chen You Liang. He was the Commander-in-chief of Chen You Liang's army defending Jianchang (now Nancheng, Jiangxi Province). Li Wen Zhong asked Li Han Er to write a letter to Wang Pu advising him to surrender. Then Wang Pu submitted himself to Li Wen Zhong. Li Wen Zhong sent some soldiers to escort Wang Pu to Yingtian to Zhu Yuan Zhang. Zhu Yuan Zhang appointed him as the Commander-in-chief of the army defending Jianchang. In the later days when Zhu Yuan Zhang attacked Jiangzhou (now Jiujiang, Jiangxi Province) and Nanchang (now Nangchang, Jiangxi Province), he was the guide for Zhu Yuan Zhang's army.

In August 1361 Zhu Yuan Zhang decided to carry out an expedition against Chen You Liang. At that time Li Ming Dao had already surrendered and was in Yingtian. Zhu Yuan Zhang asked Li Ming Dao about Chen You Liang. Li Ming Dao said, "After Chen You Liang murdered Xu Shou Hui, the generals under him were in dissension and discord. Zhao Pu Sheng was a fierce general, but Chen You Liang killed him because of his resentment of Zhao Pu Sheng. Although he still has many troops, he will be easily defeated." Zhu Yuan Zhang summoned all the generals to his office and said to them, "Chen You Liang has murdered his master and usurped the throne. Recently he invaded our territory. Many of my great generals were killed in battle against his invasion. He has done great harm to us. I have made up my mind to annihilate him. You should command the troops under you in this expedition against Chen You Liang."

On 12 August 1361 Zhu Yuan Zhang started his expedition against Chen You Liang. He sat on a huge warship on the sides of which golden colored dragons were inlaid, commanding his warships to sail up the Yangtze River. At that time more than 10,000 birds flew over Zhu Yuan Zhang's warship. On 20 August 1361 Zhu Yuan Zhang reached Anqing (now Anqing, Anhui Province). The troops under Chen You Liang defending Anqing would not come out to fight. Zhu Yuan Zhang sent some foot soldiers to attract the attention of the enemy. At the same time he sent Liao Yong Zhong and Zhang Zhi Xiong to take the navy and attack the strongholds by the Yangtze River. They destroyed them all. Then Zhu Yuan Zhang ordered his troops to attack the city of Anqing. The attack started in the morning and lasted to sunset but the troops under Zhu Yuan Zhang could not take the city. Liu Ji suggested to Zhu Yuan Zhang that he should give up the attack of Anqing and go up the Yangtze River to take Jiangzhou (now Jiujiang, Jiangxi Province), Chen You Liang's actual capital. Zhu Yuan Zhang accepted his advice and commanded his fleet to sail westward up the Yangtze River. When Zhu Yuan's fleet sailed past Xiaogu Shan (now Xiaogu Shan, Anhui Province), Ding Pu Lang and Fu You De, two generals under Chen You Liang, led all their troops to submit themselves to Zhu Yuan Zhang. Fu You De was a very brave and resourceful general. At first he joined Li Xi Xi, a leader of the uprising in Shandong (now Shandong Province) and fought his way into the area of Shu (now Sichuan Province). He was always the vanguard of the army of Li Xi Xi. Later Li Xi Xi was killed in the area of Shu. Fu You De joined Ming Yu Zhen, the local strongman in the area of Shu. But Ming Yu Zhen did not appoint him to any important position. Then Fu You De led his troops to Wuchang (now Wuchang, Hubei Province) to join Chen You Liang.

But Chen You Liang did not entrust him with any important task. So Fu You De was always unhappy. When he knew that Zhu Yuan Zhang was passing Xiaogu Shan to attack Jiangzhou, he exclaimed, "My true master has come!" When Zhu Yuan Zhang saw Fu You De, he knew that Fu You De was a capable man and promoted him to the rank of a general and put under the command of Chang Yu Chun.

On 24 August 1361 Zhu Yuan Zhang's great army reached Hukou (Jiangxi Province) which was not far from Jiangzhou. Zhu Yuan Zhang's fleet met the petrol boats of Chen You Liang's naval troops.

The petrol boats were all destroyed by Zhu Yuan Zhang's naval troops. So the information that Zhu Yuan Zhang's army had come was not reported to Chen You Liang. When Zhu Yuan Zhang's victorious army appeared on the Yangtze River outside Jiangzhou, Chen You Liang was panic-stricken. He thought that Zhu Yuan Zhang's great army had descended from Heaven. He could not arrange the resistance. At that time Liao Yong Zhong had the naval troops to lead the way. He saw that the city wall of Jiangzhou was just beside the river. He measured with his eyes the height of the city wall. Then he ordered the soldiers to build wooden bridges by the sterns of the big warships. Then he ordered the soldiers to sail the warships backwards, stern first. When the sterns of the warships got close to the city war, the bridges were connected to the top of the wall. The soldiers climbed up, and on 25 August 1361 Zhu Yuan Zhang's army took Jiangzhou. Chen You Liang escaped to Wuchang (now in Wuhan, Hubei Province) at night, taking his wife and children with him.

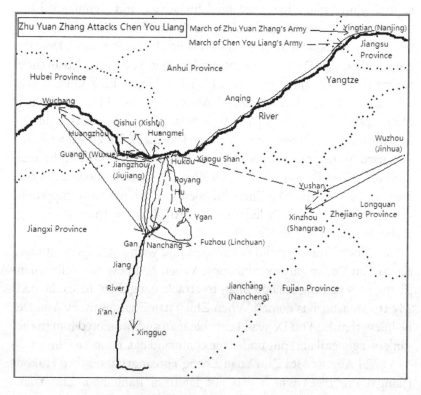

On 26 August 1361 Zhu Yuan Zhang sent troops to attack Qishui (now Xishui, Hubei Province), Huangzhou (now in Hubei Province), Xingguo (in today's Jiangxi Province), Huangmei (now in Hubei Province) and Guangji (now Wuxue, Hubei Province). They captured them all. On 3 September 1361 Wang Pu, a general under Chen You Liang defending Jianchang (now Nancheng, Jiangxi Province), who had surrendered to Zhu Yuan Zhang, presented the city to him. Zhu Yuan Zhang let him remain as general defending Jianchang. Having found out that Chen You Liang had been defeated, Wu Hong, a general under Chen You Liang defending Yugan (in Jiangxi Province), Peng Shi Zhong, another of Chen You Liang's generals, this time defending Longquan (now in the western part of Zhejiang Province) and Zeng Wan Zhong, a general under Chen You Liang defending Ji'an (in what is now Jiangxi Province), sent envoys to Zhu Yuan Zhang to negotiate the terms for their surrender. Zhu Yuan Zhang accepted their surrender and their cities.

In November 1361 Zhu Yuan Zhang sent Deng Yu to attack Fuzhou (now Linchuan, Jiangxi Province). At that time Deng Ke Ming, another of Chen You Liang's generals, was defending Fuzhou. Deng Yu stationed his troops in Pingtang (in the area of Linchuan, Jiangxi Province) and had General Wu Hong command his troops to attack Fuzhou. But Wu Hong was defeated by Deng Ke Ming and ran back. Deng Ke Ming pretended that he would surrender and sent an envoy to Deng Yu to negotiate the terms. Deng Yu knew that Deng Ke Ming could not have been sincere; so during the night of 19 November 1361, Deng Yu and his troops carried out a surprise attack on Fuzhou. All his soldiers took off their armor so that they could advance faster. They moved very quickly along the mountain roads in the dark. At dawn the next morning, they took the outer city wall of Fuzhou. Deng Ke Ming singly rode a horse through the south gate of the city. It became clear that it would be very difficult to make an escape, so he surrendered to Deng Yu.

In December 1361 Zhu Yuan Zhang decided to take Nanchang (now in Jiangxi Province). Hu Ting Rui, the Governor of Jiangxi Province appointed by Chen You Liang, was defending. Zhu Yuan Zhang sent an envoy to demand his surrender along with the city of Nanchang. Hu Ting Rui knew that Chen You Ling had already been defeated. So on 22 December 1361 Hu Ting Rui sent Zheng Ren Jie, one of his generals, as his emissary to Jiangzhou to talk to Zhu Yuan Zhang about his surrender, with one request: "After I surrender, please don't disband my army and distribute my officers and men under the command of other generals." At these words Zhu Yuan Zhang hesitated; he found it difficult to accept this condition. Liu Ji was sitting beside him. He kicked Zhu Yuan Zhang's chair as a signal that he should accept this condition. Zhu Yuan Zhang realized what Liu Ji meant, and he wrote a letter to Hu Ting Rui.

The letter read, "Zheng Ren Jie has come. He has conveyed your sincere intention to submit to me and render your service to me. This shows that you are a man of understanding. And you worry that the officers and men under you would be disbanded and distributed to other generals. This is an unnecessary worry. I have been in revolt for ten years. Many persons of unusual talent and ability have come to join me from all directions of the realm. Many of them have the ability to judge the right time to do the right thing and to predict the development of the situation. They have come to submit to me because they want to make great contributions to the nation in their lifetime and be remembered by the generations to come. When two true men meet with each other, they are frank and open to each other. With a hearty laugh they will become good friends. They will treat each other with sincerity. I will assign those who have come to join me to suitable position according to their ability. If he has just a few soldiers, I will increase the number of soldiers. If he is low in rank, I will promote him to a higher rank. If he is in want of money, I will grant him money. This is the way I treat my generals and officers. I will certainly not disband his army and distribute his officers and men to other generals. If I do that, those who have joined me will lose heart. Chen You Liang's fierce general Zhao Pu Sheng was under suspicion and Chen You Liang killed him. Chen You Liang has no trust or confidence in his generals. He is such a suspicious man that he will not be able to accomplish anything. Recently in the battle of Longjiang, Chen You Liang's generals Zhang Zhi Xiong and Liang Xuan surrendered. I let them command the troops originally under them and I treat them equally with my own generals without any discrimination. Later Zhang Zhi Xiong took part in the battle to destroy the strongholds by the Yangtze River in Anqing; and Liang Xuan took part in the battle to take the area north of the Yangtze

River. Both of them made great contributions and they both were granted rich awards. I treat even Zhang Zhi Xiong and Liang Xuan in such a way; let alone you who are willing to submit to me with a big city! Chance comes rarely. You should seize the chance and don't let it slip through your fingers. You should make up your mind as soon as possible." When Hu Ting Rui got the letter, he sent Kang Tai, one of his generals, to Jiangzhou to ask Zhu Yuan Zhang to accept his surrender.

On 4 January 1362, Hu Ting Rui surrendered to Zhu Yuan Zhang and presented the city of Nanchang to him.

Style Names

Zhu Yuan Zhang went by the style name of Zhu Guo Rui, so after Hu Ting Rui surrendered he changed his name to Hu Mei. Traditionally, it was prohibited in China to presume to address anyone by his real name unless the speaker was of distinctly higher station, nor would anyone use part of an emperor's name. Equals would address each other by their style names. But even the style name was protected from "over use" by one's social inferiors. (Further information on these conventions is available at http://kongming.net/novel/names/.)

Here, in a gesture of humility, Mr. Hu made sure not to trammel upon Zhu Yuan Zhang's style name. The Chinese characters for Zhu Guo Rui are 朱國瑞. 朱(Zhu) is the family name; 國(Guo) means "national"; 瑞 (Rui) means "propitious omen". When 國 (Guo) and 瑞 (Rui) are put together, it means "national propitious omen". The Chinese characters for Hu Ting Rui are 胡廷瑞. It is clear that the third character in Hu Ting Rui's name is the same as the third character 瑞 (Rui) in 朱國瑞. So Hu Ting Rui changed his name to Hu Mei (胡美).

A person's style name was used to explain his real name. The name Zhu Yuan Zhang means "the greatest jade tablet." In Chinese tradition, jade tablet was a propitious omen for the nation. Thus his style name Zhu Guo Rui (national propitious omen) explains the meaning of his less public name.

The Chinese characters for Zhu Yuan Zhang are 朱元璋. The first part, 朱 (Zhu), is the family name; 元 (Yuan) means "the first" or "number one," "the greatest" or "the best"; 璋 (Zhang) means "jade tablet." When 元 (Yuan) and 璋 (Zhang) are put together, the meaning is "the number one jade tablet" or "the best jade tablet."

Our man Zhu Yuan Zhang decided to go to Nanchang himself, and on 8 January 1362 he set out. On 12 January Zhu Yuan Zhang reached Qiaoshe (now situated thirty kilometers north of Nanchang, Jiangxi Province). Hu Ting Rui sent an envoy to meet him in Qiaoshe to hand over the seal of the Governor of Jiangxi Province, given by Chen You Liang, with a detailed and itemized lists of the amounts of grain stored by the army and the people in the city of Nanchang. When Zhu Yuan Zhang arrived in Nanchang on 14 January, Hu Ting Rui led all his generals and officials to the north gate to meet and have an audience with Zhu Yuan Zhang. The next day, Zhu Yuan Zhang entered the city of Nanchang. He first visited the Temple of Confucius and paid his respects. Then he ordered that the grain storehouses be opened to provide food to the poverty-stricken people. He abolished Chen You Liang's decrees. All the people in Nanchang were very happy with the new regime.

In February Zhu Yuan Zhang started his journey back to Yingtian, and he allowed Hu Ting Rui to go with him. Before he left Nanchang, he appointed Deng Yu as the Governor of Jiangxi Province to defend Nanchang.

When Hu Ting Rui and Zhu Yuan Zhang left Nanchang, Zhu Zong and Kang Tai, two of Hu Ting Rui's generals, remained in Nanchang. They were unhappy with Wu Ting Rui's surrender, and he sensed their resentment. So he secretly suggested to Zhu Yuan Zhang that they were likely to rebel. At that time Xu Da and his army were chasing Chen You Liang to Wuchang (now in Hubei Province). He stationed his men in Dunkou (now in Hanyang, Wuhan, Hubei Province). Zhu Yuan Zhang sent an envoy to Nanchang to order Zhu Zong and Kang Tai to lead their troops to Wuchang and to put themselves under the command of Xu Da. When the naval ships under Zhu Zong and Kang Tai sailed to Nu'ergang Harbor (in Poyang Hu Lake near Hukou, Jiangxi Province), the two commanded their troops to rebel. At that time a ship loaded with valuable textiles was sailing by their warships. They took away all the cloth and made banners with it. Then they sailed south back to Nanchang.

They reached the foot of the Nanchang city wall on 17 March 1362. In the evening the rebellious soldiers broke into the north gate. Wan Si Cheng and Ye Shen, the officials in charge of Nanchang, were captured and then killed. When Deng Yu got news that Zhu Zong and Kang Tai had rebelled, he fled from the city with about thirty men. They met with the rebel soldiers on their way. Most of the followers were killed. Deng Yu's horse slipped and fell. Deng Yu had to change to another horse but that horse also slipped and fell. At last his adopted son offered his horse to him and he successfully made his escape through Fuzhou Gate (the southern gate of Nanchang) back to Yingtian. Zhu Yuan Zhang did not punish him because Deng Yu had made such great contributions to their success in the past.

When Xu Da learned that there had been a rebellion in Nanchang, he brought his army to come from Dunkou of Hanyang to suppress it. Zhu Zong escaped to Xingan (in Jiangxi Province) and was killed by Deng Zhi Ming, the general in charge. Kang Tai escaped to Guangxin (in Shangrao, Jiangxi Province). Zhu Yuan Zhang spared Kang Tai because he was Hu Ting Rui's nephew. When Zhu Yuan Zhang heard that Xu Da had recovered Nanchang, he was very glad and said, "Nanchang is strategically important. It controls the areas of the southern part of Hubei Province and northern part of Jiangxi Province. It provides us protection in the southwest. Since I have got Nanchang, I have cut away one of Chen You Liang's arms. I must send one of my close relatives to defend that city." He selected his nephew Zhu Wen Zheng to be commander-in-chief and he put Zhao De Sheng, Xue Xin and Deng Yu under his command to defend Nanchang.

(4) The Rebellions of the Miao Nationality Generals and the Death of Hu Da Hai and Geng Zhai Cheng

A terrible and unfortunate event took place in February 1362; the roots of the situation reached back to September 1358. When Yang Elezhe, the Marshal of the army of the Miao Nationality, was killed, his generals Jiang Ying, Liu Zhen and Li Fu led their Miao Nationality soldiers to surrender. They were put under the command of Hu Da Hai, who was at that time Commander-in-chief of the army defending Wuzhou (now Jinhua, Zhejiang Province). He liked these Miao generals because they were brave and good fighters, and he treated them very well. He never suspected that they would rebel.

But they did. In February 1362 these three generals plotted together. At first Liu Zhen hesitated out of respect for Hu Da Hai. But Li Fu convinced him to go along, saying, "Hu Da Hai really treats us very well. But as long as he is the commanding general and holds all the military power in his hands, he is in our way — if we don't kill him, we will not be able to accomplish our cause. Now we are carrying out our great cause. We must forget his kindness to us." They agreed with him and decided to kill Hu Da Hai.

They sent letters to Li You Zhi and He De Ren in Chuzhou (now Lishui, Zhejiang Province), who were former generals of the Miao army, to tell them that they were planning to start a rebellion on 7 February; they asked Li You Zhi and He De Ren to act in cooperation with them. On that fateful day, while Hu Da Hai was working in his office, Jiang Ying went in to invite him to Bayong Tower (in the southeast part of the city of Jinhua) to watch an archery show at the foot of the tower. Hu Da Hai stepped outside of his office and was preparing to mount his horse when a soldier instigated by Jiang Ying stepped forward. He knelt down before him and said, "Jiang Ying wants to kill me." Hu Da Hai was surprised to hear these words and turned back to look at Jiang Ying. At this, Jiang Ying took a big hammer from his sleeve. He raised his hammer, pretending that he was going to kill that soldier, but instead he struck Hu Da Hai hard on the head and killed him.

That was just the start. He cut Hu Da Hai's head off his dead body, mounted his horse (holding the head in his hand), and went to show it to Zhang Bin, an official, and forced him to join the rebellion. Then Jiang Ying killed Hu Da Hai's son Hu Guan Zhu, while the other rebel generals arrested Wang Kai, Hu Da Hai's advisor. But Wang Kai, too, had been very kind to the generals of the Miao Nationality, and Liu Zhen wanted to spare his life and take him to the west with them. Now, Wang Kai shouted at the generals, "It is my duty to defend our territory. I am willing to die for a righteous cause. How can I submit to you rebels and join in your rebellion!" At the same time, Wu De Zhen, one of the rebel generals, still held some grudges against Wang Kai from the past and he wanted to put him to death. He said, "If we spare him now, he will cause great trouble to us." So in the end, the generals killed both Wang Kai and his son Wang Yin.

Li Bin, Hu Da Hai's secretary, escaped by getting down the city wall by a rope, taking the provincial official seal with him. He hurried to Yanzhou (now Jiande, Zhejiang Province) to tell Li Wen Zhong, the commanding general defending Yanzhou, about the rebellion in Wuzhou. Li Wen Zhong sent General He Shi Ming and General Guo

Yan Ren to take a great army to confront the generals of the Miao Nationality. When the great army reached Lanxi (in today's Zhejiang Province), Jiang Ying and the other generals were very much afraid. They looted the people in the city and forced the women and children to head westward to surrender to the army under Zhang Shi Cheng.

General He Shi Ming and his army entered the city of Wuzhou. Zhang Bin and Wu De Zhen came to surrender. He Shi Ming understood that Wang Kai had been killed because Wu De Zhen said something against him. That made He Shi Ming very angry and he ordered his soldiers to tie him up; he was going to have him killed. But his partner in rebellion Zhang Bin stopped him, saying, "If Wu De Zhen is killed, the rebels who want to surrender will be terrified. Then there will be no one who dares come to surrender." Thinking it over, He De Ren set Wu De Zhen free.

When Hu Da Hai's adopted son heard that Hu Da Hai had been killed, he took an army to Wuzhou from Xinzhou, and Li Wen Zhong also took an army to Wuzhou. They put down the unrest there, and peace and order were restored in the city of Wuzhou.

On 11 February, Li You Zhi and He Ren De, Miao generals in Chuzhou (now Lishui, Zhejiang province), heard that Jiang Ying had killed Hu Da Hai and they also held a rebellion. Word of this came to Geng Zai Cheng, the commanding general defending Chuzhou, as he was having his meal with a friend. He immediately jumped up, called for his horse and gathered all the soldiers he could gather. Only twenty soldiers responded fast enough, so Geng Zai Cheng in his haste took just twenty soldiers to meet the rebellious soldiers of the Miao Nationality. He yelled to the rebels, "You renegades! We have been very kind to you. Why have you rebelled?" But they responded shamelessly, stabbing at him with long spears. Geng Zai Cheng broke several of these spears with his sword, but one hit him at the neck and blood spilt out. He fell to the ground from his horse. He did not stop cursing the rebels until he died.

Sun Yan, one of his generals, was also captured by the rebels. He Ren De tried to force him to surrender but Sun Yan refused and shouted curses at the rebels. He De Ren drew out his sword and ordered Sun Yan to take off his purple-colored robe. Sun Yan said, "This robe was granted to me by the Duke of Wu. I will die with this purple-colored robe on." And they killed him.

Li Wen Zhong, who recently had gone to secure Wuzhou, sent troops to Jinyun (now in Zhejiang Province), to the northeast of Chuzhou as a move toward preparing to put down the rebellion in Chuzhou. Incidentally Geng Tian Bi, Geng Zai Cheng's son, was sent to Chuzhou to call up the Miao Nationality army. On his way, he learned that they had rebelled and his father had been killed. He hurried to Yanzhou to Li Wen Zhong's army camps. Zhu Xun, one of Geng Zai Cheng's generals, also sent his troops to Yanzhou. Geng Tian Bi took command of this army. Shao Rong, the Manager of Governmental affairs, took another great army to Chuzhou to pacify the rebellion. On 4 April 1362 Geng Tian Bi commanded his troops to join forces with Shao Rong. Wang You and Hu Shen, two generals under Shao Rong, commanded their troops to attack the northeast gate of the city and their soldiers set fire to this gate and broke in. Li You Zhi killed himself. He De Ren was defeated and fled toward Jinyun. But he was captured by the peasants there and put into a cage and escorted to Yingtian, where he was executed.

When Zhu Yuan Zhang heard that the rebellions of the Miao generals in Wuzhou and Chuzhou had been put down, he appointed Li Wen Zhong Governor of East Part of Zhejiang Province, responsible for the military affairs of Yanzhou (now Jiande, Zhejiang Province), Quzhou, Chuzhou (now Lishui, Zhejiang Province), Xinzhou (now Shangrao, Jiangxi Province) and Zhuquan (now Zhuji, Zhejiang Province).

Hu Da Hai had been a man of strategy. He had strictly disciplined his subordinates. He often said, "I am a warrior. I am not a man of letters. I only insist on three things: do not kill innocent people, do not loot the people, do not to burn the houses." He was highly respected by the people around. When he died, people shed tears for him. Zhu Yuan Zhang granted him the title of Duke of the State of Yue posthumously.

Geng Zai Cheng was a strict general. His soldiers never took anything from the people. Zhu Yuan Zhang granted him the title of Duke of the State of Si posthumously.

(5) The Great Battle in Poyang Hu Lake

In January 1363 Zhang Shi Cheng sent troops to attack Anfeng (now Shouxian, Anhui Province) where Liu Fu Tong and Han

Lin Er, the Emperor of the State of Song, were staying. Zhang Shi Cheng appointed Lü Zhen as the commander of the vanguard army. Zhang Shi Cheng himself commanded the main force to go behind the vanguard army. When Lü Zhen reached Anfeng, he laid siege to the city. The siege lasted for a long time. The food supply in the city ran short. Liu Fu Tong sent an envoy to Yingtian to ask Zhu Yuan Zhang for help. Zhu Yuan Zhang said, "If Anfeng is lost and falls into the hands of Zhang Shi Cheng, Zhang Shi Cheng will become more powerful. We have to rescue Anfeng." Liu Ji said, "Liu Fu Tong and Zhang Shi Cheng are now trying to find out the weak points of the other so as to defeat him. It would be improper for you to take a great army to rescue Anfeng." But Zhu Yuan Zhang would not take his advice. Not long later Lü Zhen took Anfeng. Liu Fu Tong was killed. Han Lin Er ran away to Chuzhou (now Chuzhou, Anhui Province). On 1 March 1363 Zhu Yuan Zhang commanded Xu Da and Chang Yu Chun to take a great army to rescue Anfeng.

At that time Lü Zhen set up his camps outside the city of Anfeng. He ordered his soldiers to erect logs and build a fence around the camps. And he ordered his soldiers to dig deep trenches outside the city. General Wang attacked one of the strongholds and took it, but the left army and the right army were defeated and they could not come out — they could not get past the deep trenches. Zhu Yuan Zhang ordered Chang Yu Chun to charge Lü Zhen's battle formation. Three battles were fought, and Chang Yu Chun won all three. Lü Zhen's army was disastrously defeated. Many of his soldiers were killed or captured. Zuo Jun Bi, a local strongman in Luzhou (now Hefei, Anhui Province), took an army to reinforce Lü Zhen, but Chang Yu Chun defeated him, too. Lü Zhen and Zuo Jun Bi escaped to Luzhou. Zhu Yuan Zhang ordered Xu Da to head up a great army to attack Luzhou; then Zhu Yuan Zhang came back to Yingtian.

Chen You Liang felt indignant because his territory had been greatly reduced. He was determined to recover his territory. He ordered several big warships to be built. These big warships were over ten meters tall and were painted with bright red. There were three decks on each one, with a shed for horses on each deck. There were more than thirty watch towers on each ship. Iron plates were installed outside each watch tower.

In April 1363 Chen You Liang heard that Zhu Yuan Zhang had gone to Anfeng to fight Zhang Shi Cheng's army. He decided to take this moment to start an offensive on Nanchang (now in Jiangxi Province). The big warships conveyed Chen You Liang, his wife and children, all the military and civil officials and 600,000 officers and soldiers from Hanyang (now in Wuhan, Hubei Province) down the Yangtze River. They sailed past Hukou (now in Jiangxi Province) into Poyang Hu Lake (now in Jiangxi Province). Then the fleet sailed into Gan Jiang River. On 23 April 1363 Chen You Liang's great fleet reached the city of Nanchang.

Chen You Liang had planned to get his big warships very close to the city wall when river was at high tide and let the soldiers to climb up the city wall from the sterns of the big ships. But to his great disappointment, he found that Zhu Yuan Zhang's troops had rebuilt the city wall and now the wall was thirty feet away from the river. The big warships could not get close at all. Chen You Liang ordered his soldiers to build a lot of equipment for attacking cities, including ladders, movable watch towers, shields made of bamboo.

Zhu Wen Zheng, the Commander-in-chief of Zhu Yuan Zhang's army at Nanchang, discussed with all his generals a plan to defend the city. He decided to assign the generals to defend the city gates. Deng Yu was responsible for Fuzhou Gate (the south gate); Zhao De Sheng was responsible for Gongbu Gate, Shibu Gate and Qiaobu Gate (the three north gates); Xue Xian was responsible for Zhangjiang Gate and Xincheng Gate (the two west gates); Niu Hai Long, Zhao Guo Wang, Xu Gui, Zhu Qian and Cheng Guo Sheng were responsible for Liuli Gate and Dantai Gate (the two east gates). Zhu Wen Zheng stayed in the center of the city to supervise the defense. He put 2,000 select troops under him and was ready to send these troops to reinforce whichever place was most under threat.

On 27 April 1363 Cheng You Liang personally led his troops to attack Fuzhou Gate. Each of his soldiers carried a shield made of bamboo to protect him against the arrows and stones shot down from the top of the city wall. They attacked fiercely. The city wall of about seventy meters long was destroyed. Deng Yu ordered his soldiers to fire shotguns to beat back the enemy. Then he ordered the soldiers to erect wooden logs to build a fence along the destroyed part of the city wall. Chen You Liang's soldiers tried their best to break the fence, but Zhu Wen Zheng inspired the generals to resist the attack, and he organized the soldiers to repair the destroyed part of the city wall. The soldiers worked all through the night and the city wall was repaired. In this battle, Generals Li Ji Xian, Niu Hai Long, Zhao Guo Wang, Xu Gui and Zhu Qian were killed in action.

On 1 May 1363, Chen You Liang sent generals to attack Ji'an (now in Jiangxi Province). One of the generals defending Ji'an, Li Dao Ming, had a grudge against Zeng Wan Zhong, his Commanding General. He defected and opened the city gate to let Chen You Liang's army into the city.

Zeng Wan Zhong was killed in action. Liu Qi and Zhu Shu Hua were captured by Chen You Liang's soldiers. Not long later Chen You Liang's army took Linjiang (Linjiang Town, Zhangshu, Jiangxi Province). Zhao Tian Lin, the general defending Linjiang, was captured. On 8 May 1363 Chen You Liang and his troops attacked Xincheng Gate (one of the west gates of Nanchang). Xue Xian, the general in charge of that gate, commanded his select troops to rush out and they charged the enemy battle formation. He killed two top generals of Chen You Liang's army. On 14 June 1363 Chen You Liang ordered his soldiers to repair the siege towers, battering rams and other weapons, and then they started a fierce attack on Fuzhou Gate. He wanted to destroy the fence and enter the city. Zhu Wen Zheng sent his most robust soldiers to defend the fence. These soldiers used long spears to thrust at the enemy soldiers through the fence — but the enemy soldiers grabbed some of the spears and managed to shake them out of the grasp of the defending soldiers. The enemy pressed on. Zhu Wen Zheng ordered his workmen to make long spears with iron handles. Before these spears were used, the sharp ends were put to the fire. Now, when the soldiers poked these spears through the fence, the men who grabbed at them lost their hands that were burned and seared. So they had to retreat.

Chen You Liang saw that Zhu Wen Zheng's troops were resolute to defend Nanchang and it was clearly going to be difficult to take the city by storm. He thought of a way to destroy the determination of the defenders. He ordered the captives to be brought forth: Liu Qi, Zhu Shu Hua and Zhao Tian Lin, who had been captured in Ji'an and Linjiang. They were brought to the foot of the city wall and shown to the defenders. Chen You Liang shouted, "Surrender now! Otherwise I will kill them all!" Zhu Wen Zheng and the other generals were upset and angry; but they suppressed their emotions and became more determined. Liu Qi, Zhu Shu Hua and Zhao Tian Lin would rather die than surrender in shame, and they were killed before their comrades.

In sunset that day Chen You Liang sent troops to attack Gongbu Gate and Shibu Gate. Zhao De Sheng, the general in charge of their defense, was leading his troops in resisting the attack. An archer of Chen You Liang's army saw Zhao De Sheng and aimed at him. He let fly the arrow and hit Zhao De Sheng at his waist. The arrow penetrated as deep as six inches. Zhao De Sheng pulled out the arrow and said with a long sigh, "Since I joined the army at the prime of my life, I have been wounded many times by arrows and stones. But none of them was as serious as this time. As a true man, I will die without anything to regret. I only regret that I will not have a chance to take part in the battles to recover Central China." And then he died. He was thirty-nine years old. Later Zhu Yuan Zhang made Zhao De Sheng Duke of the State of Liang posthumously.

Nanchang had been under siege for a long time. The city was completely isolated. Zhu Wen Zheng sent Zhang Zi Ming, an officer, to Yingtian to report the situation to Zhu Yuan Zhang and ask him for urgent help. Zhang Zi Ming stole out of the city from the northwest gate at night. He found a fishing boat in Gan Jiang River and crossed the river to Shitoukou, on the west bank. He rested in the daytime and traveled at night. It took him half a month to reach Yingtian. Zhu Yuan Zhang asked him, "How powerful is Chen You Liang's army?" Zhang Zi Ming answered, "Chen You Liang's army is powerful, but many of his soldiers have been killed in battle. Now the water in the Gan Jiang River has become shallow. Chen You Liang's big warships are constricted in their movements. His army has stayed outside Nanchang for a long time. Their food supplies must have gotten short. If our relief troops arrive, we will surely defeat his army." Zhu Yuan Zhang said, "Go back and tell Zhu Wen Zheng that if he can defend Nanchang firmly for a month, I will surely defeat Chen You Liang." He sent Zhang Zi Ming to go back to Nanchang. When Zhang Zi Ming arrived at Hukou (now Hukou, Jiangxi Province), he was captured by Chen You Liang's soldiers. He was brought before Chen You Liang. Chen You Liang said to him, "If you can seduce Zhu Wen Zheng to surrender, I will not kill you and you will enjoy wealth and high rank."

Zhang Zi Ming pretended to accept his conditions for surrender. Then Chen You Liang brought Zhang Zi Ming to the foot of the city wall of Nanchang. Zhang Zi Ming shouted to Zhu Wen Zheng and the other generals who were standing at the top of the city wall, "Our Master has ordered you to defend the city resolutely. The great rescuing army will come very soon!" Chen You Liang was so angry that he waved his sword and killed Zhang Zi Ming.

At that time Xu Da and Chang Yu Chun had commanded their troops to lay siege to Luzhou (now Hefei, Anhui Province) and to attack Zuo Jun Bi. Zuo Jun Bi ordered his soldiers to build drawbridges on the top of the city wall to hang down the soldiers to the foot of the city wall at night and started a surprise attack on the camps of Xu Da's army. But the surprise attack was not successful. Zuo Jun Bi had to run back to the city of Luzhou. The siege to Luzhou lasted for three months but Xu Da and Chang Yu Chun still could not take it. Zhu Yuan Zhang sent an envoy to Luzhou to tell them, "If we lose Nanchang because we concentrated our army to take Luzhou, the loss will outweigh the gain even if we take Luzhou." Then Xu Da and Chang Yu Chun lifted the siege on Luzhou and commanded their troops to go back to Yingtian.

On 6 July 1363 Zhu Yuan Zhang personally took command of a great army and went to rescue Nanchang. All his troops gathered in Longjiang (now Xiaguan, Nanjing, Jiangsu Province). Before the army started their march, a ceremony of offering sacrifice to the flags was held. They killed goats and pigs and spilt their blood to the flags. There were 200,000 naval soldiers in all. Generals Xu Da, Chang Yu Chun, Feng Guo Sheng, Yu Tong Hai and Liao Yong Zhong, and civil officials Liu Ji, Tao An and Xia Yu went with Zhu Yuan Zhang. On 16 July 1363 Zhu Yuan Zhang's great army reached Hukou (now in Jiangxi Province). He sent Commander Dai De to lead an army to station in Jingjiangkou (by the Yangtze River in the south of Susong, Anhui Province) and sent some troops to guard Nanhuzui situated in the northwest part of Hukou to cut Chen You Liang's retreat route. At the same time he sent an envoy to Xinzhou (now Shangrao, Jiangxi Province) to ask Hu De Ji to send an army to Wuyangdu (southeast of Nanchang County, Jiangxi Province) to prevent Chen You Liang from escaping to the southeast.

Chen You Liang had laid siege to the city of Nanchang for eighty-five days. When he found out that Zhu Yuan Zhang was bringing a great army to relieve Zhu Wen Zheng, he immediately raised the siege. His great fleet sailed eastward into Poyang Hu Lake to meet Zhu Yuan Zhang. Zhu Yuan Zhang and his army entered Poyang Hu Lake from Songmen (now in the south of Duchang, Jiangxi Province) and on 20 July 1363 they met with Chen You Liang's fleet near Kanglangshan (now Kangshan, situated in an island in the southwest part of Poyang Hu Lake, Jiangxi Province). Chen You Liang arranged his warships in a line to prevent Zhu Yuan Zhang from advancing.

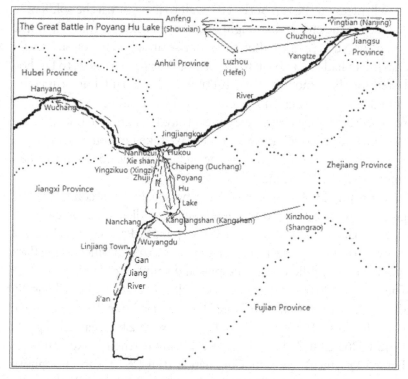

When Zhu Yuan Zhang saw that Chen You Liang's big warships had been linked together bow and stern, he said to his generals, "It would be very difficult for them to move forwards or backwards. I have a way to defeat them." He arranged his naval troops into eleven teams. Some teams used guns. Some teams used bows and arrows. Some teams used spears and swords. Zhu Yuan Zhang instructed his generals, "When you get close to the enemy ships, use fire power.

When you get closer, use bows and arrows. When you get right up to the ships, use spears and swords."

On 21 July 1363 Xu Da, Chang Yu Chun and Liao Yong Zhong commanded their boats to get close to the enemy big warships. Xu Da took the lead in charging the enemy. He commanded his troops to defeat Chen You Liang's vanguard army. They killed 1,500 enemy soldiers and captured one big warship. Yu Tong Hai ordered his soldiers to fire cannons and more than twenty enemy ships were destroyed. Many enemy soldiers were killed this way and many were drowned. Xu Da and the other generals fought for a very long time. Xu Da's ship caught fire. The enemy took the chance to attack, but Xu Da's men extinguished the fire and continued to fight. Zhu Yuan Zhang sent warships to reinforce Xu Da, and the enemy had to retreat.

Not long later Zhang Ding Bian, Chen You Liang's fierce general, came directly to attack Zhu Yuan Zhang's warship. The warship ran aground on the sand. The enemy ships surrounded Zhu Yuan Zhang's warship in three rings. Cheng Guo Sheng and Chen Zhao Xian fought very bravely to defend their leader. Han Cheng, a general under Zhu Yuan Zhang, said to him, "In ancient times people would sacrifice themselves for a just cause. I am willing to die for Your Highness." Then he put on Zhu Yuan Zhang's hat and robe and walked to the bow of the ship to show that he was Zhu Yuan Zhang. He jumped into the water in front of the enemies and was drowned to death.

The enemies believed that Zhu Yuan Zhang had died and they slowed down the attack. Cheng Guo Sheng and Chen Zhao Xian also died in this battle. The situation was tense. Chang Yu Chun came to rescue Zhu Yuan Zhang. He saw Zhang Ding Bian and pulled his bow and shot an arrow at him. Zhang Ding Bian was seriously wounded and had to retreat. Yu Tong Hai commanded his soldiers on warships to recue Zhu Yuan Zhang. The great waves made by the fast sailing boats moved Zhu Yuan Zhang's warship away from the sand and it was out of danger. Yu Tong Hai and Liao Yong Zhong took fast boats to pursue Zhang Ding Bian; they managed to hit him with many arrows and he had to escape.

It was sunset. Zhu Yuan Zhang gave the order to beat the gongs to signal a recall of the troops. He summoned all the generals to his warship and demanded them to maintain discipline over their troops in battle. The leader was worried that Zhang Shi Cheng would take his chance, now that Zhu Yuan Zhang and all the generals were fighting in Poyang Hu Lake and the defense of Yingtian was weak, to attack that city. So he sent Xu Da to lead his troops to go back to Yingtian.

In this battle, the generals fought with all their might regardless of their personal danger. Cheng Guo Sheng was originally the general under Zhu Wen Zheng defending Nanchang. In defending Fuzhou Gate he was struck by an arrow and fell down from the city wall into the water. Zhu Wen Zheng and the defenders thought that he had died, so a memorial service was performed in Nanchang. But actually Cheng Guo Sheng did not die; and he got away. He joined in the battle in Kanglangshan in Poyang Hu Lake and laid down his life in this battle. So another memorial service was performed in Kanglangshan, for those who died in this battle, including Cheng Guo Sheng.

On 22 July 1363 Zhu Yuan Zhang ordered the soldiers to blow their horns to send signals to all the troops to assemble. Zhu Yuan Zhang personally arranged the battle formation. Chen You Liang arranged all his big warships in a line. All the big warships were linked with one another like a small mountain. Zhu Yuan Zhang's warships were small. It was unfavorable for the small boats to attack the tall boats. Zhu Yuan Zhang ordered his soldiers to move forward. But the soldiers did not dare to go forward. The troops on the right even move backwards. Zhu Yuan Zhang was very angry and ordered to execute more than ten captains of the right army. But he still could not stop them from retreating. Marshal Guo Xing Jin said to Zhu Yuang Zhang, "The troops did not dare to advance because the enemy ships are much bigger than ours. If we want to defeat the enemy, we will have to use fire to destroy them." Zhu Yuan Zhang accepted his advice. He ordered Chang Yu Chun to gather fishing boats, and he collected seven of them. Bundles of reeds were stacked on the fishing boats and then gunpowder was added.

At sunset, a strong northeast wind rose up. Zhu Yuan Zhang ordered his men to put human figurines tied together with rice straw on the seven fishing boats; these figurines were equipped with armor and held weapons in their hands. He assigned "dare-to-die" soldiers to row these boats, each towing another small boat behind so they might make their get-away. Taking advantage of the northeast wind, the dare-to-die soldiers rowed the fishing boats southwestward to the big warships of Chen You Liang's army. When they got close, they set fire to the gunpowder on the reeds, jumped onto the smaller boats and escaped. The seven flaming fishing boats were blown by the strong wind and quickly drifted towards Chen You Liang's army. The flaming boats hit their targets and in just a moment, the big warships were on fire. Since all the warships were linked together, they were all on fire. The great flames and smoke rose very high. More than two hundred big warships were burned to the waterline and more than half of Chen You Liang's soldiers were burned to death, including his two younger brothers Chen You Ren and Chen You Gui. Zhu Yu Zhang ordered his troops to attack, and then 2,000 more enemy soldiers were killed.

5. The Great Battle in Poyang Hu Lake

The battle went on heatedly. Suddenly the mast of Zhang Zhi Xiong's ship broke and the ship could not move. The enemy soldiers found him trapped and they sailed their boats in very close. They used long spears to attack. Seeing that he could not escape, Zhang Zhi Xiong killed himself with his own sword. Ding Pu Lang, a member of the Privy Council, was wounded more than ten times in the battle. He fought very bravely in a very unfavorable situation. Suddenly his head was cut off— even so, his dead body without head was still standing upright with his weapon in his hands as if he was still fighting. In this battle, Generals Yu Xu, Chen Bi and Xu Gong Fu were killed in action.

Chen You Liang noticed that the mast of Zhu Yuan Zhang's warship was white. He planned to concentrate all his warships to attack this warship with the white mast. Somehow Zhu Yuan Zhang heard about this plan, and at night on 23 July 1363, he ordered the soldiers to paint the masts of all his warships white. At sunrise Chen You Liang found all those white masts and he could not identify which ship Zhu Yuan Zhang was on. This made him disheartened.

On 24 July 1363 Zhu Yuan Zhang commanded all his warships into battle. The battle raged on. At eleven o'clock in the morning, Zhu Yuan Zhang was sitting on a chair issuing orders to command his troops in the battle. Liu Ji was standing behind him. Suddenly Liu Ji jumped up with a loud shout. Zhu Yuan Zhang jumped up from the chair and looked back. Liu Ji was holding up his two hands and shouting, "The disaster star is coming! Go to another boat!" Zhu Yuan Zhang and Liu Ji immediately jumped into another boat. The boat sailed away quickly. Before Zhu Yuan Zhang could find a steady seat on the boat, shells fired by the enemy cannons came raining down on the warship where they had been on and blew it to pieces.

Chen You Liang was sitting on the top of his own big warship. He was overjoyed when he saw that Zhu Yuan Zhang's warship was blown to pieces; but very soon Zhu Yuan Zhang ordered his warships to start an overall attack. Liao Yong Zhong, Yu Tong Hai, Wang Xing Zu and Zhao Rong commanded their troops on six fast boats to go among the enemy's big ships. Sometimes these six fast boats disappeared and sometimes they came out from behind another ship. They sailed among the enemy ships like a dragon swimming in the water. When Zhu Yuan Zhang's generals and men saw this, they became more courageous. Their loud cheers shook the sky. Then the generals commanded their troops to besiege the enemy big warships. The soldiers of Zhu Yuan Zhang's army climbed up and killed all the soldiers on the first deck of the big warships. The soldiers rowing on the lower decks did not know this and they still pulled hard at their oars. Then Zhu Yuan Zhang's soldiers set fire to the ships and all the enemy soldiers were burned to death.

At noon Chen You Liang's army collapsed, and their flags and weapons sank in the lake. Liao Yong Zhong, Yu Tong Hai, Wang Xing Zu and Zhao Rong came back victoriously. Zhu Yuan Zhang highly praised them, saying, "Your heroic deeds have brought about today's great victory!"

Seeing that the situation was not favorable for him, Chen You Liang wanted to retreat to Xie Shan (now Xie Shan, an island in Poyang Hu Lake five kilometers south to Hukou, Jiangxi Province) for protection. But Zhu Yuan Zhang had already sent an army to Yingzikou (situated to the south of Xingzi, Jiangxi Province) to intercept Chen You Liang en route to Xie Shan. Chen You Liang could not escape. He had to gather all his warships together for self-protection. Zhu Yuan Zhang ordered the troops to sail to Chaipeng (situated thirty-five kilometers southeast to Duchang, Jiangxi Province). Zhu Yuan Zhang's warships were three kilometers away from Chen You Liang's warships.

Zhu Yuan Zhang sent an envoy to Chen You Liang to challenge him in battle. But Chen You Liang did not dare to take up the challenge. Zhu Yuan Zhang's generals wanted to retreat so as to let the soldiers to have a rest. Zhu Yuan Zhang said, "Now two hostile armies are locked in a stalemate. It is not wise for us to retreat first." Yu Tong Hai asked Zhu Yuan Zhang for permission to move the warships to the upstream of the Yangtze River because the water of Poyang Hu Lake was too shallow. Liu Ji secretly suggested to Zhu Yuan Zhang that they should move the warships to Hukou where they would fight a decisive battle on a day which he predicted was favorable for them; and Zhu Yuan Zhang followed his advice.

The watercourse was narrow for the warships, and two could not pass side by side. Zhu Yuan Zhang worried that Chen You Liang would seize the moment and start an attack, so at night he ordered the soldiers to hang a lantern at the stern of each warship as a signal to guide the following ship. Then they all began to sail along one after another through the dark. At daybreak they passed the shallows and were anchored in Zuoli (an island twenty-five kilometer northwest to Duchang, Jiangxi Province). Chen You Liang moved to Zhuji (situated to the south of Xingzi, Jiangxi Province), and the two hostile armies were locked in a stalemate for three days.

6. Cannons used by Zhu Yuan Zhang's army

Chen You Liang had two Grand Generals: the Left Grand General and the Right Grand General. Chen You Liang asked them for stratagems to cope with the present situation. The Right Grand General said, "Now we have suffered great setbacks. It is very difficult for our warships to sail out of Poyang Hu Lake. I think it would be better for us to burn all the ships and go by land. We may go to the areas south to the lake and start all over again there." The Left Grand General said, "Although we have suffered setbacks, we still have many troops. We may carry out a decisive battle with the remaining troops against Zhu Yuan Zhang's army. We still have a chance to win. Why should we burn all our warships to show that we are weaker than our enemy? If we disembark and go by land, our enemy will send foot soldiers and cavalrymen to pursue us. In that case we cannot go forward and we cannot turn back either. We are doomed to lose. How can we start all over again?"

Chen You Liang hesitated, unsure which advice he should take. After a moment he said, "The suggestion put forward by the Right Grand General is correct." When the Left Grand General heard these words, he was afraid that Chen You Liang would punish him for his suggestion. So he led all his soldiers to surrender to Zhu Yuan Zhang. The Right Grand General saw that the situation was desperate and he also led his troops to surrender.

That certainly made Chen You Liang's force weaker. Zhu Yuan Zhang sent an envoy with a letter to Chen You Liang. The letter read, "In the past I tried my best to keep peace with you. But you adopted the wrong policy and invaded my territory. So I had to fight back and took your eleven prefectures including Chiyang, Jiangzhou and Nanchang. But now you still insist on your wrong doings. You started the war again. You were stuck before the city of Nanchang. Later you were defeated in Kanglangshan. Your two younger brothers were killed in that battle. More than 30,000 of your generals and men died. You have not gained anything in these battles. This is because you have acted against the will of Heaven and you have lost the support of the people. You have a great army on huge warships which cannot move flexibly to confront my army. As a man of quick temper, you should have fought a decisive battle with me. But now you follow my actions slowly as if you were acting under my command. Is this what a true man should do? I hope you will make up your mind soon." Having read the letter, Chen You Liang was furious. He detained the envoy and did not let him go back. Then he ordered that all of Zhu Yuan Zhang's soldiers that were captured in battle be killed. When Zhu Yuan Zhang heard this, he ordered that all of Chen You Liang's soldiers that had been captured be set free. He had medicine given to the wounded soldiers. All the captured soldiers were sent back to Chen You Liang's army. And he issued an order: "From now on, don't kill any soldiers captured from Chen You Liang's army." Zhu Yuan Zhang ordered a memorial service for Chen You Liang's two younger brothers and all the generals and men of Chen You Liang's army who had died in battle.

Zhu Yuan Zhang ordered his troops to sail all the warships to Hukou (now Hukou, Jiangxi Province) which was situated at the estuary of the Yangtze River where the water of the Poyang Hu Lake flew into the Yangtze River. He ordered Chang Yu Chun and Liao Yong Zhong to command the navy to line up the warships on the lake to prevent Chen You Liang's fleet from sailing out of the lake. He ordered soldiers to erect wooden posts on the bank to prevent Chen You Liang's troops from landing. Zhu Yuan Zhang's army controlled the estuary for fifteen days. But Chen You Liang did not dare to come out.

In August 1363, Zhu Yuan Zhang again sent an envoy to Chen You Liang. The letter read, "Last time when I was confronted with you in the area of Zhuji, I sent an envoy to you. Till now my envoy has not yet come back. What a narrow-minded man you are! A true man should fight for the whole realm. What profound hatred do you have that you should detain my envoy? In the areas of the Yangtze River and the Huai River there are only two heroes, that is, you and me. Why should we kill each other? I have got all your territory. It is impossible for you to recover your territory even if you and all your remaining troops fight a decisive battle with my army. If you are so lucky as to be able to escape back to Wuchang, you should give up the title of emperor and wait for your true master to come. Otherwise all the members of your clan will be extinguished. By that time it will be too late for you to have any regrets." Having read the letter, Chen You Liang was very angry. He did not give any reply to Zhu Yuan Zhang.

Chen You Liang had run out of food. He sent troops by ship to Nanchang, where they plundered the villages to get food. Zhu Wen Zheng sent troops to burn their boats. The situation became even worse for Chen You Liang. Finally, he decided to escape back to Wuchang (now Wuchang, Wuhan, Hubei Province). He commanded more than a hundred big warships to sail to Nanhuzui (northwest of Hukou, Jiangxi Province) and on 26 August 1363 he tried to make a breakthrough. He wanted to go into the Yangtze River through Hukou, but Zhu Yuan Zhang's troops blocked the way and prevented Chen You Liang's ships from entering the Yangtze River. Zhu Yuan Zhang's soldiers rowed boats and rafts with reeds and gunpowder to attack the enemy ships with fire, and many enemy warships were destroyed. Chen You Liang's army fought desperately. The battle went on from morning till night. Chen You Liang and his troops set off for Jingjiangkou (a place by the Yangtze River in the south of Susong, Anhui Province), but General Dai De commanded his troops to attack him.

Not long later that day a soldier of Chen You Liang's army came to surrender. He told Zhu Yuan Zhang that in the battle in Jingjiangkou a stray arrow had struck Chen You Liang in one of his eyes and the arrow went through his head and killed him. When Zhu Yuan

Zhang's troops got the news, they cheered loudly and they fought more bravely. They captured Chen Shan Er, Chen You Liang's eldest son and the Crown Prince of the State of Han, and Yao Tian Xiang, one of the Managers of Governmental Affairs of the State of Han. On 27 August Chen Rong, another Manager of Governmental Affairs of the State of Han, led all the naval troops, 50,000 in all, to surrender. Zhang Ding Bian rowed a small boat, taking Chen Li, the younger son of Chen You Liang, and carrying the dead body of Chen You Ling in the boat at night and escaped back to Wuchang (now Wuchang, Wuhan, Hubei Province). He put Chen Li on the throne of the State of Han.

After Chen You Liang had been defeated, Zhu Yuan Zhang said to Liu Ji, "I did not take your advice; I personally led a great army to rescue Anfeng. I made a serious mistake. If Chen You Liang had taken the chance when I was away and the defense of Yingtian was weak to command his fleets down the Yangtze River to attack Yingtian, I would have been put in a very awkward situation. I could not achieve anything when I went forward and I would not have been able to turn back either. My great cause of unifying the whole realm would not be realized. But Chen You Liang also made a mistake. He did not attack Yingtian. Instead he attacked Nanchang. This was his worst plan. He is doomed to perish. Now that Chen You Liang has died, it will not be difficult for me to pacify the whole realm."

On 1 September 1363 Zhu Yuan Zhang started from Hukou to go back to Yingtian. On 6 September he reached Yingtian. Zhu Yuan Zhang granted awards to his generals according to their contributions in the battles in Poyang Hu Lake. He granted landed properties to Chang Yu Chu and Liao Yong Zhong. He granted gold and silver to those generals and officers who had contributed greatly to his success.

On 16 September Zhu Yuan Zhang ordered Li Shan Chang and Deng Yu to defend Yingtian. He commanded Chang Yu Chun, Kang Mao Cai, Liao Yong Zhong and Hu Mei with a great army to carry out an expedition against Chen Li. On 7 October 1363 Zhu Yuan Zhang and his great army reached Wuchang. Zhu Yuan Zhang ordered Chang Yu Chun to send troops to the four gates of Wuchang to erect great wooden posts to build fences to block the four gates. Zhu Yuan Zhang's troops established their camps outside the city of Wuchang. He ordered the troops to line up the warships to form a long stronghold to prevent Chen Li's reinforcing army from entering Wuchang. He sent troops to take Hanyang (now Hanyang, Wuhan, Hubei Province) and De'an (now Anlu, Hubei Province). The governors of the prefectures in the area of Hubei surrendered to Zhu Yuan Zhang.

On 1 December 1363 Zhu Yuan Zhang left Wuchang for Yingtian. Before he left, he said to Chang Yu Chun, "Chen Li is now like a lonely little pig. If he is kept inside the pigsty for a long time, he will be tired out and will submit. If he wants to make a breakthrough, don't fight with him. You may just order your troops to hold fast to their camps and the wooden fences. Our enemy will collapse. We shall surely take Wuchang." On 19 December Zhu Yuan Zhang went back to Yingtian.

(6) Zhu Yuan Zhang Ascends the Throne of King of Wu

Zhu Yuan Zhang had performed great deeds and contributed to bringing peace to the realm. His generals and officials suggested many times that he should make himself king. But he would not take their suggestions. He said, "The war has not yet ended. The destruction brought about by the war has not been repaired. We are not sure whom Heaven has appointed as the true ruler of this realm. The people are still living in suffering. It would be quite premature for me to ascend the throne. It would be better to wait until the whole realm is at peace." But Li Shang Chang and the other officials insisted, and at last Zhu Yuan Zhang accepted their suggestion.

On 1 January 1364 Zhu Yuan Zhang took the throne as the King of Wu. He appointed Li Shang Chang as Right Premier, Xu Da as Left Premier, and Chang Yu Chun and Yu Tong Hai as Managers of Governmental Affairs. He made his eldest son Zhu Biao Successor to the Throne. Zhu Yuan Zhang said to Li Shan Chang, "We have just founded our state. The most important thing is to reform the state law and the legal system. The officials in the court of the Yuan Dynasty were corrupt. The Emperor of the Yuan Dynasty was fatuous. The legal system collapsed. Power was not in the hands of the emperor but in the hands of the officials. This led to confusion and chaos in the whole realm. I hope you and all the officials will draw lessons from the failure of the Yuan Dynasty. You should unite together and work hard to make our state prosperous."

Zhu Yuan Zhang also told his generals and officials, "Rules of etiquette form an important part of the legal system. If the rules of etiquette are established, the people will be able to live in tranquility. If the leaders at higher levels and their subordinates work in harmony, the society will be in peace and good order. We have just founded our state. Our most important task is to establish rules of etiquette. When I rose in revolt in Haozhou, I found that many generals were lawless. They ignored laws and rules. They were only after personal gain. They committed all kinds of ruthless acts. They did not know how to control their subordinates. This led to their destruction. Today all the marshals and generals I have appointed have fought side by side with me and have made great contributions. Since they came to submit to me, I have given titles to them and stated to them clearly all the rules that they should observe. So they all observe my orders. You are my ministers and assist me in managing the state. You should also observe these rules."

(7) The Final Destruction of the State of Han

Zhu Yuan Zhang's army surrounded the city of Wuchang for a long time but could not take it. On 1 February 1364 Zhu Yuan Zhang started from Yingtian to Wuchang to supervise the attack. On 17 February he reached Wuchang. He urged the generals to launch their attack.

Gaoguanshan Mountain, to the east of the city, was a dominating height. Some troops of the State of Han were stationed there. Zhu Yuan Zhang asked his generals, "Who will take that mountain for me?" The generals looked at each other but no one would accept the challenge. Finally, Fu You De offered to undertake the task. He commanded several hundred soldiers to attack the troops of the State of Han on the mountain. He took the lead in climbing up the mountain. An arrow struck him on the face but he insisted on going forward in spite of the pain. He at last took the mountain.

Chen Tong Qian, a fierce general of the State of Han, suddenly dashed into Zhu Yuan Zhang's command tent with a long spear in his hands. At that time Zhu Yuan Zhang was sitting on a chair. In this critical moment he shouted, "Guo Ying, kill him for me!" Guo Ying ran forward, spear in hand, with a loud shout. He thrust his spear at Chen Tong Qian and killed him. Zhu Yuan Zhang exclaimed, "You are as brave and as quick as Yuchi Jing De!" He took off his battle robe and put it on Guo Ying as a reward. He compared Guo Ying to Yuchi Jing De, the hero who had saved Li Shi Min, Emperor Taizong of the Tang Dynasty, in a very dangerous situation.

Chen Li and Zhang Ding Bian saw that the situation was very unfavorable for them. They sent soldiers to go out of the city by ropes and baskets to Yuezhou (now Yueyang, in the northeast part of Hunan Province) to ask Zhang Bi Xian, the Premier of the State of Han, for help. Zhang Bi Xian sent an army to rescue Wuchang. When Zhang Bi Xian reached Hongshan (ten kilometers away from Wuchang), Zhu Yuan Zhang ordered Chang Yu Chun to take the elite troops to attack him, and after a battle, Chang Yu Chun captured Zhang Bi Xian. Zhang Bi Xian was a fierce general. He was brought to the foot of the city wall of Wuchang. A general of Zhu Yuan Zhang's army shouted to Chen Li and Zhang Ding Bian, who were standing at the top of the city wall, "You depended on Zhang Bi Xian to recue you. Now Zhang Bi Xian has been captured by us. Who else can you depend on to rescue you?" Zhang Bi Xian shouted to Zhang Ding Bian, "I have been captured. I hope you will surrender as soon as possible." Zhang Ding Bian was so angry that he was speechless.

Several days later Zhu Yuan Zhang sent Luo Fu Ren to Wuchang to persuade Chen Li to surrender. Luo Fu Ren had been a minister under Chen You Liang. After he had worked for some time for Chen You Liang, he realized that Chen You Liang would end up in failure, so he ran away to Yingtian to serve Zhu Yuan Zhang. Luo Fu Ren said to Zhu Yuan Zhang, "Your Highness has practiced benevolence. You have granted blessings to this place. You have done your best to keep Chen Li alive so as to preserve Chen You Liang's descendents. I will do my best to accomplish my task. I will not regret even if I should die." Zhu Yuan Zhang said, "I have sufficient force to take Wuchang. I have stationed my army in this place for a long time because I am waiting for Chen Li to decide to submit to me so as to avoid deaths of both sides in the battle to take the city. You just go and do your best to accomplish your task." When Luo Fu Ren reached the foot of the city wall, he cried bitterly. Chen Li was greatly surprised to this. He summoned Luo Fu Ren into the city. After Luo Fu Ren had entered the city, he cried bitterly again. Chen Li asked him why he was so sad. Luo Fu Ren conveyed Zhu Yuan Zhang's intention in earnest words to Chen Li. All the generals, even Zhang Ding Bian, knew that it was impossible for them to hold out any more.

On 19 February 1364 Chen Li came out of the city of Wuchang without wearing his upper garment and with a piece of jade in his mouth, leading Zhang Ding Bian and all his generals and officials to the gate of the camps of Zhu Yuan Zhang's army, to surrender. When Chen Li saw Zhu Yuan Zhang, he immediately knelt down in front of him and was trembling all over. He did not dare to look up at the great man. Zhu Yuan Zhang saw that Chen Li was young and weak. He helped Chen Li up. Holding Chen Li's hands Zhu Yuan Zhang said, "Don't be afraid. I will not punish you." He sent eunuchs into the palace to tell Chen You Liang's father and mother that they were allowed to take all the treasures in the official treasure house. He ordered the soldiers to escort the officials to leave the palace batch by batch. Zhu Yuan Zhang ordered them to provide clothes to the wives and children of the officials and they went away together. Zhu Yuan Zhang ordered soldiers to escort Chen Li, Chen You Liang's father and mother and all the officials to Yingtian.

Zhu Yuan Zhang's great army had laid siege to the city of Wuchang for six months and at last brought Chen Li to submission. After Chen Li had surrendered, no soldiers of Zhu Yuan Zhang's army were allowed to go into the city. There was peace and order. It seemed that the people in the city did not know that a great army was stationed outside the city. Some of the people in the city suffered from hunger. Zhu Yuan Zhang ordered rice to be distributed to the hungry people. He summoned the elders of the city to his office and comforted them. The people were all very happy. From then on the prefectures in the areas of Hanyang (now Hanyang, Wuhan, Hubei Province), Mianyang (now Xiantao, Hubei Province), Jingzhou (now Jingzhou, Hubei Province) and Yuezhou (now Yueyang, in the northeast part of Hunan Province) surrendered to Zhu Yuan Zhang. Zhu Yuan Zhang established the Office of Government of Huguang (meaning Hubei Province, Hunan Province and Guangdong Province). He appointed Yang Jing, a member of the Privy Council, as the Governor of Huguang.

On 1 March 1364 Zhu Yuan Zhang turned back to Yingtian. On 2 March he made Chen Li Marquis of Guide.

On 3 April 1364 Zhu Yuan Zhang issued an order to build a Temple of Loyal Generals and Officials in Kanglangshan (now Kangshan,

Jiangxi Province) by Poyang Hu Lake to memorize the thirty-six generals and officials who had laid down their lives in the battle in Poyang Hu Lake including Ding Pu Lang, Cheng Guo Sheng, Zhang Zhi Xiong, Chen Zhao Xian, Han Cheng and Song Gui. Zhu Yuan Zhang also issued an order to build a Temple of Loyal Generals and Officials in Nanchang to memorize the fifteen generals and officials who had laid down their lives in defending Nanchang including Zhao De Sheng, Li Ji Xian, Niu Hai Long, Zhao Guo Wang, Xu Gui, Zhu Qian, Liu Qi, Zhu Shu Hua and Zhao Tian Lin.

(8) Actions to Take the Rest of the State of Han

Although the State of Han had been destroyed, Xiong Tian Rui, a general under Chen You Ling, still occupied Ganzhou (now Ganzhou, in the southern part of Jiangxi Province). On 1 August 1364 Zhu Yuan Zhang ordered Chang Yu Chun who had just taken Luzhou (now Hefei, Anhui Province), and Deng Yu who was in Yingtian to lead their troops to take Ganzhou. Deng Yu commanded his troops to march from Yingtian to Luzhou to join forces with Chang Yu Chu's troops. On 6 August the troops under Chang Yu Chun and Deng Yu reached Ji'an (now Ji'an, Jiangxi Province). Chang Yu Chun sent an envoy to Ji'an to tell Rao Ding Chen, the commander-in-chief of the Han army defending Ji'an, "I am now going to take Ganzhou. You may come out of the city to go with me."

Rao Ding Chen did not dare to go out of the city. He sent his youngest son to go out of the city to see Chang Yu Chun. Chang Yu Chun was sitting on a chair in his tent, drinking wine. He invited Rao Ding Chen's son to sit by the table and drink with him. Then he sent him back to the city of Ji'an, saying, "Go back and say this to your father: 'What are you planning to do? You want to hide in the city and not to come out? I am leaving. I will not stay in Ji'an just for you. You may make a proper arrangement.'" When his son conveyed Chang Yu Chun's words to him, Rao Ding Chen was very afraid. That night, he gave up the city and ran away to Anfu (now in Jiangxi Province) in the dark. The next morning, Chang Yu Chun took Ji'an. Next, Chang Yu Chun commanded his troops to march to Ganzhou and laid siege to the city.

On 24 August, Zhu Yuan Zhang ordered Xu Da and Yang Jing to command a great army to attack Jiangling (now Jiangling County,

Hubei Province). Zhang Jue, a Manager of Governmental Affairs of the State of Han, surrendered and presented the city of Jiangling to Xu Da. Zhang Jue said, "The one who should be executed is me. The people of the city are innocent." Xu Da highly praised his words and issued an order to prohibit his soldiers from killing and looting the people. When the defenders of the prefectures nearby heard about this, they surrendered and presented the prefectures to Xu Da.

Chang Yu Chun had laid siege to Ganzhou for about two months but he could not take the city. Zhu Yuan Zhang sent an envoy to tell Chang Yu Chun, "Xiong Tian Rui is now defending an isolated city. He is like a bird in a cage and an animal in a trap. He can do nothing. What I am worrying about is when the city is taken too many people would be killed. You should keep this in mind: when the city is taken, you should do your best to protect the lives and properties of the people. If you can do this, you will make great contributions to the realm; and this will also be an example to convince those who are defending other cities to surrender; and this will bring fortune to your generations to come. General Deng Yu of the Han Dynasty never killed innocent people. His descendants were flourishing. You may learn from him. In the great battle in Poyang Hu Lake, Chen You Liang was defeated. We captured many of his soldiers. Till today, these soldiers are fighting for us. Even if some of them have escaped, they are now our people. If we get the land and there are no people on the land, what is the use of the land?"

At that time Xiong Tian Rui defended the city resolutely. Chang Yu Chun ordered the soldiers under him to erect piles of wood to build a fence to keep the enemy from escaping. One day Xiong Yuan Zhen, Xiong Tian Rui's adopted son, secretly went out of the city to spy on the camps of Chang Yu Chun's troops. Incidentally Xiong Yuan Zhen came across Chang Yu Chun as he was coming out of his camp on a horse with several cavalrymen, but he did not recognize him until Chang Yu Chun came back. When Xiong Yuan Zhen realized that the man was Chang Yu Chu, he started a surprise attack. Chang Yu Chun sent a warrior to fight with him. The warrior waved his two broadswords to meet Xiong Yuan Zhen's attack. Xiong Yuan Zhen raised his hammer to resist the two broadswords. He retreated while fighting. When Chang Yu Chun saw this, he exclaimed, "What a strong man he is!" Then he ordered the warrior to let him go.

The siege of the city of Ganzhou lasted for five months from August 1364 to January 1365. The army under Xiong Tian Rui ran out of food. On 10 January 1365 Xiong Tian Rui sent his adopted son to go out of the city first to tell Chang Yu Chun that he would surrender. Not long later he went out of the city without wearing any clothes on his upper body. He walked to the gate of the camps of Chang Yu Chun's army and presented all the places he was in charge of defending such as Nan'an (now Dayu, Jiangxi Province), Xiongzhou (now Nanxiong, in northern Guangdong Province) and Shaozhou (in now Shaoguan) to Chang Yu Chun. Chang Yu Chun sent a party of soldiers to escort Xiong Tian Rui to Yingtian.

When Zhu Yuan Zhang learned that Chang Yu Chun had not killed a single person when Ganzhou was taken, he was extremely glad. He sent an envoy to praise him and tell him, "I hear that an army which practices benevolence is invincible. The general who does not practice benevolence is incapable. Now you have defeated the army defending Ganzhou without killing a single person. When I got the report of the victory, I would send my hearty congratulation to you. Even Chao Bin, the great general of the Song Dynasty, did not do as well as you when he took Jinling of the State of Jiangnan! Your great deeds have spread far and wide. I am very glad that I have such a great general to accomplish all kinds of difficult tasks!"

When Xiong Tian Rui ruled over Ganzhou, he levied heavy taxes on the people. After Ganzhou had been taken, Zhu Yuan Zhang ordered a reduction in taxes on the people and exemptions for those poor people who were unable to pay.

On 13 January 1365 Chang Yu Chun and his troops entered Nan'an (now Dayu, Jiangxi Province). He sent generals to Shaozhou (now Shaoguan, in the northern part of Guangdong Province) and Xiongzhou (now Nanxiong, in northern Guangdong Province) to summon the generals defending such cities to surrender. Then Zhang Bing Yi, the general of the Han army defending Shaozhou, and Sun Zu Rong, the general of the Han army defending Xiongzhou, came to Nan'an to surrender bringing all their troops and all the food supplies for the army. Chang Yu Chun ordered Commander Wang Yu to defend Xiongzhou; Zhang Bing Yi, the general originally defending Shaozhou for the State of Han, to defend Shaozhou. Then Chang Yu Chun commanded his main force to return to Yingtian triumphantly.

Having taken Jiangling, Xu Da commanded his army to march to Baoqing (now Shaoyang, Hunan Province) and took it. The officials of Jingzhou (now Jingzhou Miaozu Dongzu Zizhixian, in the southwest part of Hunan Province) surrendered. From then on the areas of Hubei Province and Hunan Province had been pacified. Xu Da also commanded his main force to return to Yingtian triumphantly.

3. ZHU YUAN ZHANG PACIFIES ZHANG SHI CHENG'S STATE OF WU

(1) Zhang Shi Cheng Proclaims Himself King of Wu

In August 1363 Zhang Shi Cheng took a chance when Zhu Yuan Zhang had gone to the west to carry out an expedition against Chen You Liang to force Dashitemuer, the Governor of Jiangsu-Zhejiang Area of the Yuan Dynasty, to ask the court of the Yuan Dynasty to make him king. Dashitemuer had to write letters to the court of the Yuan Dynasty asking the court to make Zhang Shi Cheng king. But the court did not give any reply. So Zhang Shi Cheng proclaimed himself King. He changed the name of his state from the State of Dazhou to the State of Wu. He ordered workmen to build palaces in Suzhou (now Suzhou, Jiangsu Province).

At that time Zhang Shi Cheng still claimed that the State of Wu was under the Yuan Dynasty. But when the court of the Yuan Dynasty sent officials to Suzhou to demand that Zhang Shi Cheng make tribute to the court, he refused to give any. Yu Si Qi, an official under Zhang Shi Cheng, said, "We were outlaws before. It was alright for us not to make any tribute to the court. But now we are officials of the court of the Yuan Dynasty. Is it proper for us to refuse to make tribute to the court?" At these words Zhang Shi Cheng was so angry that he knocked the table to the ground and went into an inner room. Yu Si Qi saw that Zhang Shi Cheng was going to finally end up in failure, so he resigned and went back home.

Chen Ji, one of the advisers of Zhang Shi Cheng, had tried to persuade Zhang Shi Cheng not to proclaim himself king. Zhang Shi Chang was very angry and wanted to kill him. But later he changed his mind and appointed Chen Ji as the Head of the Secretariat in charge of writing letters and documents. Chen Ji did not want to be of service to Zhang Shi Cheng, but he could not find a chance to run away.

In August 1364 Zhang Shi Cheng sent an official to see Dashitemuer to list all the mistakes Dashitemuer had made, and he forced him to resign the position of the Governor of Jiangsu-Zhejiang Area on the grounds that Dashitemuer was old and sick. Zhang Shi Cheng said that the position of Governor should be given to Zhang Shi Xin, his younger brother. Zhang Shi Xin forced Dashitemuer to hand the official seal of the Governor of Jiangsu-Zhejiang Area. Then Zhang Shi Xin proclaimed himself the Governor of the Jiangsu-Zhejiang Area and he ordered soldiers to escort Dashitemuer to Jiaxing (in northeastern Zhejiang Province) and put him under house arrest.

From then on Zhang Shi Cheng had a vast territory, in the north of which there were Tongzhou, Taizhou, Gaoyou, Huai'an, Xuzhou (all in Jiangsu Province), Suzhou (now Suzhou, Anhui Province) and Sizhou (now Xuyi, Jiangsu Province), and in the south he controlled Shaoxing (in Zhejiang Province), and in the west Haozhou (now Bengbu, Anhui Province).

Zhang Shi Cheng demanded Buhatemuer, the Chief Secretary of the Zhejiang Area of the Yuan Dynasty, to write a letter asking the court of the Yuan Dynasty to make him a True King. But Buhatemuer refused. Zhang Shi Cheng sent an official to Buhatemuer to demand that he hand over the official seal of the Chief Secretary. But Buhatemuer hid the official seal in a secret place. He said, "I will not hand over the official seal to Zhang Shi Cheng even if I should die." Zhang Shi Cheng forced him to go on a boat. Buhatemuer said, "I would rather nobly die than be insulted by others." He changed his clothes calmly. Then he took some poison and killed himself. When Dashitemuer got news that Buhatemuer had committed suicide, he said, "Buhatemuer would rather die than submit. It is no use for me to live on." He also took poison and killed himself.

Since Zhang Shi Cheng had got the Jiangsu-Zhejing Area, he entrusted the power of managing this area to Zhang Shi Xin. He did not attend to the state affairs. But Zhang Shi Xin was a dissolute person. When he attained a position of power, he started large-scale construction of his office and residence. He collected many female singers and dancers in his home. Whenever he was sent out with an army to go to battle, he brought along all these female singers and dancers and all kinds of instruments for gambling and games. Zhang Shi Xin had three favorite subordinates. They were Huang Jing Fu,

Cai Yan Fu and Ye De Xin. They tried their best to please Zhang Shi Xin, and he entrusted them with great power. When Zhu Yuan Zhang got this information, he said to his ministers and officials, "Every day I spend a lot of energy attending to state affairs. I carry out the laws strictly. Still some persons have deceived me. Zhang Shi Cheng stays at home all the year round and does not attend to the state affairs. He will surely be defeated."

(2) Battles to Resist Zhang Shi Cheng's Attacks

In October 1364 Zhang Shi Cheng sent his younger brother Zhang Shi Xin to attack Changxing (in northern Zhejiang Province). Geng Bing Wen and Fei Ju, the generals defending Changxing, defeated the brother and captured his general Song Xing Zu. Zhang Shi Xin was very angry and sent more troops to lay siege to the city of Changxing. Tang He commanded troops to rescue Changxing from Changzhou (now Changzhou, Jiangsu Province). Tang He's troops attacked Zhang Shi Xin's army from outside the city and Geng Bing Wen's troops attacked Zhang Shi Xin's army from inside the city. Zhang Shi Xin was defeated and ran back to Suzhou. In January 1365 Zhang Shi Cheng commanded an army to attack Changxing again. Geng Bing Wen defeated Zhang Shi Cheng's army at the foot of the city wall of Changxing. From then on Zhang Shi Cheng did not dare to attack Changxing again. Geng Bing Wen defended the city of Changxing for ten years. He fought very bravely to defend this isolated city. The city of Changxing defended by Geng Bing Wen, the city of Changzhou defended by Tang He and the city of Jiangyin (now Jiangyin, Jiangsu Province) defended by Wu Liang formed a protective screen for Yingtian.

On 18 February 1365 Zhang Shi Cheng sent Li Bo Sheng, the Prime Minister of the State of Wu, to take command of a 200,000-man force to attack Zhuquan (now Zhuji, Zhejiang Province). Li Bo Sheng brought Xie Zai Xing with him. Xie Zai Xing was originally a general under Zhu Yuan Zhang. He had been the commanding general of Zhu Yuang Zhang's army defending Zhuquan. He had two subordinates who often travelled to Hangzhou (now Hangzhou, Zhejiang Province) to do business. They revealed military secrets to Zhang Shi Cheng. Zhu Yuan Zhang was very angry and arrested them and killed them. Zhu Yuan Zhang suspected that Xie Zai Xing had been involved in it. So he summoned Xie Zai Xing to Yingtian. So in April 1363 Xie Zai Xing rebelled and ran away to Shaoxing (now Shaoxing, Zhejiang Province) to surrender to Zhang Shi Cheng.

Li Bo Sheng and Xie Zai Xing established camps and storehouses outside Zhuquan to make preparations for a protracted war. Li Bo Sheng sent over 30,000 troops to occupy the place to the north of the city of Zhuquan to block the way from which Zhu Yuan Zhang's army would come to rescue Zhuquan. Hu De Ji, a manager of the governmental affairs of Zhejiang Province appointed by Zhu Yuan Zhang, ordered the soldiers to fortify the defense of the city of Zhuquan. At the same time he sent out envoys to Yanzhou (now Jiande, Zhejiang Province) to ask Li Wen Zhong, the Governor of Zhejiang Province appointed by Zhu Yuan Zhang, for help. Li Wen Zhong ordered Commander Zhang Bin to lead some troops to Pujiang (in Zhejiang Province) to show to the enemy that a rescuing army was coming.

Zhang Shi Cheng sent some troops to march from Tonglu (in Zhejiang Province) along Fuchun Jiang River to Diaotai (now Diaotai, fifteen kilometers south of Tonglu) to threaten Yanzhou. Li Wen Zhong ordered the naval troops to sail down Fuchun Jiang River to meet Zhang Shi Cheng's troops coming from Tonglu. He made arrangements to defend Yanzhou. Then he himself led an army with General Zhu Liang Zu to rescue Zhuquan.

On 29 February Li Wen Zhong stationed his army in a place ten kilometers away from Zhuquan. Hu De Ji sent a secret envoy to tell Li Wen Zhong, "The enemy force is very strong. We should avoid fighting with this strong army for now so as to wait for the coming of the great army of reinforcements." Li Wen Zhong said, "From the standpoint of numbers, our enemy will win. But from the standpoint of strategy, we will win. In the past, General Xie Xuan of the Eastern Jin with 8,000 men defeated one million men headed by Fu Jian, the King of the Former Qin. The most important thing for an army is that its soldiers are keen-witted and capable. The number of soldiers in this army is only secondary." Then he issued an order, saying, "The number of enemy soldiers is great, but they are arrogant and strong in appearance but weak in reality. We have fewer soldiers, but they are all very keen-witted and capable. One soldier of our army can take on ten enemies. Our elite troops will surely win against the arrogant enemy. Now the military supplies of our enemy are piled up like mountains. These military supplies are gifts Heaven has granted to us. Let's fight bravely to get them."

In the next morning, when the soldiers were having breakfast, a scout came to report to Li Wen Zhong that the enemy troops were coming. Li Wen Zhong immediately deployed his troops in battle formation. He arranged all the elite troops on the right wing and the left wing of the battle formation. He sent Generals Xu Da Xing and Tang Ke Ming to command the troops on the left wing and Generals Yan De and Wang Shao to command the troops on the right wing. He himself commanded the troops on the center of the battle formation to cope with the chariots of the enemy troops. At this time the rescuing troops commanded by General Geng Tian Bi sent by Hu Shen, the Commander-in-chief of the army defending Chuzhou (now Lishui, Zhejiang Province), arrived. The troops under Li Wen Zhong were greatly inspired. Li Wen Zhong led about thirty cavalrymen to ride very quickly to the rear of the battle formation of the enemy troops to start a fierce attack of the main force of the enemy. The commander of the enemy troops sent cavalrymen to surround Li Wen Zhong in several rings.

Li Wen Zhong was wounded several times in the knees by spears of the enemy soldiers, but Li Wen Zhong gave a loud shout and killed several generals. He was invincible. The troops of the left wing and the right wing of the battle formation charged at the enemy. Hu De Ji commanded the troops to come out of the city of Zhuquan with loud shouts and loud drum beatings. Zhang Shi Cheng's troops collapsed and escaped in all directions. The troops under Li Wen Zhong and Hu De Ji chased the enemy troops for five kilometers. They killed more than 10,000. Li Wen Zhong recalled all his troops for lunch. Then he sent Zhu Liang Zu and Zhang Bin to pursue the remaining enemy troops. In this battle over thirty enemy camps were burned. Six hundred generals and officers and 3,000 soldiers of Zhang Shi Cheng's army were captured. They got eight hundred horses. The military supplies, armors, weapons left behind by Zhang Shi Cheng's army piled up like small mountains. Li Bo Sheng and Xie Zai Xing had a very narrow escape.

When Zhu Yuan Zhang got the news of the great victory in Zhuquan, he was extremely happy. He summoned Li Wen Zhong and Hu De Ji to Yingtian. He granted them grand clothes and good horses. And he promoted Hu De Shen as the Head of the Office of the Secretariat of Zhejiang Province.

(3) Battles to Take the Important Cities of Zhang Shi Cheng's State of Wu

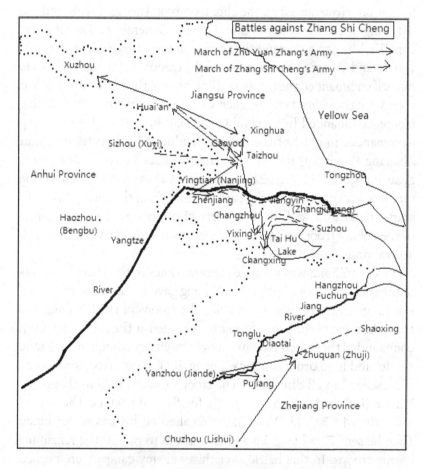

Zhang Shi Cheng had invaded Zhu Yuan Zhang's territory several times. Zhu Yuan Zhang made up his mind to carry out an expedition against him. On 14 October 1365, Zhu Yuan Zhang issued an order which read, "Zhang Shi Cheng keeps stirring up trouble. He attacked my cities of Anfeng and Zhuquan. He has sent troops to cause great disasters to my people. He has committed a serious crime which deserves death penalty. Today I will send my great army to carry out an expedition against him. My purpose is only to put Zhang Shi Cheng to death. You are not to scare the ordinary soldiers and people. Don't cause the people to desert their homes so that no one will till the land; I don't want agricultural production to be affected. I have ordered the Grand General to discipline all the officers and men. Anyone who has committed the crimes of raping women or looting the people will be punished according to military law."

Most of the action took place in Jiangsu Province. On 17 October Zhu Yuan Zhang ordered Xu Da, the Left Premier, Chang Yu Chun, a Manager of Governmental Affairs, Hu Mei, a Manager of Governmental Affairs, Feng Guo Sheng, a member of Privy Council, and Hua Gao, the Head of the Secretariat, to command cavalry, infantry and the navy to take Taizhou and Tongzhou. On 21 October Xu Da ordered his troops to lay siege to the city of Taizhou. Zhang Shi Cheng sent Marshal Wang Cheng to lead an army to rescue Taizhou from the north of the Huai River. Xu Da's troops defeated this rescuing army and captured the marshal.

On 25 October Zhang Shi Cheng sent an army from Huai'an to rescue Taizhou. Chang Yu Chun defeated them, then he sent an envoy to the city of Taizhou to persuade the defending generals to surrender. But Zhang Shi Cheng's generals, Yan Zai Xing, Xia Si Zhong and Zhang Shi Jun, refused to surrender. They resisted the attacks resolutely. Xu Da had to increase the troops surrounding the city.

On 1 of the second October, Kang Mao Cai, the general defending the naval camps by the Jiangyin section of the Yangtze River (on the south bank), sent an envoy to Yingtian to report to Zhu Yuan Zhang urgently, "Zhang Shi Cheng has sent troops on more than four hundred ships to come along the Yangtze River. The ships have reached Fancaigang. He has also sent troops on smaller boats to Gushan; now they are sailing back and forth along the River. Please get ready to repel an attack by Zhang Shi Chang's army."

When Zhu Yuan Zhang got Kang Mao Cai's report, he analyzed the enemy's actions carefully and saw through Zhang Shi Cheng's plan. He sent an envoy to tell Xu Da, "The enemy troops are now stationed in Fancaigang. I think this is a deceptive move. Now these enemy troops are hesitating and dare not sail up the Yangtze River. This makes it more clear that it is merely a deception. Zhang Shi Cheng is not planning to attack. His purpose is to get us to send troops to repel them, so that our force will be dispersed. Now you should order Liao Yong Zhong to lead some troops to defend the naval camps by the river. The main force will just stay where it is and should not be moved anywhere. The enemy is now sailing back and forth along the Yangtze River. They will be tired out soon and will lose their concentration. We may take this chance to storm the city of Taizhou. If we take Taizhou, the enemy troops on the Yangtze River will collapse. The only thing we should do is to prepare well."

On 26 of the second October, Xu Da and Chang Yu Chun took Taizhou. They captured Yan Zai Xing, the Commander-in-chief of Zhang Shi Cheng's army defending Taizhou. Zhu Yuan Zhang ordered Xu Da to make arrangements to defend Taizhou and to take the surrounding prefectures and counties. Xu Da sent Commander Liu Jie to lead some troops to attack Xinghua. Li Qing, a commander of Zhang Shi Cheng's army defending Xinghua, surrendered.

On 8 November Xu Da commanded an army to attack Gaoyou. Zhu Yuan Zhang was afraid that Xu Da would go too deep into the enemy territory and could not act in coordination with other generals. So he ordered Feng Guo Sheng and his troops to pin down Zhang Shi Cheng's troops in Gaoyou so that Xu Da could lead his great army to go back to Taizhou and prepare to attack Huai'an, Haozhou (now Bengbu, Anhui Province) and Sizhou (now Xuyi, Jiangsu Province). It happened that Zhang Shi Cheng sent an army to attack Yixing. Xu Da commanded his top troops to rescue Yixing. Xu Da commanded his troops to cross the Yangtze River. His army reached Yixing and defeated Zhang Shi Cheng's army. They captured 3,000 enemy soldiers, and the siege was lifted.

On 1 January 1366 Zhang Shi Cheng sent his naval forces to station themselves by Junshan (a mountain situated in the northern outskirt of Jiangyin, by the Yangtze River). They sailed more than three hundred ships to Matuosha (a sandy beach) which was not far from Jiangyin. They were on their way up the Yangtze to attack Zhenjiang. Zhu Yuan Zhang personally took to the field with a great army to meet the enemy. His troops marched on land and traveled by water to Zhenjiang. Zhang Shi Cheng's troops set fire to the city of Guazhou and looted Xijin (where the Yangtze River can be crossed) and then retreated. Zhu Yuan Zhang ordered Kang Mao Cai, the general defending the naval camps on the southern bank of the

Yangtze River at Jiangyin, and Wu Liang, the Commander-in-chief of Zhu Yuan Zhang's army defending Jiangyin, to pursue the retreating enemy along the Yangtze River.

When they reached Fuzimen (now Wushangang Port of Zhangjiagang, Jiangsu Province), Zhang Shi Cheng used five hundred ships to block the estuary of the Yangtze River. The enemy warships started an attack when the Yangtze was at high tide. Wu Liang and Kang Mao Cai commanded their troops to fight bravely against the enemy. The enemy troops on the front line could not get help from the troops on the rear. So the enemy troops were disastrously defeated. Some gave up their ships and went by land. But they fell into an ambush by the foot of Jiangyin Mountain. Two thousand enemy soldiers were captured.

In this battle, Kang Mao Cai commanded his naval troops and won a great victory. Wu Liang and his troops pursued the enemy to Fuzimen. He had to build his defense line while fighting against the enemy troops. So he won the victory in a very difficult situation. Zhu Yuan Zhang came to the battlefront to convey his greetings to the victorious troops. He made a tour to the battlefields. He saw that strongholds had been built by Wu Liang's troops while they were fighting against the enemy. He exclaimed, "Wu Liang is really as great as General Wu Qi, the renowned strategist of the Period of the Warring States!" Wu Liang had been in Jiangyin for ten years. During these ten years he was always on the alert. He spent the nights in the tower of the city wall. When he slept, he lay in bed with his head pillowed on his spear waiting for daybreak. In the daytime he invited scholars to give talks on classical works and strategies and tactics. He established schools in Jiangyin. He ordered his troops to reclaim wasteland for cultivating food grains. The city of Jiangyin was in good order. The strongly defended Jiangyin provided a protection for Yingtian.

During this period, Feng Guo Sheng's troops laid siege to the city of Gaoyou. On 17 February 1366 Yu Tong Qian, the commanding general of Zhang Shi Cheng's army defending Gaoyou, sent an envoy to see Feng Guo Sheng telling him that he would surrender and telling him that he would push down the outer wall of the city as the signal for his surrender. Feng Guo Sheng believed him. On that night he sent Commander Kang Tai to lead several hundred soldiers into the city first. When Kang Tai and his soldiers entered the city, the enemy soldiers immediately closed the gate and killed them all. When Zhu Yuan Zhang heard of this, he was outraged. He summoned Feng Guo Sheng and sentenced him to be beaten ten times with a big rod. Then Zhu Yuan Zhang ordered him to walk back to Gaoyou. Feng Guo Sheng felt ashamed and was determined to take Gaoyou.

Xu Da commanded his army to go back to Gaoyou from Yixing. On 21 February Xu Da asked Zhu Yuan Zhang's permission to let Commander Sun Xing Zu defend Huai'an (now Huai'an, Jiangsu Province) and Chang Yu Chun to command the naval troops to sail up Gaoyou Hu Lake (now Gaoyou Hu Lake, Jiangsu Province) to support Feng Guo Sheng's troops attacking Gaoyou. Zhu Yuan Zhang agreed. He sent an envoy to say to Xu Da, "Zhang Shi Cheng started his career from Gaoyou. He occupied the areas of Wu and Yue from Gaoyou. Gaoyou is his most important base. Now our armies are attacking Gaoyou. He will certainly send troops to rescue this city. We have heard that Zhang Shi Cheng has sent his premier Xu Yi to command a great army with warships to sail out to sea and then into the Yangtze River to rescue Gaoyou. Zhang Shi Cheng has sent out troops from several places as well. You must be well prepared." He ordered Xu Da to station his troops in Taizhou to prepare for Zhang Shi Cheng's attack.

On 8 March 1366 Xu Da led his troops to march to Gaoyou from Taizhou to join forces with the troops under Feng Guo Sheng. On 14 March the armies under Xu Da and Feng Guo Sheng stormed the city of Gaoyou and took it. They killed Yu Tong Qian, the general who had pretended to surrender and lured Feng Guo Sheng's troops into the city and killed them all.

On 25 March Zhu Yuan Zhang ordered Xu Da to lead his victorious army to take Huai'an. On 5 April Xu Da and his troops reached Huai'an. Xu Da learned that the naval troops under Xu Yi, the premier of Zhang Shi Cheng's State of Wu, were stationed in Maluogang (a port situated in the northeast of Huai'an, Jiangsu Province). Xu Da start a surprise attack on the naval camps at night and defeated the enemy troops. Xu Yi fled by boat to the sea.

Xu Da commanded his troops to press on to the foot of the city wall of Huai'an. Mei Si Zu, the governor of Huai'an, sealed all the treasury houses and made a list of all the generals and men. Then he opened the city gate to surrender to Xu Da. He presented four prefectures under his jurisdiction. Zhu Yuan Zhang highly praised Mei Si Zu for his actions to protect the safety of the people. He appointed Mei Si Zu as the Deputy Head of the Office of Provincial Military Governor. Zhu Yuan Zhang ordered Commander Cai Xian and Hua Yun Long to lead their troops to defend Huai'an. On 7 April Xu Da marched his army from Huai'an to Xinghua and took it. Then Xu Da's troops attacked Xuzhou (now Xuzhou, Jiangsu Province) and took it. From then on the areas in the northern part of Jiangsu Province were basically pacified.

(4) Zhu Yuan Zhang Pays a Visit to Haozhou, His Hometown

After Guo Zi Xing left Haozhou in July 1354 and Sun De Ya left Haozhou in March 1355, Li Ji, a general under Zhang Shi Cheng, occupied Haozhou. In April 1366 Zhu Yuan Zhang ordered Li Shan Chang to write a letter to urge Li Ji to surrender. But Li Ji did not give any reply. Zhu Yuan Zhang said, "Haozhou is my hometown, but it is now occupied by Zhang Shi Cheng. Now I own a state but I have no home!" So he ordered Han Zheng, a manager of Governmental Affairs, to lead General Gu Shi and a great army to attack Haozhou. When they reached Haozhou, they stormed the moon shaped fortress outside the city and the west gate of the city. Han Zheng ordered his soldiers to fire cannons on the city wall and then ordered his soldiers to climb up the city wall with long ladders. On 9 April 1366 Li Ji opened the city gate and surrendered. When Zhu Yuan Zhang got the news, he rejoiced.

On 13 April Zhu Yuan Zhang started his journey to Haozhou from Yingtian. He would go back to his hometown to hold a memorial ceremony for his ancestors. He ordered Xu Cun Ren, a scholar, and Wang Wei, the official in charge of recording the activities of the royal family, to go to Haozhou with him. On 16 April Zhu Yuan Zhang reached Haozhou. Zhu Yuan Zhang was always sad when he thought that when his parents died, no funerals were held for them because he was so poor. He asked Xu Cun Ren what kind of mourning apparel he should wear in the funeral ceremony. Xu Cun Run suggested fine linen. But Zhu Yuan Zhang thought that fabric would be too light, and he decided on coarse white linen. At that time there was a saying which goes, "The supernatural power of Heaven and Earth will congregate in an emperor's place of origin; it's better not to move the graves of the ancestors of an emperor, so that the supernatural power will not leave the place." Zhu Yuan Zhang agreed with this saying and decided not to move his ancestors' graves. He ordered workmen to add earth to the tops of the graves to make them higher, and he appointed twenty families to tend his ancestral graves.

On 17 April the elders of Haozhou came to visit Zhu Yuan Zhang. Zhu Yuan Zhang gave a banquet to entertain them. At the banquet Zhu Yuan Zhang told the elders, "I have been away my hometown for more than ten years. I have experienced all kinds of hardships and more than a hundred battles. At long last I can come back to my hometown to sweep the graves of my ancestors to pay respect to them. And I have the chance to meet you again. The pity is I cannot stay with you for long. I hope you will teach your children to be filial and to work hard to till the land and increase food production. Don't let them leave the land and engage in trade. Now the people in the prefectures in the areas along the Huai River are still suffering from looting by the enemy. You should take good care of yourselves." All the elders knelt down and touched their heads to the ground to express their thanks to Zhu Yuan Zhang.

On 27 April Zhu Yuan Zhang was going back to Yingtian. Before he left, he went to the graveyard to say good-bye to his ancestors. He summoned the twenty families who had been appointed by Zhu Yuan Zhang to take care of the graves of his ancestors and granted them silk and food to express his thanks to them. Zhu Yuan Zhang said to the elders of Haozhou, "I have ordered the officials concerned not to levy your land taxes. One or two years later I will come back to see you." On 3 May Zhu Yuan Zhang came back to Yingtian.

(5) Battles to Cut the Reinforcements to Suzhou

On 27 July 1366 Zhu Yuan Zhang summoned all the officials and generals to his office to discuss the matter of the expedition against Zhang Shi Chang. Zhu Yuan Zhang said, "Zhang Shi Cheng uses Suzhou as his base and has invaded our territory many times. He is our die-hard enemy. We must carry out an expedition against him. Now you may express your ideas freely." Li Shan Chang said, "We should really launch a punitive expedition against Zhang Shi Cheng. But as I see, although Zhang Shi Cheng has been defeated by us many times, he still has a great army. The soil of the lands in Zhang Shi Cheng's territory is fertile. The people there are rich. He has stored up a lot of materials in his storehouses. I am afraid that it would be difficult for us to defeat him in a short time. It would be better for us to wait patiently for our chance to come." Zhu Yuan Zhang said, "Zhang Shi Cheng is fatuous and self-indulgent. He has invaded our territory many times. If we don't get rid of him now, he will cause great trouble to us later. His territory has been greatly reduced. The areas along the Yangtze River and Huai River have been taken by us. If I send my victorious army to attack him, we will surely destroy him. There is evidence that Zhang Shi Cheng will be surely defeated. There is no need to wait for another opportunity." Xu Da said, "Zhang Shi Cheng is arrogant and high-handed. He is brutal and leads a luxurious life. He is doomed to perish. His generals such as Li Bo Sheng and Lü Zhen are mean persons. They hold great military powers to secure their own interests. Zhang Shi Cheng depends on his three advisers Huang Jing Fu, Cai Yan Tian and Ye De Xin. These three people are pedantic scholars. Their suggestions are just impractical talk. They have no military knowledge at all. With the mighty reputation and great power of Your Highness, our troops will be invincible and the areas occupied by Zhang Shi Cheng will be pacified in a short time." Zhu Yuan Zhang was glad to hear Xu Da's words. He praised him, saying, "The opinions of other people are limited by their understanding of the situation. But I see the situation the same way you do. With you in command, we shall be victorious." Then he ordered the generals to train their troops well and prepare for battle.

On 8 August 1366 Zhu Yuan Zhang appointed Xu Da as the Grand General and Chang Yu Chun as the Deputy Grand General to lead 200,000 troops to carry out an expedition against Zhang Shi Cheng. He summoned all the generals and high officers to his office and said to them, "Since rebellions broke out in the realm, persons of exceptional ability rose everywhere. The nation was torn apart by such people. Chen You Liang occupied the west part of the realm. Zhang Shi Cheng occupied the east part of the realm. Each of them owned a territory of over five hundred square kilometers and a great army of over 300,000 men. Our state was situated between the two of them. We have been fighting against them for more than ten years. These two men were not fighting for the interests of the people. They are only fighting for their own interests. Now Chen You Liang has been defeated and killed. Only Zheng Shi Cheng still remains. He has a vast territory which includes the areas of the west part of Zhejiang Province and areas along the Yangtze River and Huai River. He sent armies to invade our territory many times. In these years you have been fighting very hard to take the areas along the Yangtze River and the Huai River. Now only Suzhou and other several prefectures have not been taken. This is the reason why I have sent you to carry out an expedition against Zhang Shi Cheng. You must discipline the troops under you. Looting the people, killing innocent people, opening graves and destroying houses — these are strictly prohibited. I hear the grave of Zhang Shi Cheng's mother is at the outskirts of the city of Suzhou. Don't destroy this grave. You must observe this discipline strictly. You generals must be in concord with each other. Don't let your subordinates humiliate the soldiers. Any general has to rely on his soldiers in fighting battles. You should treat your soldiers well. Our purpose in fighting battles is to win victory. Anyone who wants to be a virtuous man must show his benevolence widely. Always keep my words in mind." All the generals bowed to Zhu Yuan Zhang to indicate that they would obey his orders.

Before the great army started, Zhu Yuan Zhang summoned Xu Da and Chang Yu Chun to his office. He asked them, "Which place should we attack first?" Chang Yu Chun answered, "If we want to drive away an owl, we must destroy its nest. If we want to drive a rat away, we must fumigate its hole with smoke. In this expedition, we should attack Suzhou directly so as to destroy the den of Zhang Shi Cheng. If we have taken Suzhou, other cities can be taken without much fighting." Zhu Yuan Zhang said, "That is not the right way. Zhang Shi Cheng was originally a salt smuggler. Zhang Tian Qi and Pan Yuan Ming were his good friends. They are valiant generals. Now Zhang Tian Qi is defending Huzhou and Pan Yuan Ming is defending Hangzhou. If we attack Suzhou and the situation for Zhang Shi Cheng is dangerous, Zhang Tian Qi will come from Huzhou and Pan Yuan Ming will come from Hangzhou to rescue Suzhou. When all the rescuing armies come, it will be very difficult for us to take Suzhou. It would be better for us to attack Huzhou first. Then Zhang Shi Cheng will have to do his best to rescue Huzhou. When Huzhou is taken by us, no more rescuing army from Huzhou will come. Then Suzhou will be isolated and we can take it in a short time." Zhu Yuan Zhang asked his attendants to leave the room. Then he said secretly to Xu Da and Chang Yu Chun, "I want to let Xiong Tian Rui go with you. He was forced to surrender in Ganzhou. Actually he did not want to surrender, and now he is always sad. Just now I discussed with you the strategies to attack Zhang Shi Cheng. You should tell the generals under you not to let Xiong Tian Rui know our true decision. You should just let Xiong Tian Rui know that we shall attack Suzhou directly. When Xiong Rui hears this, he will find a chance to defect to Zhang Shi Cheng and report to him that we shall attack Suzhou directly. In this way Zhang Shi Cheng will fall into our trap."

On 25 August Xu Da's great army reached Sanliqiao (a place situated in the east outside the city of Huzhou, Zhejiang Province). Zhang Tian Ji, the Right Premier of Zhang Shi Cheng's State of Wu, sent out troops to resist Xu Da's army. Huang Bao, a Governmental Manager of Zhang Shi Cheng's State of Wu, commanded his troops to resist Xu Da's troops attacking the city from the south; Tao Zi Shi, a general under Zhang Tian Ji, commanded his troops to resist Xu Da's troops attacking the city from the east; and Zhang Tian Ji commanded his troops to resist Xu Da's troops attacking the city from the north; Tang Jie, a general under Zhang Tian Ji, commanded his troops to stay behind as the reserve troops. Xu Da sent Chang Yu Chun to lead his troops to attack Huang Bao from the south; Xu Da sent Wang Bi to lead his troops to attack Zhang Tian Ji from the north. Xu Da himself commanded his troops to attack Tao Zi Shi from the east. He sent Wang Guo Bao to lead his troops to cut the return routes of the enemy. Chang Yu Chun's troops and Huang Bao's troops met. After a fierce battle, Huang Bao was defeated and turned back trying to get into the city from the south gate. But when he reached the moat, he found that the suspension bridge over the moat had been destroyed and he could not get across the moat. So he had to turned back to fight. But very soon he was captured. At this time Zhang Tian Ji and Tao Zi Shi did not dare to fight any more. So they all retreated into the city of Huzhou.

Zhang Shi Cheng sent Li Bo Sheng to command an army to rescue Huzhou from Suzhou. Li Bo Sheng led his troops to sneak into Huzhou from Digang (south of Huzhou, Zhejiang Province). Xu Da's army laid siege to the city of Huzhou. Li Bo Sheng and Zhang Tian Ji shut the

gates tight and defended the city resolutely. Xu Da sent Wang Guo
Bao to attack the west gate of the city of Huzhou. Xu Da himself took
a great army to coordinate the attack. Tao Zi Shi and Yu De Quan, a
member of the Privy Council of Zhang Shi Cheng's State of Wu, came
out of the city to fight. But very soon they were defeated and escaped
back into the city.

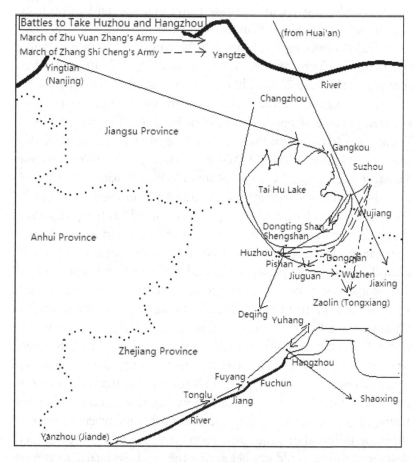

Zhang Shi Cheng sent Zhu Xian, a manager of Governmental
Affairs, Lü Zhen, a member of the Privy Council, and the Fifth Crown
Prince, Zhang Shi Cheng's adopted son, to command 60,000 men
to rescue Huzhou. This great army was stationed in Jiuguan (in
Zhejiang Province), eighteen kilometers east of Huzhou. At that time
Tang He with his army came from Changzhou to join forces with Xu
Da's army. The troops under Xu Da, Chang Yu Chun and Tang He

were stationed in Gusaoqiao of Dongqian Town which was situated to the east of Jiuguan. These troops built ten strongholds to cut the route from which Zhang Shi Cheng's army would come from the east to rescue Zhu Xian, Lü Zhen and the Fifth Crown Prince. Pan Yuan Shao, Zhang Shi Cheng's son-in-law, stationed his troops to the east of Wuzhen (in Zhejiang Province) to support the troops under Zhu Xian, Lü Zhen and the Fifth Crown Prince in Jiuguan. One night Xu Da sent some troops to start a surprise attack on Pan Yuan Shao's troops. Pan Yuan Shao ran away. Xu Da ordered his troops to cut the food transportation lines to Huzhou. When Zhang Shi Cheng saw that the situation was very unfavorable to him, he personally led a great army to rescue Huzhou. When Zhang Shi Cheng reached Zaolin (three kilometers northwest of Tongxiang, Zhejiang Province), Xu Da sent a great army to meet the enemy in Zaolin. Zhang Shi Cheng's army was disastrously defeated. Zhang Shi Cheng had to run back to Suzhou.

In September 1366 Zhang Shi Cheng sent Xu Zhi Jian, a member of the Privy Council, to lead the naval troops on boats to sail near Dongqian to pry into Xu Da's army stationed in Dongqian and plan to attack Gusaoqiao. When Chang Yu Chun saw that the enemy had come, he sent elite troops on several hundred small boats to attack the coming enemy. It happened that there was a rainstorm and it got very dark, very early. Chang Yu Chun's troops rowed their boats hard and attacked the enemy troops fiercely. They captured Xu Zhi Jian and 2,000 enemy soldiers.

On 16 September Zhu Yuan Zhang ordered Li Wen Zhong, the Governor of Zhejiang Province, to lead his army to attack Hangzhou (now Hangzhou, Zhejiang Province) from Yanzhou (now Jiande, Zhejiang Province) and he ordered General Hua Yun Long to attack Jiaxing (now Jiaxing, Zhejiang Province) from Huai'an (now Huai'an, Jiangsu province) so as to pin down Zhang Shi Cheng's troops in these two places.

On 26 September General Liao Yong Zhong and General Xue Xian commanded their troops to attack the camps of Zhang Shi Cheng's troops stationed in Deqing (now Deqing, Zhejiang Province) which was situated to the south of Huzhou. They captured Zhong Zheng, the commanding general of Zhang Shi Cheng's army defending Deqing, and forty enemy ships.

Since Xu Zhi Jian was defeated and captured, Zhang Shi Cheng was very afraid. He sent Xu Yi, his Right Premier, to Jiuguan to observe the situation. Xu Yi went to Jiuguan and completed his task. When he was about to return to Suzhou to report to Zhang Shi Cheng what he had observed, Chang Yu Chun commanded some troops to cut his way back. Xu Yi could not leave Jiuguan. He sent a man to sneak out of Jiuguan to ask Zhang Shi Xin to send an army to join forces with the troops in Jiuguan to attack Xu Da's troops. Zhang Shi Cheng sent Pan Yuan Shao to command the naval troops on red dragon boats to sail towards Jiuguan to rescue Xu Yi. Then Xu Yi got on board a red dragon boat and escaped. Xu Yi and Pan Yuan Shao anchored the red dragon boats in Pingwang, a port in Tai Hu Lake by Wujiang (now Wujiang, Jiangsu Province). Then Xu Yi and Pan Yuan Shao and some troops took small boats to Wuzhen, planning to rescue the troops in Jiuguan. Chang Yu Chun commanded the naval troops to sail on Tai Hu Lake and reached Pingwang. The troops under Chang Yu Chun set fire to the red dragon boats. The soldiers on the red dragon boats ran away for their own lives. From then no more troops could be sent to rescue the troops in Jiuguan. Zhang Shi Cheng's troops in Jiuguan ran out of food. Many soldiers ran out of Jiuguan to surrender.

On 4 October 1366 Chang Yu Chun commanded his troops to attack Wuzhen. Xu Yi and Pan Yuan Shao were defeated and ran away. Chang Yu Chun commanded his troops to pursue the defeated enemy troops to Shengshan (east of Huzhou). They destroyed six camps of Zhang Shi Cheng's troops under Wang Cheng, a manager of Governmental Affairs. The rest of the enemy troops ran into Jiuguan to join forces with the troops there. Dai Mao, a member of the Privy Council of Zhang Shi Cheng's State of Wu, surrendered. At night the same day Wang Cheng also surrendered to Chang Yu Chun.

On 16 October Li Wen Zhong commanded Zhu Liang Zu and Geng Tian Bi to attack Tonglu (now Tonglu, Zhejiang Province). Dai Yuan Shuai, Zhang Shi Cheng's general defending Tonglu, surrendered. Then Li Wen Zhong sent Generals Yuan Hong and Sun Hu to attack Fuyang (now Fuyang, Zhejiang Province). They captured Li Tian Lu, the general defending Fuyang. Then Li Wen Zhong commanded all his troops to lay siege to Yuhang (now Yuhang, Zhejiang Province).

On 30 October Xu Da commanded his troops to attack the naval camp in Shengshan. General Gu Shi led his troops on several small boats to go around the enemy big boats. The enemy soldiers on the big boats laughed at the soldiers on the small boats. General Gu Shi found that the enemy soldiers were slack. He commanded his troops to jump onto the enemy big boats with load shouts and attacked the enemy soldiers fiercely. The soldiers on the other small boats followed their example and jumped on the enemy big boats to fight. The Fifth Crown Prince came to rescue them with a great army. Chang Yu Chun saw that the enemy troops come ferociously. So he led his troops to retreat a little bit. Xue Xian commanded his naval troops to fight head on with the coming enemy. His troops burned the enemy ships. Fire rose high into the sky. The enemy troops collapsed. The Fifth Crown Prince, Zhu Xian and Lü Zhen handed over Jiuguan to Xu Da and surrendered. After the battle, Chang Yu Chun told Xue Xian, "You are the one who has contributed the most to win today's victory. I am not as good as you are."

On 6 November Xu Da sent Lü Zhen and Wang Cheng to the foot of the city wall of Huzhou to persuade Li Bo Sheng to come out of the city to surrender. Li Bo Sheng stood in the tower of the city wall and said loudly, "Zhang Shi Cheng has been very kind to me. How can I betray him?" Then he drew out his sword and was going to kill himself with it. The generals standing by him held him tightly and not to let him kill himself. A general said to him, "No rescuing army will come. We have come to a dead end. What can we do except for surrendering?" Li Bo Sheng lowered his head and could not say anything. On this day Zhang Tian Ji surrendered and delivered the city of Huzhou to Xu Dan. Li Bo Sheng also surrendered.

On 13 November Li Wen Zhong's army attacked Yuhang (now Yuhang, Zhejiang Province) and took it. Then he commanded his army to march to Hangzhou (now Hangzhou, Zhejiang Province). Pan Yuan Ming, a manager of Governmental Affairs of Zhang Shi Cheng's State of Wu and the commanding general defending Hangzhou, was very afraid. He sent Fang Yi, an official under him, as his envoy to the gate of the camps of Li Wen Zhong's army to see Li Wen Zhong to talk about the conditions for his surrender. Li Wen Zhong told Fang Yi, "My army has just arrived here. It is very difficult to predict who will win. Now you have suddenly come to talk about the conditions for your surrender. Are you playing a trick to trap me?" Fang Yi answered, "Your troops have arrived so suddenly as if you have descended from

Heaven. Your troops are powerful and cannot be resisted. Anyone who wants to resist this great army will be destroyed. Hangzhou is an isolated city. There are more than one million people in it. We are truly considering the interest of the people in the city. We hope that your troops will preserve the lives of the people." Li Wen Zhong saw that he was sincere and led him into his command tent. They made a plan for Pan Yuan Ming's surrender and for Li Wen Zhong's troops to enter the city. Then Li Wen Zhong let Fang Yi go back into the city. Li Wen Zhong ordered his troops to stay inside their camps waiting for Pan Yuan Ming to surrender. In the afternoon the next day, Pan Yuan Ming went out of the city of Hangzhou to surrender, holding the lists of the number of lands, amount of the money in the treasury houses, number of households in the city, amount of food supplies, and number of the soldiers. He arrested Jiang Ying and Liu Zhen, who had murdered Hu Da Hai in February 1362 and had escaped to Hangzhou, and brought them out. Pan Yuan Ming knelt down on his knees by the left side of the road leading to the city gate. Then Li Wen Zhong came and accepted Pan Yuan Ming's surrender. His army entered the city with great discipline. Zhu Yuan Zhang still appointed Pan Yuan Ming as a manager of Governmental Affairs and the general of the army defending Hangzhou because Pan Yuan Ming had handed over the city of Hangzhou without a battle and the city was preserved intact. He put Pan Yuan Ming under the command of Li Wen Zhong. When Jiang Ying and Liu Zhen were escorted back to Yingtian, Zhu Yuan Zhang ordered to hold a memorial ceremony for Hu Da Hai. In the ceremony, a portrait of Hu Da Hai was hung up on the wall. Then Jiang Ying and Liu Zhen were executed before the portrait and the blood from the dead bodies of Jiang Ying and Liu Zhen was used as a sacrificial offering to Hu Da Hai.

On 22 November Li Wen Zhong commanded his troops to attack Shaoxing (now Shaoxing, Zhejiang Province). Li Si Zhong, the general of Zhang Shi Cheng's army defending Shaoxing surrendered. On 23 November Hua Yun Long who had marched from Huai'an took Jiaxing (now Jiaxing, Zhejiang Province).

(6) The Final Destruction of Zhang Shi Cheng

After Xu Da had taken Huzhou, he commanded all his generals and men to start their march towards Suzhou on 23 November. When his army reached Nanxun (34 kilometers to the east of Huzhou), Wang Sheng, Zhang Shi Cheng's general defending Nanxun, surrendered. Then Xu Da's great army continued its march to Wujiang (now Wujiang, Zhejiang Province). Li Fu, Zhang Shi Cheng's general defending Wujiang, surrendered. On 24 September Xu Da's great army reached Nianyukou which was situated to the south of the city of Suzhou. Dou Yi, Zhang Shi Cheng's general defending Nianyukou, was defeated and ran away. Kang Mao Cai with his troops came from Huzhou to Yinshanqiao Bridge (a bridge south of Suzhou). His troops met with Zhang Shi Cheng's troops there. A battle broke out. Kang Mao Cai, holding his big halberd in his hand, commanded his troops in battle and he himself fought very bravely and killed many enemy officers and soldiers with his halberd. The enemy troops were defeated. Kang Mao Cai's troops destroyed more than 1,000 enemy warships.

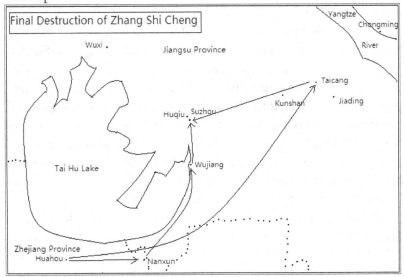

On 25 November Zhu Yuan Zhang's great armies laid siege to the city of Suzhou. Xu Da stationed his troops outside Fengmen Gate (the east gate of Suzhou); Chang Yu Chun stationed his troops in Huqiu Hill (situated in the northwest outskirt 3.5 kilometers away from Suzhou); Guo Xing stationed his troops outside Loumen Gate (the northeast gate of Suzhou); Hua Yun Long stationed his troops outside Xumen Gate (the southwest gate of Suzhou); Tang He

stationed his troops outside Changmen Gate (the northwest gate of Suzhou); Wang Bi stationed his troops in Panmen Gate (another gate on the southwest side of the city wall of Suzhou); Zhang Wen stationed his troops outside the west gate; Kang Mao Cai stationed his troops outside the north gate; Geng Bing Wen stationed his troops to the northeast corner of the city wall; Chou Cheng stationed his troops to the southwest corner of the city wall; He Wen Hui stationed his troops to the northwest corner of the city wall. A wall was built around the city of Suzhou. A tall wooden tower of three layers was built. From the top of the wooden tower Xu Da's soldiers could observe the movements of Zhang Shi Cheng's troops. On each layer of the wooden tower there were cannons, fire guns and arrows. The cannons fired shells into the city. All the enemy soldiers were scared.

Mo Tian You, the commander-in-chief of Zhang Shi Cheng's army defending Wuxi, had a general named Yang Mao. Yang Mao could swim very well. Mo Tian You ordered him to enter Suzhou to get in touch with Zhang Shi Cheng. Yang Mao tried to slip into Suzhou by swimming in the river running though Changmen Gate, but he was captured. He was brought before Xu Da. Xu Da released him and used him as his spy. At that time Suzhou was strongly defended and could not be taken in a short time. Mo Tian You's army in Wuxi was ready to reinforce Suzhou. Xu Da let Yang Mao go between Wuxi and Suzhou freely and Xu Da got all the secret information passed between Mo Tian You and Zhang Shi Cheng. Xu Da used this secret information to make his plans to attack Suzhou.

Yu Tong Hai had taken part in Xu Da's actions to take Huzhou. After Huzhou had been taken, he commanded his troops to attack Taicang (in Jiangsu Province). On his way, the people welcomed his army, presenting wine and meat to the soldiers. Yu Tong Hai expressed his thanks to the people but he did not accept the wine and meat presented by the people. His troops marched in great discipline. His troops did not cause the slightest trouble to the people. All the people were very happy. When Yu Tong Hai's troops reached Taicang, Chen Ren, the commanding general of Zhang Shi Cheng's army defending Taicang, surrendered with several hundred big ships. The defenders of Kunshan (in Jiangsu Province), and both Chongming and Jiading (in Shanghai Municipality) surrendered.

In February 1367 Xu Da had laid siege to Suzhou for a long time but could not take the city. He sent an envoy to Yingtian to ask Zhu Yuan Zhang for instructions. Zhu Yuan Zhang personally wrote a letter to comfort Xu Da. The letter read, "Since ancient times, when an emperor started his career, he was assisted by persons of outstanding ability. You joined me long ago. You have been devoted and righteous. You are resolute and resourceful. You have conquered many powerful enemies with your ability and wit. You have performed great deeds that no one can surpass. Actually the matters for which you have asked instructions can be handled by yourself. You have taken everything into consideration and will not make any imprudent decisions. This is a blessing for the realm. But it is pointed out in "The Book on the Art of War," 'a general in the field is not bound by orders from his sovereign.' From now on, all matters on the battlefield will be handled by you." When the letter was brought to Xu Da by an envoy, Xu Da knelt down and received the letter personally.

In April 1367 Xu Da sent an envoy to inform Yu Tong Hai that he should command his troops to join in the siege to Suzhou. When Yu Tong Hai reached Miedu Bridge (situated outside Fengmen Gate of the city wall of Suzhou), his troops defeated the enemy troops there. He marched his troops to Taohuawu (a place situated in the northeast outskirt of Suzhou), and there they attacked Zhang Shi Cheng's camps. Unfortunately he was struck by an arrow and was seriously wounded. He entrusted all his troops to a general and ordered him to lead the troops to join forces with Xu Da's army. Then he ordered some soldiers to carry him back to Yingtian. Zhu Yuan Zhang visited him in his home. Zhu Yuan Zhang said sadly, "Do you know that I have come to visit you?" Yu Tong Hai was so seriously ill that he could not say anything. Zhu Yuan Zhang shed tears and went out of the room. On 10 April Yu Tong Hai died at the age of thirty-eight. Later Zhu Yuan Zhang granted him the title of Duke of the State of Guo posthumously.

On 4 June 1367 Zhang Shi Cheng wanted to make a breakthrough. He went up to the top of the city wall and looked out of the city. He found that Xu Da's troops on the left side were in gallant array. He did not dare to make a breakthrough from this part of the army. He sent Xu Yi and Pan Yuan Shao to command their troops to sneak out of the city from the west gate and then move to the northwest. Xu Yi and

Pan Yuan Shao intended to start a surprise attack on the camps of the troops under Chang Yu Chun. Chang Yu Chun found that the enemy troops were coming and he sent some troops to the northern ditch by Changmen Gate (the northwest gate) to cut off their retreat route. Chang Yu Chun sent generals and men to fight with the troops under Xu Yi and Pan Yuan Shao. The battle lasted for a long time but neither side could defeat the other. Zhang Shi Cheng sent a general to lead a thousand men to reinforce the troops under Xu Yi and Pan Yuan Shao. He himself took an army to Shantang (situated near Huqiu Hill) to rescue the troops under Xu Yi and Pan Yuan Shao.

The road in Shantang was narrow. The troops under Zhang Shi Cheng were stuck there and could not move forward. Zhang Shi Cheng ordered his soldiers to retreat a little bit. Chang Yu Chun patted General Wang Bi on the back and said, "All the officers and men in the army say that you are a fierce general. Can you eliminate these enemy troops for me?" Wang Bi said, "Yes, I can." He jumped on his horse and dashed into the enemy battle formation, waving his two broadswords in his two hands. The enemy troops retreated. Chang Yu Chun commanded his great army to fall upon the enemy soldiers. The enemy troops were disastrously defeated. Many enemy soldiers fell into Shapentan canal (running outside Changmen Gate) and were drowned. Zhang Shi Cheng's bodyguards also fell in and were drowned. Zhang Shi Cheng's horse was startled and threw Chang Shi Cheng into the water. The generals did their best to save him from the water and carried him back into Suzhou in a sedan. Zhang Shi Cheng was greatly frustrated and was at a total loss as to what he should do next.

Li Bo Sheng was a former general under Zhang Shi Cheng and he had surrendered to Xu Da in Huzhou. He knew that Zhang Shi Cheng was at the end of his resources, and he wanted to persuade him to submit to Zhu Yuan Zhang, so he sent a man who had once served under Zhang Shi Cheng as an envoy. The envoy went to the city gate and told the gate guards that he had some important things to tell Zhang Shi Cheng. Zhang Shi Cheng let him into the city, and asked the envoy, "What do you want to say?" The envoy said, "I have come to tell you the strategies that affect the rise and fall of your state. I hope you will listen to me patiently." Zhang Shi Cheng said, "Well, I will listen to you patiently."

The envoy said, "Do you know anything about the Will of Heaven? In the past Xiang Yu was the most powerful man among the leaders who had risen up against the rule of the Qin Dynasty. He had experienced more than a hundred battles and had won all of them. But in the end he was defeated by Liu Bang in Gaixia and had to kill himself. The whole realm belonged to Liu Bang who established the Han Dynasty. Why? This was the Will of Heaven. You went into Gaoyou with eighteen followers. The court of the Yuan Dynasty sent a million men to surround the city of Gaoyou. At that time you were like a tiger which had fallen into a trap. You were in great danger. But suddenly there was a conflict among the court officials of the Yuan Dynasty and the army surrounding Gaoyou collapsed and ran away. You took this chance to lead your troops to take the areas of Wu. You secured a territory of over five hundred square kilometers and your army expanded to an army of over 300,000 men. You made yourself King of the State of Wu. At that time you were as powerful as Xiang Yu. At that time if you had not forgotten the difficult spell in Gaoyou, and you had worked hard and recruited persons of outstanding abilities and appointed them to proper positions; if you had let the people live in peace; if you had trained your troops well and you had had a good way to command your generals, the people of the State of Wu would have submitted themselves to you and your State of Wu would have been able to survive, and you may have been able to pacify the whole realm." Zhang Shi Cheng said, "You did not say these words to me at that time. What is the use of saying these words to me now?" The envoy said, "At that time although I already had this advice in mind, I could not get to see you and offer this advice. Why? You were always with your sons and brothers, your relatives and generals. You led a luxurious life. Beauties always danced before you. You held banquets day and night. Those who commanded your troops thought that they were as great as General Han Xin in the Han Dynasty and General Bai Qi in the Qin Dynasty. Your advisors thought they were as resourceful as Xiao He and Cao Shen in the Han Dynasty. They were all very proud and conceited. At that time you just stayed in the palace. You did not attend to the state affairs. You did not know when your army had been defeated and you did not know when one of your cities had been lost. This is the reason why the situation has developed as bad as now." Zhang Shi Cheng said with a long sigh, "I deeply regret for what I had done in the past. But it is too late for regrets now. What shall I do?" The envoy said, "I have a suggestion. But I am afraid you will not be willing to accept it."

"The worst thing for me is death," Zhang Shi Cheng replied. The envoy said, "If your death is good for the realm and for your descendants, it will be a worthy death. Otherwise you will die in vain. Have you ever heard about Chen You Liang? He owned the vast areas of Hubei Province, Jiangxi Province and Hunan Province. He had an army of over a million men. He and Zhu Yuan Zhang fought in Poyang Hu Lake. He wanted to burn Zhu Yuan Zhang's ships with fire, but a great wind rose and blew the fire to burn Chen You Liang's ships. Chen You Liang was defeated and killed. Why? This is the Will of Heaven. Human beings can do nothing against the Will of Heaven. This time when you hoped that the rescuing army would come from Huzhou, Huzhou fell; when you hoped the rescuing army would come from Jiaxing, Jiaxing fell; when you hoped that a rescuing army would come from Hangzhou, Hangzhou fell. You are defending this isolated city. And you swear that you will fight until you die. I think the best thing for you to do is to submit to the Will of Heaven. You may just send an envoy to Yingtian to convey your intention to submit to Zhu Yuan Zhang so as to spare the lives of the people in this city. You may open the city gate and surrender. I think Zhu Yuan Zhang will make you marquis enjoying the tax from 10,000 households. Zhu Yuan Zhang once said that he would treat you as nicely, as Emperor Taizu of the Song Dynasty treated Qian Ti, King of the State of Yue, who willingly submitted to him. All your places have been taken from other people. Now if you lose them all as in gambling, it will not do much harm to you." Zhang Shi Cheng lowered his head and thought for a long time. Then he said, "You may take a rest now. I will think it over carefully." But Zhang Shi Cheng hesitated and could not make his final decision.

On 7 June 1367 Zhang Shi Cheng commanded his troops to go out of Xumen Gate, and they fought fiercely. Chang Yu Chun's troops could not resist the attack by Zhang Shi Cheng's army. They retreated a bit. Zhang Shi Xin, Zhang Shi Cheng's younger brother, stood at the top of the city wall to supervise the battle. Suddenly he shouted, "The soldiers are now very tired! Let them have a rest." Then he beat the gong to send the signal to retreat. Chang Yu Chun took the chance to pursue the enemy troops, and Zhang Shi Cheng's men were seriously defeated. Chang Yu Chun's troops pursued them to the foot of the city wall. They built strongholds around the city. From then on Zhang Shi Cheng did not dare to send his troops out of the city anymore.

On that day, Zhang Shi Xin ordered his men to set up a tent on top of the city wall. He held a banquet to entertain the generals under him. He sat on a silver chair. One of his subordinates handed him a peach. Zhang Shi Xin was about to eat the peach, when suddenly a shell from a cannon fired by Xu Da's soldiers struck him right on the head and killed him.

Xiong Tian Rui, the man who had defected to Zhang Shi Cheng, taught Zhang Shi Cheng's soldiers to make stone and wood launchers to attack Xu Da's troops. All the stones and wood in the city were used for these stone and wood launchers. Then they destroyed the temples and the houses to get stones and wood for the launchers. Xu Da ordered his soldiers to make shelters in the shape of houses made of wood with wheels. They put bamboo on top the shelters. On 8 September 1367 Xu Da ordered the soldiers to get inside the house-shaped shelters, and then they were pushed forward. Protected from the stones and wood launched by Zhang Shi Cheng's troops Xu Da's forces got close to Fengmen Gate (the east gate of Suzhou). Chang Yu Chun's troops destroyed Zhang Shi Cheng's camps by Changmen Gate (the northwest gate of Suzhou), got across the bridge and reached the foot of the city wall. Tang Jie, a member of the Privy Council of Zhang Shi Cheng's State of Wu, went up to the top of the city wall to resist the attack. Zhang Shi Cheng stationed his troops inside the city gates. He ordered Xie Jie and Zhou Ren, two generals, to erect wooden posts to build a fence so as to repair the destroyed part of the city wall.

Tang Jie could not resist Xu Da's fierce attack. So he ordered his soldiers to lay down their weapons and surrendered. Then Zhou Ren, Xu Yi and Pan Yuan Shao also surrendered. By sunset Zhang Shi Cheng's troops were disastrously defeated. Xu Da's troops bravely climbed up the city wall by ladders and took the city of Suzhou.

Zhang Shi Cheng ordered Liu Yi, a general under him, to gather the remaining soldiers. He got 30,000 of them. Zhang Shi Cheng commanded them to carry out a street fight. But very soon these troops were defeated. Liu Yi surrendered. Zhang Shi Cheng ran back home. His wife Lady Liu had already ordered soldiers to stack firewood under a tower. When the city of Suzhou fell, she asked an old lady to take her two young sons and escape. She went up the tower and ordered the soldiers to set fire to the firewood, and she was burned to death by the flames.

Zhang Shi Cheng himself sat alone in his home. Xu Da sent Li Bo Sheng to get him and persuade him to surrender. It was already dark. Zhang Shi Cheng shut the door of the room and put a silk rope over a beam and tried to kill himself by hanging. Li Bo Sheng broke the door open and took Zhang Shi Cheng down from the rope. When he regained consciousness, Xu Da sent Pan Yuan Shao to persuade him to surrender. Li Bo Sheng and Pan Yuan Shao talked to him for a long time, but Zhang Shi Cheng just closed his eyes and did not say a single word. Then Li Bo Sheng ordered the soldiers to carry Zhang Shi Cheng on an old shield out of Fengmen Gate. They put Zhang Shi Cheng on a door plank and carried him on board of a ship. They escorted him, Xu Yi and several officials of the Yuan Dynasty back to Yingtian. Xiong Tian Rui was captured and was executed in Suzhou.

The massive armies under Xu Da and Chang Yu Chun entered the city of Suzhou with great discipline. Xu Da's troops were stationed in the east part of the city; Chang Yu Chun's troops were stationed in the west part of the city. The city was in great peace and order. The people lived peacefully.

On the way to Yingtian, Zhang Shi Cheng just lay on the ship and refused to eat anything. When the ship reached Longjiang (now Xiaguan District, Nanjing), he refused to get up. The soldiers had to carry him to the Office of the Secretariat. Li Shan Chang, the Premier, talked to him, but Zhang Shi Cheng turned a deaf ear to what Li Shan Chang had said. Suddenly Zhang Shi Cheng began to shout abuses at Li Shang Cheng. Li Shang Chang was very angry and shouted back. Zhu Yuan Zhang's intention had been to spare Zhang Shi Cheng, but he hanged himself in jail. Zhu Yuan Zhang granted him a coffin and Zhang Shi Cheng was duly buried.

On 28 September all the generals returned to Yingtian triumphantly. Zhu Yuan Zhang personally came to the gate of the palace to hold a ceremony to grant rewards to his officials and generals. He made Li Shang Chang Duke of the State of Xuan, Xu Da Duke of the State of Xin, and Chang Yu Chun Duke of the State of E. Zhu Yuan Zhang granted other generals and officials very handsome rewards according to their contributions in the pacification of Chen You Liang's State of Han and Zhang Shi Cheng's State of Wu. Zhu Yu Zhang told all the generals and officials, "You have established very great contributions in destroying the State of Han and the State of Wu. You have surpassed all the most famous generals and officials since ancient times. Now we are going to carry out a northern expedition to pacify Central China. I hope you will do your best in this northern expedition."

The next day, all the generals and officials came to the palace to express their thanks to Zhu Yuan Zhang. Zhu Yuan Zhang asked them, "When you went back home yesterday, did you hold a banquet and drink wine to celebrate the happy moment?" They answered, "Since we have had the rewards granted by Your Highness, we did hold banquets and drink wine to celebrate this happy moment." Zhu Yuan Zhang said, "But I did not hold a banquet to entertain you in this happy moment. Peace has not been brought to Central China. It is not time for you to enjoy yourselves yet. Zhang Shi Cheng has set a negative example for you. When he got power, he drank wine all day and did not attend to state affairs. I hope you will always be on guard against such wrong doings."

4. FANG GUO ZHEN SURRENDERS

Fang Guo Zhen occupied Qingyuan Prefecture (now the area around Ningbo, Zhejiang Province), Taizhou Prefecture (now the area around Taizhou, Zhejiang Province) and Wenzhou Prefecture (now the area around Wenzhou, Zhejiang Province). He was appointed by the court of the Yuan Dynasty as a senior official of Zhejiang Province. In January 1358 Zhu Yuan Zhang's army took Wuzhou (now Wuyuan, in the northeast part of Jiangxi Province). In December 1358 Zhu Yuan Zhang sent Liu Chen, a senior official, as his envoy to persuade Fang Guo Zhen to submit to him. Fang Guo Zhen discussed this matter with his younger brothers. Fang Guo Zhen said, "Now the Yuan Dynasty is falling. Heroes all over the realm have risen up against the Yuan Dynasty. The most powerful man is Zhu Yuan Zhang. He is a capable leader. His army is invincible. Now he has taken Wuzhou. We are not able to resist him. We already have strong enemies: Zhang Shi Cheng in the east and Chen You Ding in the south. It would be better for us to show our submission to Zhu Yuan Zhang so that we can get support from him."

On 25 March 1359 Fang Guo Zhen sent Zhang Ben Ren as his envoy to see Zhu Yuan Zhang in Yingtian. Zhang Ben Ren presented fifty catties of gold, one hundred catties of silver and one hundred bolts of silk to Zhu Yuan Zhang. He told Zhu Yuan Zhang that Fang Guo Zhen would offer Wenzhou, Taizhou and Qingyuan to Zhu Yuan Zhang. In order to show his sincerity, Fang Guo Zhen had asked Zhang Ben Ren to bring Fang Guan, his second son, to Yingtian as a hostage. Zhu Yuan Zhang said, "The reason for hostage is that one suspects that the other would not keep his promise. Now I do not suspect Fang Guo Zhen's true intention. There is no need for a hostage." He granted a handsome award to Fang Guan and sent him back. At that time Fang Guo Zhen was waiting for the outcome of the fight between Zhu Yuan Zhang and Zhang Shi Cheng. He still hesitated as to whether he should submit to Zhu Yuan Zhang.

Although Fang Guo Zhen had promised to hand over the three prefectures of Wenzhou, Taizhou and Qingyuan to Zhu Yuan Zhang, he had never really done it. He only said that to put pressure on the court of the Yuan Dynasty. In September 1366 the court of the Yuan Dynasty appointed Fang Guo Zhen as the Premier of Zhejiang Province. His younger brothers Fang Guo Zhang, Fang Guo Ying, Fang Guo Min, and his son Fang Ming Shan were appointed as the managers of Governmental Affairs of Zhejiang Province.

Fang Guo Zhen became more and more proud. He sent troops to occupy the counties along the seashore of Zhejiang Province. He refused to be submitted to Zhu Yuan Zhang. At that time Zhu Yuan Zhang was fighting against Chen You Liang and Zhang Shi Cheng. He did not have the time to deal with Fang Guo Zhen. He sent Xia Yu, a scholar, to persuade Fang Guo Zhen to submit to him. But Fang Guo Zhen was still hesitating as to which side he should take. When Zhu Yuan Zhang learned about this, he laughed and said, "Just let him alone for now. When I have taken Suzhou, it will be too late for him to submit to me."

Fang Guo Zhen changed his mind frequently. He once sent an envoy to Zhu Yuan Zhang to tell him that he would hand over the three prefectures to Zhu Yuan Zhang after Hangzhou was taken. But when Zhu Yuan Zhang's army had taken Hangzhou, he still would not hand over the three prefectures. He sent envoys to present tribute to Zhu Yuan Zhang. The purpose of the envoys was to observe the situation in Yingtian so that Fang Guo Zhen could decide whether he should submit or not. Zhu Yuan Zhang wrote a letter to Fang Guo Zhen to list twelve mistakes Fang Guo Zhen had made. In the letter Zhu Yuan Zhang said, "I have taken Hangzhou for a long time. But you have not fulfilled your promise to hand over the three prefectures to me. Zhang Shi Cheng's State of Wu just borders your territory on the north. It would be very easy for Zhang Shi Cheng to occupy your territory. But Zhang Shi Cheng did not dare to do so because of me. I will take Suzhou very soon. Then I will send an army to attack you. By that time you may carry out a desperate fight. That will show that you are a true hero. Or you may choose to go out to sea. But since ancient times no one could stay on the sea till he got old. I hope you will think it over carefully."

When Fang Guo Zhen got the letter, he was certainly intimidated. He discussed this matter with his younger brothers and his generals and officials. Zhang Ben Ren, one of his advisers, said, "Zhu Yuan Zhang is now fighting Zhang Shi Cheng. The outcome is still pending. I think Zhu Yuan Zhang will not be able to attack us, because Zhang Shi Cheng's State of Wu lies between Zhu Yuan Zhang's State of Wu and our territory."

Liu Xi, another adviser, said, "Zhu Yuan Zhang has foot soldiers and cavalrymen. His troops can fight on land but they cannot fight our navy."

Qiu Nan, an official, said to Fang Guo Zhen, "None of their suggestions will benefit Your Highness. Making decisions depends on wisdom. Ruling a state depends on good faith. Commanding an army depends on honesty. In the past, persons of exceptional ability rose up in arms in the areas between the Yangtze River and the Huai River. Every one of them thought that he would become an emperor. But the strongest states were Chen You Liang's State of Han, Zhang Shi Cheng's State of Wu and Zhu Yuan Zhang's State of Wu. Chen You Liang was a brave man. He fought against Zhu Yuan Zhang, but he was killed in battle and his State of Han was conquered. Now Zhang Shi Cheng is like a rat in a trap. It is very clear that he will be defeated. Zhu Yuan Zhang's army shows great discipline and is very powerful. His troops do not do the least harm to the people when they go past a place. When they have made a conquest, they seal all the treasury houses and hand them over to the government. Zhu Yuan Zhang is now carrying out a punitive expedition. He will surely own the whole realm. He has conquered Chen You Liang's State of Han and is going to take Zhang Shi Cheng's State of Wu. Your Highness has been in the east part of Zhejiang Province for more than ten years. You only own three prefectures. You are not wise if you don't make the decision right now; you are not trustful when you have made a promise to hand over the three prefectures to Zhu Yuan Zhang but have gone back on your own words. If you don't keep your promise, Zhu Yuan Zhang will send troops to attack us. It would be better for you to hand over the three prefectures to Zhu Yuan Zhang." But Fang Guo Zhen refused to accept his advice.

In September 1367 Zhu Yuan Zhang sent Zhu Liang Zu to lead a great army of foot troops, cavalrymen and naval soldiers to attack Fang Guo Zhen in Zhejiang Province. Zhu Liang Zu commanded his troops to start from Hangzhou. Meanwhile, on 21 September, Zhu Liang Zu's troops reached Tiantai. Yin Tang Pan, Fang Guo Zhen's general defending Tiantai, surrendered.

Then Zhu Liang Zu commanded his troops to march to Taizhou. Fang Guo Ying, Fang Guo Zhen's younger brother, was defending Taizhou. When he heard that Zhu Liang Zu was coming with a great army, he wanted to run away. At that time Fang Guo Zhen was in Qingyuan (now Ningbo, Zhejiang Province). He was gathering his troops there to rescue Taizhou. He sent an envoy to order Fang Guo Ying to defend Taizhou resolutely. Fang Guo Ying had to obey the order and commanded his troops to go up the city wall to defend the city. But the soldiers were very afraid and many of them ran away.

Zhu Liang Zu stormed the city. On 28 September Fang Guo Ying saw that the city was about to fall, so he took his wife and children to embark a big warship and sailed out of Taizhou to Huangyan at night. Then Zhu Liang Zu led his troops into Taizhou.

By October 1367, Zhu Liang Zu had reached Huangyan and was ready to continue his attack. Fang Guo Ying left Ha'erlu, a Yuan general, to defend Huangyan and again packed up his wife and children to sail out to sea. Ha'erlu simply surrendered to Zhu Liang Zu.

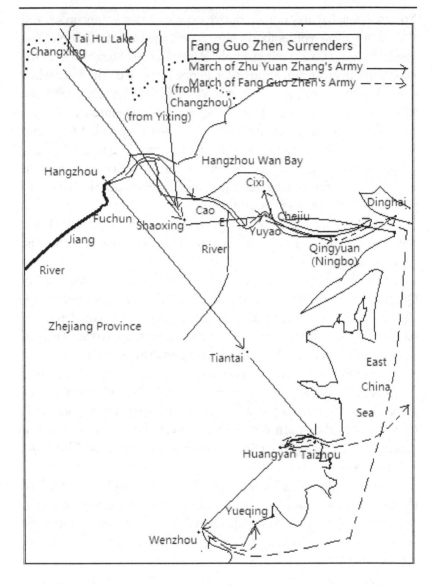

On 11 October 1367 Zhu Yuang Zhang appointed Tang He as the Grand General of the Southern Expedition and Wu Zhen as the Deputy Grand General of this expedition to command the troops in Changzhou (now Changzhou, Jiangsu Province), Changxing (now Changxing, in the north part of Zhejiang Province), and Yixing (now Yixing, Jiangsu Province) to carry out an expedition against Fang Guo Zhen in Qingyuan. Before they started, Zhu Yuan Zhang said to them,

"You are going to carry out a punitive expedition under my order. You should not allow your subordinates to kill the innocent people. You should take Xu Da as your example. When he took Suzhou, he let the people live in great peace and order. I hope you will do the same when you take Qingyuan." In November, Wu Zhen commanded his naval troops on warships to sail from Hangzhou Wan Bay into Cao E River (now Cao E River, Zhejiang Province). Then they sailed to Chejiu (now Chejiu, 17 kilometers southeast to Yuyao, Zhejiang Province). There, one of Fang Guo Zhen's soldiers came to surrender. He told Wu Zhen that Fang Guo Zhen had commanded his fleet to sail out to sea. Wu Zhen sent his navy after them.

Tang He commanded his troops to march from Shaoxing. He led them across Cao E River and they marched to Yuyao. Li Shu, the governor, surrendered.

Then Tang He commanded his troops to march to the city of Qingyuan. He ordered his troops to attack the west gate of the city. On 9 November Xu Shan, the governor of Qingyuan, surrendered and handed the city over to Tang He. Tang He sent troops to take Dinghai (now Dinghai, in Zhoushan Island, Zhejiang Province) and Cixi.

Fang Guo Zhen commanded his fleet to sail south to Wenzhou. Zhu Liang Zu commanded his troops to march from Huangyan to attack Wenzhou. He deployed his troops in battle formations three kilometers to the south of the city of Wenzhou. Fang Guo Zhen ordered his son Fang Ming Shan to lead an army to resist Zhu Liang Zu's troops.

After a battle, Fang Ming Shan was defeated and ran back into the city of Wenzhou. Zhu Liang Zu commanded his troops to attack the city. Fang Guo Zhen and his son Fang Ming Shan escaped by sea to Panyu Shan Mountain (twenty five kilometers southwest of Yueqing). Then Zhu Liang Zu took Wenzhou.

Tang He sent envoys to Fang Guo Zhen urging him to surrender. Then Fang Guo Zhen sent his son Fang Guan to Yingtian to see Zhu Yuan Zhang, taking a letter of surrender with him. The letter of surrender read, "I hear that Heaven covers everything under it and the Earth carries everything on it. A monarch follows the examples of Heaven and the Earth. He tolerates all kinds of people. I have been accorded a lot of kindness granted by Your Highness. I dare not be alienated from Heaven and the Earth. This is the reason why I have written this letter to express my feelings. I was originally a mediocre person. It happened that the whole realm was in chaos. I rose up in arms from an island. I did it all by myself. I did not have the intention to make myself an emperor. Your Highness is powerful. When the army of Your Highness reached Wuzhou, I sent my son to Yingtian as a hostage. At that time I already knew that Your Highness would become my monarch. I just hope that the brightness of Your Highness will shine on me like the sun and the moon. Your Highness has been very frank to me and let me hold my prefectures and counties. I have obeyed the orders of Your Highness and did not dare to do anything else. But my subordinates did something against the will of Your Highness and this brought about the punitive army sent by Your Highness. When the punitive army sent by Your Highness came, I should have come out to welcome it. But at last I chose to sail out to sea. Why? When a devoted son is beaten by his father with a small rod, he will accept the beating. But when his father is going to beat him with a big rod, he has to run away. This is the reason why I had run away to the sea. I wanted to be bound and be brought before Your Highness. But I was afraid that I would be executed. The people in the realm do not know what great crime I have committed and they will think mistakenly that Your Highness cannot tolerate me. I do not want to bring harm to the great fame of Your Highness."

Having read the letter of surrender, Zhu Yuan Zhang had pity on Fang Guo Zhen. He wrote a letter to him which read, "You have gone against my orders. You did not submit to me right away when I issued my order. You have gone out to sea. You have been ungrateful to my kindness shown to you. Now you are at the end of your resources and you have presented your letter of surrender. The words in the letter are sad, honest and sincere. I will believe your sincerity and forgive all your wrong doings in the past. So don't hesitate."

On 24 November 1367 Fang Guo Zhen, his son Fang Ming Shen and his subordinates went to Huangyan to surrender. They were escorted to Yingtian. Fang Guo Zhen was brought before Zhu Yuan Zhang. Zhu Yuan Zhang scolded him by saying, "You have come really too late!" Fang Guo Zhen knelt down, touched his head to the ground and begged Zhu Yuan Zhang to pardon him. Zhu Yuan Zhang set him free and appointed him as the Left Premier of the Government of Guangxi Province. He did not have to go to Guangxi to take up his position. He simply enjoyed the emoluments for this position.

5. PACIFICATION OF FUJIAN PROVINCE

Chen You Ding was a leading official of Fujian Province appointed by the court of the Yuan Dynasty. In 1364 he established his office in Yanping (Yanping District, Nanping). He was devoted to the Yuan Dynasty. Every year he sent tribute to the court by sea. Emperor Toyan Temür of the Yuan Dynasty issued an imperial order to praise him.

In February 1365 Chen You Ding commanded an army to invade Chuzhou (now Lishui, Zhejiang Province). Hu Shen, Zhu Yuan Zhang's general defending Chuzhou, sent them packing. Chen You Ding retreated to Pucheng (in Fujian Province). Then Hu Shen persued Chen You Ding to Pucheng. On 1 April 1365 Hu Shen attacked Songxi (now Songxi, Fujian Province) and took it. Zhang Zi Yu, the general of Chen You Ding's army defending Songxi, was captured. The rest of the troops of Chen You Ding's army fled to Chong'an (now Wuyishan City, Fujian Province).

Hu Shen requested Zhu Yuan Zhang to send troops from other places to take Fujian Province. Zhu Yuan Zhang ordered Zhu Liang Zu, the commander-in-chief of the army in Xinzhou (now Shangrao, Jiangxi Province), to have his troops march from Xinzhou to go past Yanshan (in Jiangxi Province) into Fujian Province. Zhu Yuan Zhang also ordered Wang Pu, the Governor of Jianchang (now Nanchang, Jiangxi Province) to command his troops to start from Shanguan (in Guangze, Fujian Province) to join forces with Hu Shen's army. In May 1365 Hu Shen attacked Pucheng and took it. Then he marched his troops to Chong'an to meet Zhu Liang Zu's troops. In June the troops under Zhu Liang Zu and Hu Shen took Chong'an. Then they marched southward to attack Jianyang (in Fujian Province) and took that place, too.

In June 1365 Zhu Liang Zu and Hu Shen commanded their men to march to Jianning (now Jianning, Fujian Province). Their troops were stationed outside the city of Jianning. Zhu Liang Zu wanted to attack the city right away. But Hu Shen sensed something ominous. He told Zhu Liang Zu, "Heaven has shown signs of danger. There will be a disaster. We should not fight with our enemy for now." Zhu Liang Zu said, "Why do you use natural disasters as the excuse not to attack the enemy? Our troops have come here. Why should we delay our attack? The signs shown by Heaven are obscure. The streams of the air in the mountain change frequently. These signs cannot be used to predict anything."

Then Zhu Liang Zu forced Hu Shen to lead his troops to storm the city. Hu Shen still hesitated. Accidentally Yuan De Rou, the commanding general of Chen You Ding's troops defending Jianning, sent 40,000 troops to get close to the rear of Hu Shen's troops. Zhu Liang Zu scolded Hu Shen and urged him to attack the city. Hu Shen had to command his troops to storm the city. Yuan De Rou commanded all his troops to surround Hu Shen in several rings. Hu Shen fought very bravely. It was already late in the afternoon. Hu Shen made his breakthrough. But when he was going back, he fell into an ambush and was captured.

He was brought before Chen You Ding. Chen You Ding treated him politely. He did not want to kill Hu Shen. But at that time an envoy sent by the court of the Yuan Dynasty came. He forced Chen You Ding to kill him. Then Hu Shen was executed. On the day Hu Shen was killed, Liu Ji saw a black spot in the sun. Liu Ji went to see Zhu Yuan Zhang and said to him, "A great general in the southeast has been killed." Very soon it was reported that Hu Shen had been killed. Zhu Yuan Zhang was very sad. He made Hu Shen the Earl of Jinyun Prefecture posthumously.

In August 1366 the court of the Yuan Dynasty appointed Chen You Ding as the Governor of Fujian Province because he had defeated Hu Shen in Jianning.

On 21 October 1367 Zhu Yuan Zhang appointed Hu Mei as the Grand General of the Southern Expedition; He Wen Hui, the Left Premier of Jiangxi Province, as the Deputy Grand General. They should command their troops to take Fujian Province. Zhu Yuan Zhang ordered Dai De, the Governor of Hunan Province and Guangdong Province, to go with them. Before Hu Mei left, Zhu Yuan Zhang told him, "You came over to me when you were the Premier of Chen You Liang's State of Han. You have served under me for several years. You have been very devoted to me and have not made any mistakes. This is the reason why I have appointed you as the Grand General to command the whole expedition army to take Fujian Province. He Wen Hui is your deputy. Dai De is put under your command. He Wen Hui and Dai De are good friends of mine. But if they go against your order, you should punish them according to military laws as if they were ordinary persons. In the past when I was an ordinary soldier, I saw that the generals could not control their subordinates. I thought that they were doing the wrong thing. Later I held some military power. Most of the soldiers under my command were men who had recently surrendered. I commanded my troops to fight in the battlefield. Two of my soldiers went against my orders. I immediately executed them before all the rest. All of the soldiers were frightened. From then on, no one would defy my orders. If you are determined, you may accomplish your task. I know that you once attacked Fujian Province when you were a general under Chen You Liang. You know the geography of Fujiang Province. Now you are going as commander of a great army to take the Province. Attack the places which you can surely take. I now entrust you with the task of bringing order to Fujian Province." Hu Mei accepted the command and left.

On 30 November 1367 Hu Mei and his troops headed out into Fujian Province, past Shanguan, and conquered the city of Guangze. On 7 December they took Shaowu. Li Zong Mao, the Yuan Dynasty commander of the army defending Shaowu, surrendered. On 15 December Hu Mei took Jianyang. Cao Fu Chou, the defending commander, surrendered.

On 16 December Zhu Yuan Zhang appointed Tang He as the Grand General of the Southern Expedition and Liao Yong Zhong as the Deputy Grand General of the Southern Expedition to take charge of the naval troops and conquer Fuzhou (in Fujian Province) by sea, and Tang He, Liao Yong Zhong and Wu Zhen set sail from Qingyuan (now Ningbo, Zhejiang Province) towards Fuzhou.

Originally, Chen You Ding had personally commanded his army while defending Fuzhou. He had ordered his soldiers to build forts around the city wall. But when Hu Mei's army passed Shanguan, he ordered Lai Zheng Sun, Xie Ying Fu and Deng Yi to set 20,000 soldiers to defend Fuzhou while he, himself, took command of the elite troops defending Yanping (in Fujian Province).

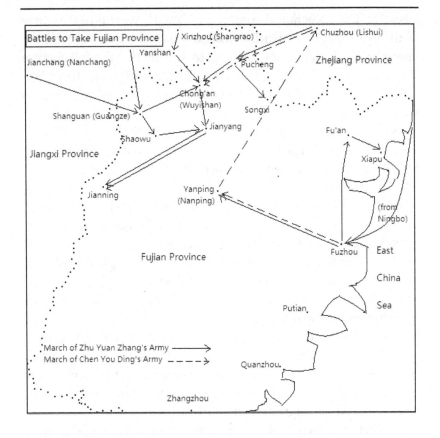

Several days later Tang He's great naval troops reached Fuzhou. On 28 December Tang He sent an envoy into the city of Fuzhou to demand that the defenders surrender. Kuchun, one of the defending Yuan generals, killed the messenger. Upon that, Tang He ordered his troops to leave their ships and go ashore. Tang He ordered his troops to lay siege to the city. Kuchun sent his troops out from the southern gate to meet Tang He's troops. Xie De, a general under Tang He, commanded his troops to fight Kuchun, and they defeated him. Kuchun ran back into the city. That night Yuan Ren, an official in Fuzhou, secretly sent an envoy out of the city to tell Tang He that he would surrender. In the early morning of 29 December Tang He commanded his troops to attack Fuzhou fiercely. Yuan Ren opened the southern gate of the city. Tang He's troops rushed into the city. Deng Yi resisted this onslaught but he was killed. Lai Zheng Sun and Xie Ying Fu escaped out the west gate and fled to Yanping to join

Chen You Ding. Kuchun also got away. Tang He went into the Office of the Governor of Fujian Province and issued orders to quell the unrest in the city. He sent out envoys to demand that the defenders of Xinghua (now Putian, Fujian Province), Zhangzhou (now Zhangzhou, Fujian Province) and Quanzhou (now Quanzhou, Fujian Province) surrender. And surrender, they did.

But those defending Funing Prefecture (including the areas of Fu'an and Xiapu, Fujian Province) would not surrender. Tang He sent troops to attack, and they took them. Now Tang He was ready to march to Yanping.

In January 1368 Hu Mei and He Wen Hui had their troops march to Jianning (now in Fujian Province) from Jianyang. Dalima, the defending general for the Yuan Dynasty, and Chen Zi Qi, an official of the Government of Fujian Province, gathered all the officers and officials to discuss the matter. Dalima said, "I hear that the approaching soldiers are very brave. Since they passed Shanguan, they have captured many places. They are irresistible. Now, we have more than 10,000 soldiers defending this city. We have sufficient storage of food supplies. We shall just defend the city and will not go out to engage with the enemy. If they cannot take our city, they will retreat. Then we shall go out to pursue them. We shall surely win." All the officers and officials agreed with his plan.

Hu Mei and his troops laid siege to the city and challenged them to battle, but Dalima refused to come out to fight. Hu Mei set his troops to attack the city day and night. Finally, Dalima could not resist the attacks. He secretly stole out of the city at night and went to He Wen Hui's camp to surrender. Hu Mei was very angry with Dalima because he did not surrender to him but to He Wen Hui; for this affront, he wanted to kill all the people in the city. He Wen Hui brought him up short, saying, "You and I were ordered by His Highness to take this city. Our purpose is to let the people to live in peace. Now Dalima has surrendered with the city, but you want to kill the people so as to give vent to your pent-up anger. Do you think you have the right to do that?" So Hu Mei had to give up the idea of killing the people. On 21 January, Hu Mei's troops entered the city of Jianning with great discipline.

Tang He and Liao Yong Zhong marched their troops to Yanping. Tang He sent an envoy ahead to demand that Chen You Ding surrender. Of course, he simply arrested the envoy. Then he gathered all his generals to a banquet. During the banquet, Chen You Ding had envoy killed and he spilled his blood into a mug of wine. He ordered all his generals to drink the wine with the blood to swear their determination to defend the city.

Tang He's great army reached the city of Yanping. Chen You Ding arranged his troops in battle formation by the bank of a stream. Tang He arranged his troops in battle formation on the opposite bank of the stream. When the battle began, Tang He's troops crossed the stream to attack. Chen You Ding's troops were defeated and withdrew into the city. But Chen You Ding was still confident. He told his generals, "The enemy troops have come afar. They want a quick, decisive battle. If we fight with them, we shall lose more soldiers. We'd do better not to fight with them but to carry out a protracted war and wait for the right moment." All his generals agreed with him. Then they all went up to the top of the city wall to defend the city. They stayed there day and night without a moment of rest. They were very tired. They began to complain. They wanted to go out to fight. Chen You Ding did not allow them to do so.

Chen You Ding suspected that Xiao Yuan Pan and Liu Shou Ren, two of his generals, wanted to betray him. He arrested Xiao Yuan Pan and had him executed. He took away Liu Shou Ren's military power. What did Liu Shou Ren do next? He went out of the city to surrender. In fact, many soldiers climbed down the city wall to surrender. On 29 January 1368 there was a loud explosion in the storehouse of arms and ammunition. Tang He thought that there was a rebellion in the city, so he ordered his troops to attack the city fiercely and his troops broke in. Chen You Ding knew that his final moment had come. He went into his office, sat on a chair and took poison to kill himself. Tang He's troops rushed into the city and into Chen You Ding's office. They carried Chen You Ding out on a stretcher. Suddenly there was rainstorm, and in the wet and chill Chen You Ding regained consciousness.

Chen You Ding was escorted to Yingtian and was brought before Zhu Yuan Zhang. Zhu Yuan Zhang said, "The Yuan Dynasty has fallen. For whom are you fighting? You have killed General Hu Shen and many of my soldiers. You have come to the end of your life." Chen You Ding said, "All is over. Say no more. All I want is death." Then Chen You Ding was executed in the marketplace. Very soon there was peace throughout the whole province of Fujian.

6. NORTHERN EXPEDITION TO TAKE CENTRAL CHINA

On 18 October 1367 Zhu Yuan Zhang ordered the generals to carry out a Northern Expedition to take Central China. He reminded Xu Da and the other generals,

"Since the Yuan Dynasty lost its power to rule over China, the whole realm has been in chaos. People have been plunged into an abyss of misery. I rose up in arms with you. We did our best to save the people from suffering. Now we have brought peace to Chen You Liang's State of Han and Zhang Shi Cheng's State of Wu. Fujian Province, Guangdong Province and Guangxi Province will settle down soon. But the areas of Central China are in great chaos. Wang Xuan and his son Wang Xin have occupied the area of Shandong Province. Kuokuotemuer has control of Henan Province. Li Si Qi and Zhang Si Dao occupied the areas of Shaanxi Province and Gansu Province. The Yuan Dynasty will soon fall. Now I want to order you to carry out a Northern Expedition. What strategy shall we adopt?"

Chang Yu Chun said,

"The southern part of the realm is peaceful. We have sufficient military strength to attack and take the capital of the Yuan Dynasty. Our troops are battle hardened. The Yuan troops have lived in leisure for a long time; they're soft. They can be easily defeated. If we conquer the capital, our troops will be able to take the other places easily, carrying on the momentum of the victory."

But Zhu Yuan Zhang had another view. He said,

"Dadu has been the capital of the Yuan Dynasty for over a hundred years. The defense of this city must be very strong. If our troops march deep into the areas of our enemy and our troops stop in front of a strongly defended city, food and military supplies will be difficult to transport. When other armies come to attack from all sides, it will be very unfavorable for us. My plan is to take Shandong Province first. Then our troops will take Henan Province and gain control of the Tongguan Pass. By doing so, we clear all the protections for the capital of the Yuan Dynasty. Then the capital will be isolated. In this way we shall be able to take the city without much fighting. Once we take control of the capital of the Yuan Dynasty, our troops will be able to march westward with the beating of the drums to take the areas of Yunzhong, Jiuyuan, Guanzhong and Long."

All the generals agreed with his plan. On 21 October 1367 Zhu Yuan Zhang appointed Xu Da as the Grand General of the Northern Expedition and Chang Yu Chun as the Deputy Grand General of the Northern Expedition. They would lead 250,000 men to the Yellow River from the Huai River.

Before the Northern Expedition set off, Zhu Yuan Zhang summoned the generals to his office again for a bit of strategic briefing. Among other things he said,

> "The purpose of the expedition is to put down the chaos. So it is very important to appoint the right person on the right position. Now all of you are very good fighters. But the most prudent and disciplined man who can lead all the other generals to victory is Xu Da. The general who can resist a million enemy soldiers and always leads the way to destroy the enemy battle formations and win is Chang Yu Chun. Chang Yu Chun is really a very good fighter. But I worry that he might underestimate the strength of the enemy. As a general, he should not personally fight enemy soldiers like a low ranking officer."

On 24 October Xu Da set out with the great army to Huai'an (now Huai'an, Jiangsu Province). He sent an envoy ahead to Yizhou (now Linyi, Shandong Province) to demand that Wang Xuan and his son Wang Xin to surrender. Wang Xuan was originally an official of the Department of Agriculture of the Government of the Yuan Dynasty. He had done a good job to bring the Yellow River under control. The court of the Yuan Dynasty then ordered Wang Xuan and his son Wang Xin to defend Yizhou. On 28 October, after Wang Xin had received Xu Da's letter, he sent an envoy to Yingtian to negotiate the terms for surrender.

In response Zhu Yuan Zhang sent Xu Tang and Li Yi, two of his officials, to Yizhou to appoint Wang Xin as the Governor of Yizhou. All the generals and officials under Wang Xin remained on their original positions. And Zhu Yuan Zhang ordered that all the troops under Wang Xuan and Wang Xin should be put under the command of Xu Da.

But actually Wang Xin and his father Wang Xuan were not really willing to surrender. This was a double cross. While they offered to surrender, they were actually preparing to resist Xu Da's army; Wang Xuan sent his son Wang Xin to Juzhou (now Juxian, Shandong Province) to recruit soldiers. Zhu Yuan Zhang had quite a network of informants, apparently, as he soon found out what they were up to. He sent a secret messenger to tell Xu Da to take his great army to march to Yizhou to observe the actions of Wang Xuan and Wang Xin.

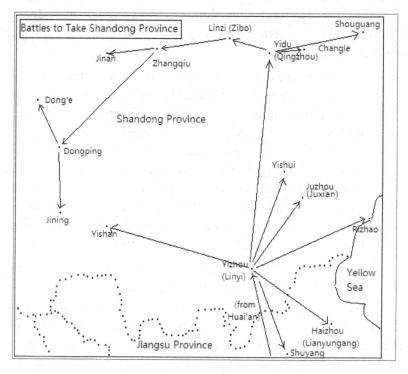

When Xu Da's great army reached Yizhou, Wang Xuan sent a team to bring wine and meat to them. After the team had come back, Wang Xuan attacked Xu Tang, Zhu Yuan Zhang's envoy, at night. Xu Tang somehow escaped and ran away to Xu Da's camps. On 10 November Xu Da ordered his troops to storm the city of Yizhou. Wang Xuan could see that he was not likely to fend off such a fierce attack. He opened the city gate to surrender. Xu Da ordered him to write a letter to his son Wang Xin, telling him to surrender. Xu Da ordered Sun Wei De, one of his generals, to take the letter to Juzhou to Wang Xin.

But Wang Xin killed Sun Wei De and slipped away to the west with his elder brother Wang De. Xu Da sent troops to take Yishan (now Yishan, Shandong Province), Juzhou (now Juxian, Shandong Province), Haizhou (now Lianyungang, in the north part of Jiangsu Province), Shuyang (now Shuyang, in the north part of Jiangsu Province), Rizhao (now Rizhao, Shandong Province) and Yishui (now Yishui, Shandong Province). Xu Da's troops took all these places.

Xu Da was very angry with Wang Xuan because he was so unreliable, and because his son Wang Xin had killed Sun Wei De. He ordered Wang Xuan arrested and put to death.

On 29 November 1367 Xu Da's army attacked and took Yidu (now Qingzhou, Shandong Province). Then Xu Da sent troops to attack more of Shandong Province. They captured Shouguang, Linzi (now Zibo) and Changle. On 6 December Xu Da commanded his great army to march to Zhangqiu. Wang Cheng, the Yuan Dynasty general defending Zhangqiu, surrendered.

Xu Da sent General Wang Xing Zu at the head of an army to march to Jining. On 7 December this army took Dongping. Then he sent Commander Chang Shou Dao to lead some troops to take Dong'e (also in Shandong Province). Wang Xing Zu and his troops marched to Jining. Chen Bing Zhi, the Yuan Dynasty general defending Jining, gave up the city and fled. So On 8 December Wang Xing Zu took Jining. On 8 December Xu Da's army reached Jinan. Duo'erji, the local general defending Jinan, surrendered.

Reports of all these losses came in to Emperor Toyan Temüer of the Yuan Dynasty; many cities in Shandong Province had fallen and now Zhu Yuan Zhang's army was approaching Dadu (now Beijing), the capital of the Yuan Dynasty.

Still grasping at straws Emperor Toyan Temüer ordered Tulu, the Governor of Shaanxi province, to command the troops under Zhang Liang Bi, Tulubu and Li Si Qi to march quickly out of Tongguan (now in Shaanxi Province) to rescue Dadu. But they refused to do so.

Chapter Four: Zhu Yuan Zhang Founds the Ming Dynasty

1. Zhu Yuan Zhang Ascends the Throne of the Ming Dynasty

On 11 December 1367, Li Shan Chang, the Premier, led the generals and officials to see Zhu Yuan Zhang. They suggested that Zhu Yuan Zhang should ascend the throne of emperor. But Zhu Yuan Zhang turned them down.

The next day, the same men came again and put forward the same suggestion. This time Zhu Yuan Zhang graciously acquiesced. A week later, the premier, generals and officials presented a plan for the throne ceremony. Zhu Yuan Zhang came to the newly built palace on 22 December. He summoned all the generals and officials to express his thanks for their suggestion for him to ascend the throne, and on that day a ceremony was held to offer sacrifices to Heaven and the gods.

On 4 January 1368 Zhu Yuan Zhang held a grand ceremony in the southern outskirts of the city of Yingtian to offer further sacrifices to Heaven and the Earth. After that, he ascended the emperor's throne in the palace.

He named the new dynasty the Ming Dynasty, the bright or brilliant dynasty. The title of his reign was Hongwu ("Hong" means "Great," and "Wu" means "Military," so together they mean "Great Militarist"). He made his wife, Lady Ma, Empress. He made his eldest son Zhu Biao the Crown Prince. He appointed Li Shan Chang Left Premier and Xu Da

Right Premier; he appointed Liu Ji and Zhang Yi as the Heads of the Supervision Office. All the generals and officials were promoted.

7. The throne on which Emperor Zhu Yuan Zhang once sat

On 6 January 1368 Zhu Yuan Zhang held a grand banquet in Fengtian Hall of the palace to entertain the generals and officials. In the banquet, Emperor Zhu Yuan Zhang said to all his officials, "When I read the biographies of the monarchs and their officials in history books, I found that some monarchs were very open to hear complaints and remonstrations from their officials, but the officials never presented any; or the officials submitted many remonstrations to the monarchs, but the monarchs refused to accept such critiques. I often express my viewpoints to my officials, but they respond in a subservient way and simply accept my viewpoints. There must be something which I should correct in how I express my views. I hope you will frankly point them out so as to help me to amend anything that I have overlooked." After the banquet, Emperor Zhu Yuan Zhang told Liu Ji, the Head of the Supervision Office, "Emperor Yao and Emperor Shun were the best emperors in ancient times. They lived in periods of peace and tranquility. But they always thought of danger in times of peace. I am not as virtuous as they were, but I am ruling over the whole realm. So I am very worried. I have ascended the throne of an emperor with the help of all of you. I am always aware that this realm is vast and there are many people in it. I have a heavy load of complex and intricate government affairs to attend to. When I think of this at night, I cannot fall asleep."

On 10 January Liu Ji and Tao An, a scholar of the Hanlin Academy, told the Emperor, "We hear that the authorities concerned have suggested that we should follow the system of the Yuan Dynasty and appoint a Head of the Secretariat. We suggest that the Crown Prince should assume this post." Emperor Zhu Yuan Zhang said, "If we want to follow the systems of the previous dynasties, we must be sure to follow good systems. If we adopt systems which are not good, it will be like climbing a high mountain and turning back halfway, and it will be like crossing the Yangtze River and turning back halfway. Then we will never be able to reach our goal. My son is still young. He has not yet learned much. He does not have enough experience. What the Crown Prince should do now is to respect his teachers, study the classic works so that he possesses a wide knowledge of things ancient and modern and knows how to do the right things at the right time. In the future, he will read all the reports of important military and civil affairs first, and then present them to me. It is not necessary to follow the system of the Yuan Dynasty and make him the Head of the Secretariat."

Tao Kai, the Minister of the Ministry of Rites, suggested that officials should be assigned as specialized officials in the Office of the Crown Prince. Emperor Zhu Yuan Zhang said, "I will appoint those court officials who are virtuous to serve concurrently as officials of the Office of the Crown Prince. If officials are appointed as specialized officials of the Office of the Crown Prince, I am afraid that they will be in conflict with the officials of the court. I will make a regulation to appoint officials of the court to be concurrently officials of the Office of the Crown Prince. In this way, father and son will become an integral whole, and the Monarch and his officials will be of one mind." Then he appointed Li Shang Chang, the Left Premier, to be concurrently Grand Tutor of the Crown Prince; Xu Da, the Right Premier, to be concurrently Grand Protector of the Crown Prince; Chang Yu Chun to be concurrently Grand Guardian of the Crown Prince. The other officials of the Office of the Crown Prince were concurrently officials of the court.

Lady Ma had shared weal and woe with Zhu Yuan Zhang all these years. When Zhu Yuan Zhang ascended the throne of the Ming Dynasty, he made her Empress. He also wanted to appoint Empress Ma's relatives to top positions, as an honor to his wife. But Empress Ma was a wise lady, and she observed, "The positions of officials should be granted to those who are virtuous and capable. My relatives are not capable enough to hold such positions. As far as I know, in the previous dynasties, many of the relatives of the empresses were haughty and decadent and did not obey the laws. Many of them were put to death. If Your Majesty wants to grant favors to my relatives, I hope Your Majesty may grant them property or wealth such that they may enjoy an adequate living, that is all. If they are not capable and are assigned to positions over their heads, they will become very proud. This will lead to their destruction. I would not like that." Emperor Zhu Yuan Zhang was persuaded by Empress Ma and gave up the idea of elevating her relatives to high official positions.

8. *Emperor Zhu Yuan Zhang (in the center), Empress Ma (second on the right), Xu Da (first on the right), Chang Yu Chun (first on the left), Li Shan Chang (second on the left)*

One day after morning court, when all the officials had left, Emperor Zhu Yuan Zhang said to Liu Ji and Zhang Yi, the two Heads of the Supervision Office, "I took up arms in the area of the Hui River, and at last I own the whole realm. During the periods of wars, many people were killed. When I think of this, I always feel sad. The people have suffered terribly during these periods. They long for peace and tranquility. If I suppress them with harsh laws, it will be like forcing medicine on a patient together with poison. They will suffer all the more." Zhang Yi knelt down, touched his head to the ground and said, "Your Majesty has considered all these. It is the blessing for the people of the whole realm."

On 13 January 1368 Emperor Zhu Yuan Zhang issued an imperial order to send one hundred and sixty four officials to the west part of Zhejiang Province to take a census verifying the actual amount of farmland. Emperor Zhu Yuan Zhang said to the officials of the Secretariat, "After the war and turmoil, the registration books of the households and the farmland in the prefectures and counties have been lost. If we impose too heavy a tax on the people, they will suffer again. It is very important for the government to treat the people well so as to let the people lead a better life. And the most important thing in letting the people lead a better life is to reduce the land taxes. I am sending officials to the west part of Zhejiang Province to set new rates for land taxes."

The land was taxed by the mu (1 mu = 666.7 square meters). In Chuzhou (now Lishui, Zhejiang Province) this tax had risen ten times since the war began and Zhang Yi had reported this to Zhu Yuan Zhang many times. Now he suggested that the taxes should be reduced to match the rate that had prevailed during the Song Dynasty plus 0.7 liter. Since he had become a specialist in this area, Emperor Zhu Yuan Zhang accepted his suggestion.

One day Emperor Zhu Yuan Zhang asked Liu Ji for ways to rejuvenate the nation in the aftermath of such widespread, major turmoil. Liu Ji answered with a general recommendation: "We should practice leniency and benevolence." But Emperor Zhu Yuan Zhang found that too vague, and said, "I think it is more important to give people tangible benefits so as to show our lenience and benevolence. I think we must do our best to increase the property of the people and reduce their financial burdens. We must do our best to reduce government expenses; otherwise we will still have to increase taxes and further impoverish the nation. We must reduce conscript labor;

otherwise the people will be too exhausted. We must educate the people; so that they will know righteousness, honesty and a sense of shame. We must prohibit corrupt practices among the officials; otherwise the people cannot live peacefully." Liu Ji knelt down, touched his head to ground and said, "Your Majesty is right. Only a benevolent Emperor can practice benevolent government."

2. Pacification of Central China

Xu Da and Chang Yu Chun continued their military operations in Shandong Province. On 12 February 1368 Chang Yu Chun and his troops attacked Dongchang (now Liaocheng, Shandong Province). Seeing that he could not resist Chang Yu Chun's great army, Shen Rong, the Yuan Dynasty's Governor of Dongchang, killed himself by hanging. Chang Yu Chun mopped up Dongchang and the counties around it. Then, leaving some troops to defend Dongchang, he himself led the main force to Jinan to join Xu Da.

Xu Da intended to attack Le'an (now Gaoqing, Shandong Province) but before he even got there, Yu Sheng, the local Yuan general, came out to surrender. Xu Da treated him with due courtesy and sent him back to Le'an. But when Yu Sheng was back in Le'an, he rebelled. By now, Chang Yu Chun was freshly arrived from Dongchang. He joined forces with Xu Da, and they commanded their troops to attack Le'an. On 25 February Zhang Zhong Yi, the Governor of Le'an, surrendered. General Yu Sheng escaped. So Xu Da and Chang Yu Chun took Le'an, and now Xu Da ordered Hua Yun Long to defend Le'an. Finally, Xu Da and Chang Yu Chun took the main force back to Jinan.

On 16 February Emperor Zhu Yuan Zhang ordered General Deng Yu to take the troops in Xiangyang (now Xiangyang, Hubei Province) and Anlu (now Anlu, Hubei Province) northward to conquer Henan Province. First they attacked and captured Tangzhou (now Biyang, Henan Province), then Nanyang (now in Henan Province). Zuo Jun Bi, the Yuan general defending Tangzhou, escaped to Anfeng (now in Anyang, Henan Province) and from there he went to Bianliang (now Kaifeng, Henan Province). General Li Ke Yi, at Bianliang, sent him to defend Chenzhou (now Huaiyang, Henan Province).

Emperor Zhu Yuan Zhang sent a letter to Chenzhou for General Zuo Jun Bi, saying, "These wars have gone on for many years. Heroic men have risen up everywhere. Each of them tried to be the strongest.

They fought bravely — not only for fame and accomplishment, but also to do their best to preserve their fathers, mothers, wives and children in troubled times. You and I fought against each other once. You were defeated and fled to an alien land, leaving your mother behind in Hefei. Now, my state is your father and mother's homeland. Hefei is your hometown. You have become a hostage in an alien land. You have made a wrong decision to abandon home for an alien land, leaving behind your old mother and your wife. They live in anxiety. For them, days wear on like years. Even if you don't care about your wife, how can you forget your mother who brought you into this world? Once your mother is lost, she will be lost forever. I hope you will think it over carefully." Zuo Jun Bi read the letter, but he still hesitated. Finally, Emperor Zhu Yuan Zhang sent a delegation to escort Zuo Jun Bi's mother to Chenzhou. Zuo Jun Bi was moved to tears.

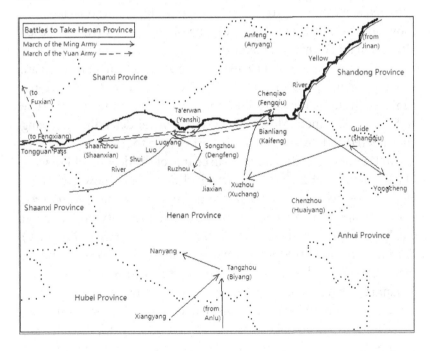

Xu Da and his great Ming Dynasty army marched to the upper reach of the Yellow River in Henan Province to Yongcheng, Guide and Xuzhou. Then they reached Chenqiao, twenty kilometers northeast of Bianliang. Li Ke Yi, the general of the Yuan army there, took off for

Luoyang. On 29 March 1368 Zuo Jun Bi led his troops to the gate of the camps of Xu Da's army to surrender.

Xu Da named General Chen De to defend Bianliang. He commanded the main force to march west to take Luoyang. On 8 April Xu Da commanded the great army to march to Ta'erwan (in Yanshi, Henan Province). Toyintemu'er, a Yuan general, arranged his troops of 50,000 men on the northern bank of Luo Shui River (now called the Luo He River). Chang Yu Chun rode into the enemy battle formation single handedly, just the kind of bold move the Emperor had cautioned against. Toyintemu'er sent twenty cavalrymen with long spears to fight him. Chang Yu Chun shot an arrow and killed the first cavalryman and then he dashed at the enemy battle formation with a loud shout. The officers and men following him rushed forward to join the attack. The Yuan battle formation collapsed and the soldiers scattered in all directions. Lucky again. Toyintemu'er gathered some of his scattered soldiers and slipped off to Shaanzhou (now Shaanxian, Henan Province). The Ming Dynasty troops chased after them for twenty kilometers.

Xu Da's army pushed forward to the outside of the northern gate of Luoyang and pitched camps there. Now Li Ke Yi (who had just run away from Bianliang to Luoyang) had to escape again, this time to Shaanxi Province. Aluwen, the Yuan general defending Luoyang, surrendered and presented the city of Luoyang to Xu Da.

Xu Da put General Zhao Yong in charge of the defense of Luoyang. On 12 April Chang Yu Chun attacked Songzhou (now Dengfeng, Henan Province). Li Zhi Yuan, the defending general, surrendered. On 14 April Chang Yu Chun's troops entered the city of Songzhou. On 21 April Chang Yu Chun took Ruzhou (still in Henan Province). Then he sent some troops to attack Jiaxian and they prevailed once more. On 22 April General Feng Sheng attacked Shaanzhou (now Shaanxian) and took it. Toyintemu'er again got away.

General Feng Sheng sent his troops to march to Tongguan Pass (now in Shaanxi Province). Li Si Qi and Zhang Si Dao, two Yuan generals, were defending Tongguan. When they saw that the great army of the Ming Dynasty was coming, Li Si Qi ran away to Fengxiang (in the west of Shaanxi Province) and Zhang Si Dao took off for Fuxian (in Shaanxi Province).

3. THE FALL OF DADU, THE CAPITAL OF THE YUAN DYNASTY

Emperor Zhu Yuan Zhang started his journey from Yingtian to Bianliang (now Kaifeng, Henan Province) on 24 April 1368. He ordered Li Shan Chang, the Left Premier, and Liu Ji, the Head of the Supervision Office, to stay in Yingtian to attend to state affairs.

The Emperor decided to make this journey because he wanted to meet Xu Da, the Grand General, to discuss plans for capturing the capital of the Yuan Dynasty. He reached Bianliang on 21 May and summoned Xu Da to come there to see him. The next day, Emperor Zhu Yuan Zhang changed the name of Bianliang to Kaifeng. (The city's name was changed more than once in accordance with the need to respect the various names of emperors.)

On that day, Chang Yu Chun and Feng Sheng came to Kaifeng to have an audience with Emperor Zhu Yuan Zhang. The Emperor granted Feng Sheng the title of the Right Deputy General of the Expedition against the Yuan Dynasty and put him in charge of the defense of Kaifeng.

On 1 June Xu Da came to Kaifeng to have an audience with Emperor Zhu Yuan Zhang. The Emperor held a banquet to entertain him. During the banquet, Emperor Zhu Yuan Zhang and Xu Da discussed the strategies they should adopt. Xu Da offered, "Since I have taken Shandong Province and Henan Province, Kuokuotemu'er has stayed in Taiyuan and did not dare to go out to rescue these places. When our army took Tongguan, Zhang Si Dao and Li Si Qi were defeated and ran away to the west part of Shaanxi Province. The generals of the Yuan army are in no position to go to each other's defense. Now we can carry on the momentum of our victory to attack the capital of the Yuan Dynasty. I am sure we can take it without much effort."

Emperor Zhu Yuan Zhang diplomatically agreed, up to a point. "What you have said is correct. But the topography in the north is flat; it is favorable for the cavalry to fight on flat land. It would be better for you to choose a general to take a vanguard of cavalrymen to march ahead of the whole army. You should have the foot soldiers and naval troops follow the vanguards. You can transfer the grain produced in Shandong Province as food supplies for the army attacking the capital of the Yuan Dynasty. And yes, if no outside forces come to reinforce them, the court of the Yuan Dynasty will collapse. Then we will surely conquer their capital."

Xu Da asked Emperor Zhu Yuan Zhang what to do about the Yuan Emperor himself. "If we attack the capital of the Yuan Dynasty and the Emperor runs away to the north, shall we go after him in hot pursuit?" Emperor Zhu Yuan Zhang said, "The Yuan Dynasty is doomed to fall. It will collapse by itself. It is not necessary to trouble our soldiers to give hot pursuit. After the emperor of the Yuan Dynasty has slipped out of the Great Wall, we must strongly defend our border areas. We must be well prepared against a surprise attack by the Yuan army." Xu Da knelt down, touched his head to the ground and accepted Emperor Zhu Yuan Zhang's order.

On 23 June Emperor Zhu Yuan Zhang was preparing to leave Kaifeng to go back to Yingtian, and Xu Da and the other generals came from Chenqiao to Kaifeng to wish him a safe journey. Emperor Zhu Yuan Zhang reiterated his main point. "The people in Central China have suffered from wars for a long time. I want to save them from suffering. This is the reason why I have ordered you to carry out the northern expedition against the Yuan Dynasty. The ancestors of the Yuan Dynasty entered Central China and became emperors. This was arranged by Heaven. But their descendants have not treated the people well and Heaven has resented them and has decided to get rid of them. The rulers were guilty. But the people were innocent. When a dynasty was replaced by another dynasty in the past, the emperor of the new dynasty killed many people as if they were his enemies. I will not allow my subordinates to harm the people. When you take a city, looting the people and burning the houses are strictly prohibited. You must make sure that the markets in the city operate as before. You must let the people live and work in peace and contentment. And you must treat the members of the royal clan of the Yuan Dynasty well. This way, we can act in accordance with the will of Heaven and my intention of punishing the rulers who have committed crimes and saving the people from suffering can be realized." Xu Da and the other generals knelt down and accepted Emperor Zhu Yuan Zhang's order.

On 28 July 1368 Emperor Zhu Yuan Zhang left Kaifeng and on 9 the second July (1368 was an intercalary year) he reached Yingtian.

By then, Xu Da's great army from Kaifeng and Chang Yu Chun's army from Ruzhou (now in Henan Province) had joined up in Heyin (now Guangwu, Henan Province). Then Xu Da sent generals to take the areas to the north of the Yellow River and General Fu You De led his troops on a march to Weihui. Zhang Long Er, the Yuan general defending Weihui, saw what was coming and abandoned the city of Weihui; he ran to Zhangde (now Anyang, Henan Province). The next day, Fu You De took Weihui. Then on 5 the second July Fu You De's troops reached Zhangde, so Zhang Long Er was still on the run. Chen Tong Zhi, a general under Zhang Long Er, surrendered and presented the city of Zhangde to Fu You De.

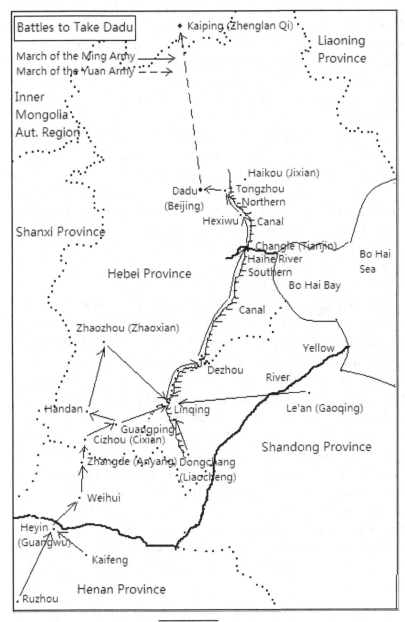

On 6 the second July Fu You De's troops were in Hebei Province. First they took Cizhou (now Cixian). Then the Ming army under Fu You De attacked Guangping. Du Wen Yu, the Governor of Handan, surrendered and handed over the city to the Ming army. The Ming army went further north and also took Zhaozhou (now Zhaoxian).

Then Fu You De sent his troops to Linqing (now in Shandong Province), beside the Nan Yunhe — the Southern Canal. On 11 the second July, Xu Da reached Linqing. He sent an envoy to Dongchang (now Liaocheng, Shandong Province) with orders for Zhang Xing Zu to command his troops to Linqing. He also sent an envoy to Le'an (now Gaoqing) with orders for Hua Yun Long to command his troops to Linqing.

On 12 the second July Xu Da ordered Fu You De to lead his foot soldiers and cavalrymen as the vanguard army marching by land. A detachment of these land troops captured two Yuan generals, and Fu You De let them act as guides. On 15 the second July, General Han Zheng and General Sun Xing Zu commanded their troops to Linqing to join forces with Xu Da's army. Then Xu Da assigned Han Zheng to stay behind to defend Linqing and Dongchang (now Liaocheng). On that day the vanguards of Chang Yu Chun's army took Dezhou, which was situated beside the Canal.

The navy sailed northward along the Southern Canal and the foot soldiers and cavalrymen marched along the embankment towards Changlu (now a district in Tianjin). On 20 the second July the general of the Yuan army defending Changlu ran away. The troops under Xu Da took the city. When they reached Zhigu River (now Haihe River), they captured seven big sailboats, made them into a floating bridge, and crossed the river. Li Shan Chang and Zhang Xing Zu led their ships along Bei Yunhe — the Northern Canal, while the foot troops and cavalrymen marched along the banks of the Canal. Yisu, the premier of the Yuan Dynasty, stationed his army near Haikou (now in Jixian, Tianjin). When he saw that the great Ming army was coming, he commanded his troops to disperse. The officials of the court of the Yuan Dynasty in Dadu (now Beijing) were shocked.

On 25 the second July, the main force of the Ming army reached Hexiwu (now in Tianjin) and defeated the Yuan army there. On 28 the second July, the Ming army reached Tongzhou (in the region of Beijing) and took it.

Emperor Toyan Temür of the Yuan Dynasty was beside himself when he heard this news. He summoned his empress and concubines and the Crown Prince to discuss what they should do. Emperor Toyan Temür said, "I do not want to be captured like Emperor Huizong and Emperor Qinzong of the Song Dynasty." He informed them that he had decided to go north to avoid being captured. Then he issued an imperial order to appoint Temu'erbuha, the King of Huai, to stay in the capital to administer state affairs.

He also appointed Qingtong as the premier to defend the capital. Many officials tried their best to persuade Emperor Toyan Temür to stay, but he would not listen to them. At midnight he slipped out the Jiande Gate, the north gate of the capital, and disappeared into the night with his empress, concubines, the Crown Prince and many officials. They went out of the Great Wall through Juyongguan Pass and ran away to Kaiping (in Zhenglan Qi, Xilin Gol, Inner Mongolia Autonomous Region, China), the Upper Capital of the Yuan Dynasty.

On 2 August 1368 Xu Da commanded the great army to Dadu (now Beijing), the capital of the Yuan Dynasty. He stationed his army outside Qihua Gate (the east gate). The Ming soldiers filled the moat with soil and crossed over to break into the city. Xu Da went up the tower on the city wall above Qihua Gate. The Ming soldiers captured Temu'erbuha, the King of Huai, as well as Qingtong, the premier, and some important officials. They said they would rather die than surrender, so they were executed. The Ming troops showed great discipline. They did not kill a single innocent person. They sealed all the treasury houses. The people in the city returned to a life of great peace and tranquility.

Xu Da sent envoys to escort the Yuan Dynasty's six princes to Yingtian and reported the great victory to Emperor Zhu Yuan Zhang. The Emperor rejoiced and changed Dadu's name to "Beiping" (meaning pacification of the north). At the same time he renamed Yingtian to Nanjing (meaning the southern capital), for use in the colder season, and, since Kaifeng would remain the northern capital, for use in warm weather, he renamed it Beijing. (That name reverted to Kaifeng ten years later when the city was made the capital of the new State of Zhou, to be ruled by the Emperor's fifth son, Zhu Su.)

4. Pacification of Shanxi Province and Shaanxi Province

In August 1368, after Xu Da had taken the capital of the Yuan Dynasty, Emperor Zhu Yuan Zhang ordered Xu Da and Chang Yu Chun to take Shanxi Province. He put Feng Sheng, Tang He and Yang Jing under the command of Xu Da and Chang Yu Chun. At that time Shanxi Province was held by Kuokuotemuer of the Yuan Dynasty. Xu Da ordered Sun Xing Zu to stay behind and defend Beiping. He sent Chang Yu Chun to command his troops to march southward in Hebei Province. On 28 August Chang Yu Chun took Baoding, then he took Zhongshan (now Dingzhou), and then he moved his troops further to Zhending (now Zhengding, Hebei Province)[1] and took that city too.

On 1 October Xu Da ordered Feng Sheng and Tang He to take their troops to attack Shanxi Province from the south, through Henan province to Shanxi Province. Feng Sheng and his troops marched from Kaifeng to Henan (now called Luoyang, Henan Province). From there the Ming army crossed the Yellow River and took Wuzhi. On 3 October they took Huaiqing (now Qinyang, Henan Province). The Ming army went over Taihang Mountains and took Zezhou (now Jincheng, Shanxi Province) and Luzhou (now Changzhi, Shanxi Province).

On 16 October Xu Da took Zhaozhou (now Zhaoxian, Hebei Province). At that time Emperor Toyan Temür had escaped to Kaiping, the Upper Capital of the Yuan Dynasty. He sent an envoy to Taiyuan to order Kuokuotemuer to command his troops to go through Yanmen Guan Pass (in Shanxi Province), then to Bao'an (now Huailai, Hebei Province), to attack Beiping. Xu Da got this information and noted to his generals, "Kuokuotemuer has sent all his troops on a long distance march to attack Beiping. The defense of Taiyuan must be very weak. Sun Xing Zu is strong enough with a great army defending Beiping. He can resist the attack. We can take the chance that the Yuan troops defending Taiyuan are not prepared to carry out a surprise attack on the city directly. The Yuan army defending Taiyuan will not be able to attack our army and cannot retreat either. There is a stratagem in the *Book on Art of War* which says, 'Control the strategic points and attack the weak point of the enemy.' If the Yuan troops which are on their way to attack Beiping turn back to rescue Taiyuan, we shall be able

---

1 The Chinese characters for Zhending are 真定; the Chinese characters for Zhengding are 正定; Zhending (真定) is the ancient name for Zhengdind (正定)

to realize our purpose and wipe out all the Yuan troops." The generals heartily agreed. And they commanded their troops to march directly to Taiyuan.

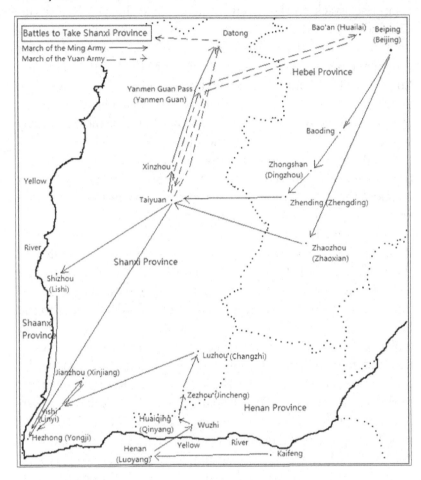

Kuokuotemuer and his troops reached Bao'an and they stationed themselves there. When he found out that the Ming army was heading to attack Taiyuan, he hurriedly commanded his troops to go back. On 30 December 1368 Xu Da's Ming troops reached Taiyuan. At the same time 10,000 cavalrymen of the vanguards of the Yuan Army under Kuokuotemuer reached the place. General Fu You De and General Xue Xian led the suicide troops to beat back the Yuan cavalrymen, but Kuokuotemuer could not enter Taiyuan. So he had to station his army to the west of Taiyuan.

Chang Yu Chun said to Xu Da, "Our cavalrymen have arrived here, but our foot troops are still on their way. If we fight with the Yuan army now, we shall surely suffer great casualties. If we launch a surprise attack on the enemy at night, we shall win." Xu Da said, "Good advice!"

It happened that night that Hubilema, a general under Kuokuotemuer, secretly sent an officer out to the Ming camp to tell Xu Da that he would surrender and he would collaborate with the Ming army from within the camps of the Yuan army. Then Xu Da selected elite cavalrymen to march to the camps of the Yuan army in silence. When they got close, they held up torches to send signals to Hubilema. When Hubilema saw the signals, he commanded his troops to attack the Yuan Army from within. Xu Da's cavalrymen attacked the Yuan camps from without. The Yuan troops were in great confusion and ran for their lives in all directions.

At that time Kuokuotemuer was reviewing the *Book on Art of War*. When the surprise attack began, he was at a total loss as to what he should do. He hurriedly jumped on a horse and rode away to Datong (now in the north part of Shanxi Province) with only eighteen cavalrymen. Hubilema led 40,000 Yuan soldiers to surrender to the Ming army. Then the Ming army attacked the city of Taiyuan and took it. Chang Yu Chun commanded some light cavalrymen to pursue Kuokuotemuer to Xinzhou (now Xinzhou, Shanxi Province), but he had gotten away. So they turned back to Taiyuan. Kuokuotemuer ran west to Gansu Province. On 4 January 1369 Fu You De and Xue Xian took Shizhou (now Lishi, in western Shanxi Province). Feng Sheng took Yishi (now Linyi, in southwestern Shanxi Province) and then took Jiangzhou (now Xinjiang, Shanxi Province). On 19 January 1369 Chang Yu Chun commanded his troops to attack Datong and took it. From then on, there was no more resistance in the whole area of Shanxi Province.

In February 1369 Xu Da's great army reached Hezhong (now Yongji, Shanxi Province). Chang Yu Chun and Feng Sheng commanded their troops to cross the Yellow River and enter Shaanxi Province first. On 1 March 1369 Xu Da also crossed the Yellow River. At that time Li Si Qi, the general of the Yuan army defending Shaanxi Province, was in Fengxiang (now Fengxiang, Shaanxi Province). Zhang Si Dao, the general of the Yuan army defending Shaanxi Province, was in Lutai (now Luyuan, Shaanxi Province) to defend Fengyuan (now Xi'an, Shaanxi Province). When he learned that the Ming army was coming, he ran away on 3 March. Three days later the Ming army entered Lutai. Xu Da sent General Guo Xing to command his troops to attack Fengyuan. The generals of the Yuan army defending Fengyuan fled. Then Xu Da commanded the Ming army to enter Fengyuan.

Emperor Zhu Yuan Zhang changed the name of Fengyuan into Xi'an (meaning tranquility in the west). At that time there was a famine in the area of Shaanxi Province. Emperor Zhu Yuan Zhang issued an imperial order to provide relief to the people in the disaster stricken areas, giving each household eight bushels of grain.

Emperor Zhu Yuan Zhang sent an envoy to Fengxiang with a letter to Li Si Qi. The letter read, "In the past you had a great army and occupied the area of Shaanxi Province which is strategically located and difficult of access. Although Zhang Si Dao and Kong Xing were also in the area of Shaanxi Province, they were no match for you. Kuokuotemuer once invaded your territory. But you beat him back. At that time you did not declare yourself king of Shaanxi area. You missed your chance to be king. Now I have occupied the whole area of Central China. Those who could rescue you have all run away. If you want to resist my great army with your isolated army, you will suffer great casualties. A virtuous man does not do that. I know very well that you are not able to defend Fengxiang. You will have to run away to the desert. The people in the desert are not of the same nationality of you. They will not obey you. If one day the officers and men who have followed you to the desert find they do not like to live in the bleak and desolate desert, they will hold a rebellion. Then you will not be able to protect your wife and children. Your hometown is Runan in Central China. The graves of your ancestors are in Runan. You should think about that. If you are sincere and submit to me, I will treat you with due consideration. Otherwise the consequences will be disastrous."

When Li Si Qi read the letter, he certainly considered surrendering. But some of his generals tried to persuade him to go west to Tubo (now Tibet Autonomous Region). Li Si Qi was quite torn. On 12 March 1369 Chang Yu Chun commanded his troops to Fengxiang. Li Si Qi was terribly afraid and fled to Lintao (now Lintao, Gansu Province).

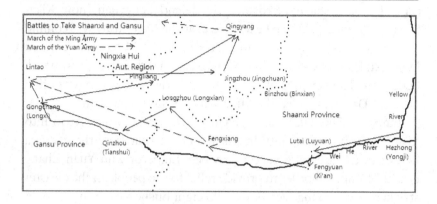

Back in February 1369 Yesu, the Premier of the Yuan Dynasty, commanded an army to attack Tongzhou (now Tongzhou, in Beijing). At that time there were only one thousand Ming troops defending Tongzhou. Yesu's 10,000 cavalrymen pitched their camps by the side of Bai He River (now Chaobai He River, Beijing). Cao Liang Chen, the general of the Ming troops defending Tongzhou, knew that his troops could not fend off an attack by the Yuan army, but he thought of a plan to defeat them. He put up a lot of flags on the boats along the Bai He River for more than ten kilometers. The soldiers in the boats beat the gongs. Yesu was scared and led his troops to retreat. In April 1369 Emperor Zhu Yuan Zhang ordered Chang Yu Chun to take his troops from Fengxiang back to Beiping area to defend the border area and make preparations to attack Kaiping, the Upper Capital of the Yuan Dynasty. He also ordered Li Wen Zhong to command his troops to join forces with Chang Yu Chun's army.

Xu Da called all his generals to discuss strategies. At that time Li Si Qi was in Lintao and Zhang Si Dao was in Qingyang (now Qingyang, in the northeast part of Gansu Province). The generals thought that Zhang Si Dao would be easily defeated, so they suggested that they should take Qingyang from Binzhou (now Binxian, Shaanxi Province). Then they would go through Gansu Province to attack Lintao.

Xu Da knew a little better. He said, "This is not the right way to defeat our enemies. The city of Qingyang is strategically located and difficult of access. The soldiers defending Qingyang are elite troops. This is not going to be easy. The Huang Shui River and the Yellow River flow through the area to the north of Lintao. However, the people of Qiang Nationality and Rong Nationality live in the areas to the west of Lintao. If we take Lintao, we can recruit sufficient new soldiers and we can get sufficient food supplies for the army from the abundant crops in these areas. If our great army presses to Lintao, Li Si Qi will have to escape to the west. Otherwise he will be captured. Once we have taken Lintao, the other prefectures will fall easily."

Xu Da dispatched generals to command troops to march to Longzhou (now Longxian, Shaanxi Province) and on 3 April 1369, the Ming army took the city. Then the Ming army attacked Qinzhou (now Tianshui, Gansu Province). Xu Da led the great army to Gongchang (now Longxi, Gansu Province), where the Yuan generals defending Gongchang surrendered. Then Xu Da sent Feng Sheng with his troops to attack Lintao; they arrived on 13 April 1369. Li Si Qi saw quite plainly that he did not have enough force to resist the great Ming army, so he surrendered and presented Lintao to the Ming army. Feng Sheng took a party of soldiers to escort him to Xu Da.

The report of victory reached Emperor Zhu Yuan Zhang. The Emperor immediately sent an envoy to tell Xu Da, "Since Li Si Qi has surrendered, go ahead and attack Qingyang and Ningxia. But be aware that Zhang Si Dao and his younger brother Zhang Liang Chen are very cunning. If they offer to surrender, you must make cautious arrangements to accept their surrender. Take great care not to fall into their traps."

On 4 May 1369 Xu Da commanded the Ming troops to attack Pingliang (now Pingliang, Gansu Province) and took it. Zhang Si Dao fled to Ningxia (now Ningxia Hui Autonomous Region) but he was captured by Kuokuotemuer. At that time Zhang Liang Chen, Zhang Si Dao's younger brother, was defending Qingyang. Xu Da sent General Zhang Huan to Qingyang to reconnoiter. When he got there, first he tried to persuade Zhang Liang Chen to surrender, and indeed on 8 May the man sent Le Ke Ren, one of his officials, to the Ming camp to offer his surrender to Xu Da. Xu Da sent General Xue Xian with 5,000 troops to Qingyang to accept Zhang Liang Chen's surrender. Zhang Liang Chen dutifully stepped out of the city and knelt on the left side of the road leading to the city gate to show that he was willing to surrender. When Xue Xian saw this, he believed that Zhang Liang Chen was truly willing to surrender.

But on the night of 15 May, Zhang Liang Chen held a mutiny. His troops launched a surprise attack on Xue Xian's troops. Zhang Huan was captured and Xue Xian was wounded. He managed to escape back to Pingliang. When Xu Da heard the report that Zhang Liang Chen had rebelled, he told his generals, "His Majesty is far-sighted. He predicted what has happened here from more than a thousand miles away. But Zhang Liang Chen's rebellion has only hastened his death. I will fight together with you to put him to death."

When Feng Sheng and Fu You De heard that Zhang Liang Chen had rebelled in Qingyang, they marched their troops from Lintao to Jingzhou (now Jingchuan, Gansu Province). In June 1369 Xu Da commanded his great army to march to Qingyang, and when they reached Qingyang, they laid siege to the city. Feng Sheng and Fu You De then joined forces with Xu Da's troops. Zhang Liang Chen sent his troops out of the city from the east gate to attack, but the Ming troops under Gu Shi beat them back. Then Zhang Liang Chen sent troops out from the west gate. But the Ming troops under Feng Sheng defeated them and drove them back. The siege lasted for more than a month, and Zhang Liang Chen ran out of food. There was no other army coming to rescue them. Zhang Liang Chen was at the end of his resources. He went up to the top of the city wall and shouted loudly to the Ming troops that he would surrender. But Xu Da ignored him. On 21 August 1369 Yao Hui, a general under Zhang Liang Chen, knowing that they had no way out, opened the city gate to let the Ming troops into the city. Xu Da sent his troops into the city of Qingyang from the north gate. Zhang Liang Chen jumped into a well, intending to commit suicide, but he was seized and was executed.

In September 1369 Xu Da ordered Feng Sheng to command an army to defend the occupied areas. Then he led the main force to go back to Nanjing, the capital of the Ming Dynasty.

5. The Final Destruction of the Yuan Dynasty

On 3 June 1369 Chang Yu Chun and Li Wen Zhong commanded their troops to start from Beiping (now Beijing) to the north to attack Kaiping (now Zhenglan Qi, Inner Mongolia Autonomous Region), the Upper Capital of the Yuan Dynasty. The great Ming army went past Sanhe went over Lu'erling Mountain (in Hebei Province).

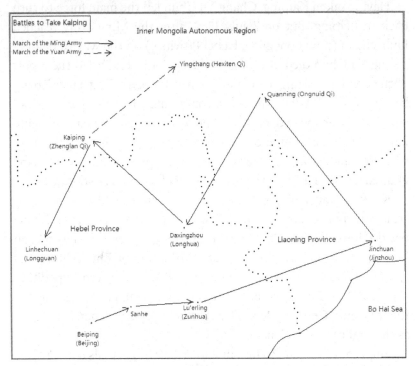

The Ming troops reached Jinchuan (near Jinzhou, Liaoning Province) and defeated Jiang Wen Qing, a general of the Yuan army. When the Ming troops reached Quanning (now Ongnuid Qi, Inner Mongolia Autonomous Region), Yisu, a general of the Yuan Dynasty, sent his troops to meet them in battle, but the Yuan troops were defeated. Then the Ming troops attacked Daxingzhou (now Longhua, Hebei Province). They laid ambushes in eight places outside the city. The Yuan general defending Daxingzhou commanded his troops to disperse at night, but they fell into the ambushes and were all captured. Then Chang Yu Chun sent the Ming army to attack Kaiping (now Zhenglan Qi, Inner Mongolia Autonomous Region), and they captured it on 17 June 1369. Emperor Toyan Temür of the Yuan Dynasty ran away to the north to Yingchang (now Hexiten Qi, Inner Mongolia Autonomous Region). The Ming troops chased after him and his followers for over a hundred kilometers but could not catch all of them. The Ming troops captured some of the members of the royal clan of the Yuan Dynasty and over 10,000 officers and soldiers of the Yuan army.

Having taken Kaiping, Chang Yu Chun led the main force to turn back to Beiping. But on 7 July 1369, after the Ming army reached Liuhechuan (now Longguan, Hebei Province) on the way to Beiping, Chang Yu Chun died of illness at the age of forty. When the report of the death of Chang Yu Chun reached Emperor Zhu Yuan Zhang, he was very sad. When the coffin containing Chang Yu Chun's dead body was transported back to Longjiang (now Xiaguan, Nanjing, Jiangsu Province), Emperor Zhu Yuan Zhang personally went there to hold a memorial ceremony for him. Emperor Zhu Yuan Zhang granted Chang Yu Chun the title of King of Kaiping posthumously.

Kuokuotemuer of the Yuan Dynasty commanded his troops to attack the border areas in the northwest. Emperor Zhu Yuan Zhang decided it was time to eliminate the remaining forces of the fallen Yuan Dynasty in the desert. On 3 January 1370 Emperor Zhu Yuan Zhang appointed Xu Da as the Grand General of the Northern Expedition Army, Li Wen Zhong as the Left Deputy General. Feng Sheng as the Right Deputy General, Deng Yu as the Left Deputy General, Tang He as the Right Deputy General.

Emperor Zhu Yuan Zhang summoned all the generals to the palace to discuss the strategic plan of the northern expedition. He pointed out, "The Emperor of the Yuan Dynasty has stayed outside the Great Wall for a long time. Recently Kuokuotemuer invaded Lanzhou with his isolated army. His intention is to establish a reputation for making military contributions for the Yuan Dynasty. He will not stop until he is eliminated." Then he said, 'Now, you are carrying out a northern expedition. Whom do you think you should attack first?" The generals answered, "The reason why Kuokuotemuer has invaded our border areas is that the Emperor of the Yuan Dynasty still exists. If our army directly marches to destroy the Emperor of the Yuan Dynasty, Kuokuotemuer will lose the purpose he is fighting for and will surrender without a fight." Emperor Zhu Yuan Zhang replied, "Now Kuokuotemuer has brought an army to invade our border areas. If we neglect him and attack the Emperor of the Yuan Dynasty in the desert, we will be ignoring the enemy close by in order to attack the enemy far away. That is not the proper way of handling things. I want to divide our army in two parts. The Grand General will command one part of the army to march out of Tongguan to Xi'an then from

Xi'an to Dingxi to attack Kuokuotemuer. The Left Deputy General will command the other part of the army to march out of Juyongguan Pass to enter the desert area to attack the Emperor of the Yuan Dynasty. Then each of them has to save himself from destruction and they will not be able to rescue each other. The Emperor of the Yuan Dynasty stays far out in the desert. He would never expect that our army would come so suddenly. He will be at a total loss when he sees our forces, like an isolated pig coming across a fierce tiger. In this way we shall surely catch him. We shall achieve two ends at once." All the generals agreed with his idea.

The strategic Tongguan Pass cuts through the mountains and opens out into the Wei River Valley, near the juncture with the Yellow River, and gives access to Shaanxi province. Xu Da and his great army marched through the high, narrow walls of the pass in April 1370 to carry out the western expedition. They reached Pingxi. Kuokuotemuer sounded a retreat, and his troops withdrew to Chedaoxian (now Chedaoling, a mountain situated to the northwest of Dingxi, Gansu Province), where they pitched camp. Xu Da's troops kept marching. From Pingxi they reached Shen'eryu (a hill situated to the north of Dingxi, Gansu Province) and Xu Da stationed his troops at the foot of the hill. The Ming army and the Yuan army faced off across the valley. They fought several battles a day. On 7 April 1370 Kuokuotemuer sent more than a thousand troops by side paths to launch an attack on the stronghold on the southeast of the Ming camps.

The Ming troops were caught completely off-guard and were in shock. Hu De Ji, the commanding general, was stunned. Xu Da sent his personal guards to meet the Yuan troops and beat them back. Xu Da arrested several generals and officers who had been charged with defending the stronghold and executed them in front of the whole army. All the soldiers were trembling. On 8 April 1370 Xu Da commanded the whole army to mount an overall attack on the Yuan army under Kuokuotemuer. The Ming troops fought fiercely and the Yuan troops were disastrously defeated, with 1,865 Yuan Dynasty officials captured, including the King of Tan, the King of Wenji, and managers of governmental affairs. More than 80,000 generals, officers and soldiers of the Yuan army were captured. Kuokuotemuer, his wife and children narrowly escaped. They fled northward to the banks of the Yellow River and crossed the river by raft. They sped across the desert as far as Karakorum (now Karakorum, Mongolia).

On 9 May 1370 Li Wen Zhong, the Left Deputy General, and General Zhao Yong commanded 100,000 Ming cavalrymen and foot soldiers from Beiping. (Beiping means "Northern Peace." The city's name was changed to Beijing, "Northern Capital", in 1403 and again in 1949.) They marched this huge force to Yehuling (now Wanquan, Hebei Province), where they captured Zhu Zhen, Manager of the Governmental Affairs of the Yuan Dynasty. From there the Ming troops marched to Luotuoshan Mountain in Chahannao'er (now Duolun, Inner Mongolia Autonomous Region). There they defeated the Yuan troops under Manzi, the Minister of War of the Yuan Dynasty. They reached Kaiping (now Zhenglan Qi, Inner Mongolia Autonomous Region), where Shangduhan, a Manager of the Governmental Affairs of the Yuan Dynasty, surrendered. Then Li Wen Zhong commanded his troops to march to Yingchang (now Hexiten Qi, Inner Mongolia Autonomous Region).

When the Ming troops were fifty kilometers from Yingchang, they captured a Yuan cavalryman and questioned him. He told Li Wen Zhong that Emperor Toyan Temür of the Yuan Dynasty had died on 28 April. Li Wen Zhong urged his troops to march to Yingchang at double speed. They encountered the Yuan troops along the way, and the Ming soldiers defeated the Yuan troops and chased them to Yingchang. There, Li Wen Zhong laid siege to the city. On 15 May, the Ming troops under Li Wen Zhong stormed the city and took it. Maidelibala, the grandson of the late emperor of the Yuan Dynasty, was taken prisoner, along with the empress and all the concubines of the late emperor and many members of the royal clan. The Ming troops got hold of the jade seal of the Yuan Dynasty and the jade seal of the Song Dynasty which the Mongolians had captured when they destroyed the Song Dynasty.

Only Aiyoushilidala, the Crown Prince of the Yuan Dynasty, had escaped with more than thirty cavalrymen to the north. The Ming troops pursued them but could not catch up with them.

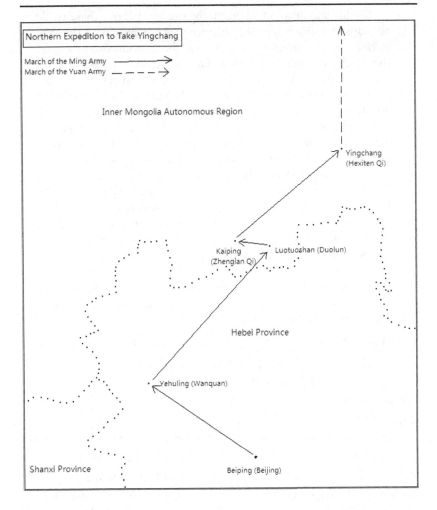

When the report of this great victory reached Nanjing, the capital of the Ming Dynasty, all the officials went to the palace to congratulate Emperor Zhu Yuan Zhang. Emperor Zhu Yuan Zhang granted Emperor Toyan Temür of the Yuan Dynasty the posthumous title of Emperor Shun (which means "be obedient to the Will of Heaven"). He granted Emperor Toyan Temür of the Yuan Dynasty this posthumous title because when the Ming army attacked Kaiping, he was obedient to the Will of Heaven and ran away to Yingchang without mounting any resistance.

Emperor Zhu Yuan Zhang wrote a funeral oration for the late emperor which read,

The life and death of a person, the rise and fall of a dynasty, do not happen incidentally. They happen in accordance with the Will of Heaven. The saints in ancient times became emperors because they knew the Will of Heaven and never had doubts about it. Your ancestors rose in the desert. They invaded the land of China with a great army and rode roughshod over the realm. They brought the people of all the nationalities into submission. They could not have done that if it had not been the Will of Heaven. But during the rule of your father and you, people rose up against the rule of the Yuan Dynasty. The whole realm was in great chaos. And your dynasty has fallen. This is the Will of Heaven. At that time, although I did not have a great army, I still managed to bring peace to the whole realm. At last I have replaced you as the emperor of the people of China. This is also the Will of Heaven. You became the master of the desert areas and I became the master of China. But you and your officials were stubborn. You incessantly sent troops to invade the border areas of my territory. Now I have learned that you have died in the desert. I regret your fate. I have sent envoys to hold a memorial ceremony for you. They will offer sacrifice to you so as to comfort your soul. I wish to draw your attention to this.

In June 1370 Li Wen Zhong sent a group of officers to escort Maidelibala, the grandson of Emperor Toyan Temür, the members of the royal clan of the Yuan Dynasty, and the jade seals of the Yuan Dynasty to the capital. Yang Xian, the Minister of Ceremonies, suggested to Emperor Zhu Yuan Zhang that a ceremony to parade the captives in public should be held in the ancestral temple to show off Maidelibala, the members of the royal clan of the Yuan Dynasty and the jade seal of the Yuan Dynasty. Emperor Zhu Yuan Zhang said, "There were many ceremonies in ancient times. When King Wu of the Zhou Dynasty conquered the Yin Dynasty, did he hold any such ceremony?" Yang Xian answered, "I don't know whether King Wu paraded his captives because he lived long ago. But Emperor Taizong of the Tang Dynasty did so."

Emperor Zhu Yuan Zhang replied, "Emperor Taizong held a ceremony in which the captives were paraded, so he could show off Wang Shi Chong. But if the captives had been members of the royal clan of the Sui Dynasty, I don't think he would have held such a ceremony. After the Mongolian emperors became the emperors of China, China entered into a period of prosperity for about a hundred years. My ancestors also enjoyed this period of prosperity. Although there have been ceremonies presenting captives, I am not hardhearted enough to do that. Just let Maidelibala and the members of the royal clan of the Yuan Dynasty come to the palace to have an audience with me in their Mongolian national costumes. After the audience I will grant them Chinese costumes. Let the concubines of the late emperor of the Yuan Dynasty come to the palace to have an audience with Empress Ma in the costumes of the Mongolian nationality. After the audience they will also be granted Chinese costumes."

On 18 May Maidelebala and the members of the royal clan of the Yuan Dynasty went to Fengtian Hall of the palace to have an audience with the Emperor. The concubines of the late Yuan emperor went to Kunning Palace to have an audience with Empress Ma. After the audiences, they were granted Chinese costumes and grand houses in Longshan (now Zijin Shan, situated just outside of Nanjing, the "Southern Capital" which was the seat of government off and on from the 3rd century AD to 1949). Emperor Zhu Yuan Zhang made Maidelibala Marquis of Chongli (meaning "the marquis who respects the rules of etiquette").

6. EMPEROR ZHU YUAN ZHANG MAKES HIS SONS KINGS

Emperor Zhu Yuan Zhang made his sons kings of different vassal states on 7 April 1370. The Emperor understood that the emperors of the Song Dynasty and those of the Yuan Dynasty, who had failed to establish vassal states, had found themselves isolated. When they were attacked, they had no one who would come to their rescue. Thus he decided to follow the examples of the ancient dynasties who did establish vassal states. That way, his sons as kings could provide protection for the emperors of the Ming Dynasty.[1]

He selected famous, big cities as the capitals of these vassal states: Xi'an (now in Shaanxi Province) as the capital of the State of Qin; Taiyuan (now in Shanxi Province) for the State of Jin; Beiping (now Beijing) for the State of Yan; Kaifeng (now in Henan Province) for the State of Zhou; Wuchang (now in Wuhan, Hubei Province) for the State of Chu; Qingzhou (now in Shandong Province) as the capital of

---

1 He made Zhu Shuang, his second son, King of the State of Qin; Zhu Gang, his third son, King of the State of Jin; Zhu Di, his fourth son, King of the State of Yan; Zhu Su, his fifth son, King of the State of Wu (later, the State of Zhou); Zhu Zhen, his sixth son, King of the State of Chu; Zhu Fu, his seventh son, King of the State of Qi; Zhu Zi, his eighth son, King of the State of Tan; Zhu Qi, his ninth son, King of the State of Zhao; Zhu Tan, his tenth son, King of the State of Lu.

the State of Qi; Changsha (now in Hunan Province) for the State of Tan; Yanzhou (now in Shandong Province) as the capital of the State of Lu.

When these princes grew up and were about eighteen years old, they were sent to their states.[1] These kings each had their own premiers and officials, and they had their guard troops of (3,000 to more than 10,000 men). Their duty was to resist foreign invaders, defend the border areas and protect the emperor in the capital of the Ming Dynasty.

7. Emperor Zhu Yuan Zhang Grants Titles of Nobility to Those Who Helped Build the Empire

On 11 September 1370 Emperor Zhu Yuan Zhang granted titles of nobility to those who had made great contributions to the good of the empire. First, he had the Ministry of War record the military contributions of the generals. Then he had the Ministry of Personnel decide on titles for the officials and generals. And when the day came, Emperor Zhu Yuan Zhang sat on his throne in Fengtian Hall. The Crown Prince and the kings stood by his side. All the officials and generals were present. In the hall, their new titles were declared: Li Shan Chang was made Duke of the State of Han; Xu Da was made Duke of the State of Wei (魏); Chang Mao, Chang Yu Chun's son, was made Duke of the State of Zheng; Li Wen Zhong was made Duke of the State of Cao; Deng Yu was made Duke of the State of Wei (衛); Feng Sheng was made Duke of the State of Song; Tang He was made Marquis of Zhongshan; and another twenty-seven men were made marquises.

On 12 September Li Shan Chang, the Left Premier, and Wang Guang Yang, the Right Premier, led all the officials and generals to the palace to express their thanks to Emperor Zhu Yuan Zhang. The

---

1 Actually, Zhu Shuang was sent to Xi'an in 1378 to be King of the State of Qin; Zhu Gang was sent to Taiyuan in 1378 to be King of the State of Jin; Zhu Su was originally made King of the State of Wu, but in 1378 he was changed as King of the State of Zhou and in 1381 he was sent to Kaifeng to be King of the State of Zhou; Zhu Di was sent to Beiping in 1380 to be King of the State of Yan; Zhu Zhen was sent to Wuchang in 1381 to be King of the State of Chu; Zhu Fu was sent to Qingzhou in 1382 to be King of the State of Qi; Zhu Zi was sent to Changsha in 1385 to be King of the State of Tan; Zhu Qi died in 1370; Zhu Tan was sent to Yanzhou in 1385 to be King of the State of Lu.

Emperor received them in Huagai Hall of the palace. He granted seats to the officials and generals and let them sit before him.

In the meeting, Emperor Zhu Yuan Zhang talked about the strategies he had used in consolidating the realm. He said,

> "I rose from the countryside. At that time my purpose was just to protect myself in the chaos. But after I had led my troops across the Yangtze River, I saw that all the powerful men were doing harm to the people. Zhang Shi Cheng and Chen You Liang were especially vicious. Zhang Shi Cheng relied on his wealth; Chen You Liang relied on his great military power.

> "I did not have anything to rely on. But I never allow my troops to kill innocent people; I am benevolent to the people; I practice thrift; I have been of one heart and one mind with you all and share weal and woe with you. When I contended with Zhang Shi Cheng and Chen You Liang, the former's State of Wu was close to our territory. It was suggested that we should deal with him first. But I considered that Chen You Liang was proud and had great ambition; Zhang Shi Cheng did not have much ambition. The one who was proud of himself would cause much trouble; the one who did not have much ambition would not be aggressive. So I decided to attack Chen You Liang first. In the battle in Poyang Hu Lake, Zhang Shi Cheng did not go out of Suzhou to rescue Chen You Liang. If we had attacked Zhang Shi Cheng first, he would have held fast to Pingjiang and Chen You Liang would have led all his troops to rescue Zhang Shi Cheng. In that case we would have been attacked from the front and from the rear.

> "In the northern expedition to pacify Central China, we took Shandong Province first and then took the areas of Kaifeng and Luoyang. Our troops marched to Tongguan Pass and stopped there. We did not attack Shaanxi Province and Gansu Province because Kuokuotemuer, Li Si Qi and Zhang Si Dao were strong enemies who had experienced a hundred battles. It was not easy to defeat them. So we did not attack them right away. Our army marched northward to take Dadu, the capital of the Yuan Dynasty. Having taken Dadu, our troops carried out a western expedition. Zhang Si Dao and Li Si Qi were very soon defeated. But Kuokuotemuer still resists our army and would not submit. If we had not taken Dadu and had fought with Kuokuotemuer instead, the outcome it is not clear who would have won."

In another gesture of respect and magnanimity, on 30 September 1370 Emperor Zhu Yucan Zhang made Wang Guang Yang, the Right

Premier, Earl of Zhongqin ("Zhong" means Devotion, "Qin" means diligent), and he made Liu Ji Earl of Chengyi ("Chengyi" means good faith).

8. EMPEROR ZHU YUAN ZHANG ADOPTS MEASURES TO BENEFIT THE PEOPLE

In January 1368 all the governors of the prefectures and counties of the whole realm went to Nanjing to have an audience with Emperor Zhu Yuan Zhang. The Emperor explained the situation thus.

"Peace has now been brought to the whole realm. But the people have nothing. They are like birds which have just learned to fly and trees which have just been planted. We must not take away the feathers of the birds's wings and we must not shake the roots the newly-planted trees. We must let the people rest and build up strength again.

"Only upright and honest officials can restrain themselves from corruption and work for the interest of the people. Greedy officials will work for their own interests and do harm to the people. Some very talented officials will fail to demonstrate their ability, because they only think of their own interests. Some officials who want to please their superiors will try their best to satisfy their interests at the cost of the interests of the people. They do all these because they are not honest and clean. You should guard against such wrong doings."

In January 1368 Emperor Zhu Yuan Zhang issued an imperial order to send a group of 164 officials to the west part of Zhejiang Province to conduct a census of farmlands there. He instructed the officials of the Secretariat-Chancellery, "After wars, most of the records on the amount of farmland and the number of households have been lost. Now we must verify all these records so that the people will not be overburdened. The most important thing for good government is to improve the life of the people. The most important thing to improve the life of the people is to reduce the land taxes. I have sent a group of officials headed by Zhou Zhu to do a census of the farmlands in the prefectures and counties so we can set the land taxes for the farmlands. This is their main task. They should not do anything else or cause trouble to the people."

One day when the Emperor was talking with Liu Ji, he asked him for ideas. "During the wars with the local warlords, the people were plunged into misery and suffering. Now the warlords have been conquered one by one. What should we do to let the people rest and build up strength?" Liu Ji said, "The most important way is to grant benevolence to the people." Emperor Zhu Yuan Zhang said, "It would be useless to talk about granting benevolence if we do not give real benefit to the people. As I see, if we want to give real benefit to the people, we must do our best to increase their wealth and save their manpower. If we do not restrain our spending, the people's resources will be exhausted. If we do not reduce the conscription of labor, the people will be exhausted. If we don't educate the people, they will not know propriety, righteousness and honesty. If we don't prohibit embezzlement, the people will live in hardship." Liu Ji knelt down, touched his head to the ground and said, "Your Majesty practices benevolent government with a kind heart."

In February 1368 Emperor Zhu Yuan Zhang ordered the officials of the Secretariat-Chancellery to remodel the system of conscript labor. Emperor Zhu Yuan Zhang was concerned there was too much conscript labor going into government construction projects and the poor people would suffer. After discussion, the officials suggested to Emperor Zhu Yuan Zhang that a household which owned six hectares of farmland should provide one conscript laborer; a household which owned less than six hectares of farmland did not need to provide a conscript laborer.

In January 1369 Emperor Zhu Yuan Zhang issued an imperial order to exempt the people in Central China from paying land tax. He particularly praised the people of Shandong Province who welcomed his armies and provided food. The people of Dadu, and areas of Shanxi Province and Hebei Province, had suffered from years of wars. Thus he spared the people in Beiping, Shandong Province and Shanxi Province from paying land tax for at least a year. Other prefectures in Henan Province and the strategic areas around Tongguan and the Yellow River, south to Tangzhou, were also exempted, along with the people in Shaanxi Province and Gansu Province who had recently changed sides.

At the same time Emperor Zhu Yuan Zhang issued an imperial order to exempt the people in the areas south of the Yangtze River from paying land tax of that year. The imperial order read, "After I had crossed the Yangtze River, I stationed my troops in Taiping. Then I took Zhenjiang and Xuancheng. After that I sent armies to carry out northern expedition and western expedition. All these expeditions were successful. When I started my career, the people in the above mentioned places had shouldered the heavy burden of providing food and money to support my armies. When I think of this, I feel pity for the people of these places. Now the whole realm is basically pacified. I have decided to exempt the people in Taiping, Yingtian and Zhenjiang from paying land tax for one year. The people in Guangde, Wuwei, Chuzhou and Hezhou will also be exempted from paying land tax for one year."

Emperor Zhu Yuan Zhang paid great close attention to projects for preventing floods and he provided relief to the people in disaster stricken areas. In July 1390 the dike of the Yellow River in Kaifeng area was breached when the river flooded. Some 150,000 houses were inundated. Emperor Zhu Yuan Zhang sent officials to provide relief to the people. In the same month more than 79,000 meters of the dike by the sea along Chongmen and Haimen (both are in Shanghai) was burst by the tide and the waves. Emperor Zhu Yuan Zhang mobilized 250,000 people to repair the dike. In August 1394 Emperor Zhu Yuan Zhang sent officials to different parts of the country to supervise water conservation projects.

9. HU WEI YONG'S CONSPIRACY

Hu Wei Yong was a man from Dingyuan (now in Anhui Province). He joined Zhu Yuan Zhang in January 1355 when he took Hezhou (now Hexian, Anhui Province). Zhu Yuan Zhang appointed him as the official in charge of reports in the Office of the Marshal. Not long later he was promoted to the position of chief secretary of Ningguo (now Ningguo, Anhui Province). Upon Li Shan Chang's recommendation, Zhu Yuan Zhang appointed Hu Wei Yong as the Governor of Ningguo. In 1364 Zhu Yuan Zhang summoned Hu Wei Yong to Yingtian to take the position of head of ministry of rites. In 1370 Hu Wei Yong was appointed as a member of the Secretariat-Chancellery.

Wang Guang Yang lived in Taiping (now Dangtu, Anhui Province). In May 1355 Zhu Yuan Zhang commanded his troops to cross the Yangtze River and they conquered Taiping. Wang Guang Yang joined Zhu Yuan Zhang there. He was appointed as an official in the Office of the Marshal and a supervisor of the army.

Wang Guang Yang worked in the army under Chang Yu Chun. In 1368 when Zhu Yuan Zhang's army took Shandong Province, Wang Guang Yang was appointed Governor there. He did a very good job in this position. The people of Shandong Province lived in peace and tranquility. In the same year Zhu Yuan Zhang appointed him to be a member of the Secretariat-Chancellery.

Yang Xian joined Zhu Yuan Zhang in 1356 when Zhu Yuan Zhang took Yingtian (now Nanjing, Jiangsu Province). He became a high official in Zhu Yuan Zhang's Office of Marshal and he was a good friend of Liu Ji. In October 1369 Left Premier Li Shan Chang wanted to retire. Emperor Zhu Yuan Zhang intended to appoint Yang Xian as a premier. He asked Liu Ji's opinion about it. Liu Ji said, "Yang Xian has the ability of a premier, but he is not a broad-minded person. A premier should be fair and impartial. When he makes judgments, he should put public interests first and should not consider his own interests. Yang Xian does not have the moral character of a premier. If he is appointed as premier, he will surely end up in failure."

Then the Emperor asked him about his friend: "What about Wang Guang Yang?" Liu Ji said, "He is a narrow minded man." Emperor Zhu Yuan Zhang asked, "What about Hu Wei Yong?" Liu Ji said, "He is just a young bull. If he is used to tow a cart, the cart will be turned over. If he is used to drag a plough, the plough will be broken." Then Emperor Zhu Yuan Zhang said, "No one would be a more suitable premier than you." Liu Ji said, "I know myself well enough. I hate injustice like poison. I cannot undertake all the miscellaneous affairs. If Your Majesty appoints me as the premier, I am afraid that I will fail to live up to your expectation. There are capable persons in the realm, but I think the persons Your Majesty mentioned just now are not suitable candidates."

But Emperor Zhu Yuan Zhang still appointed Yang Xian as the left premier. Yang Xian was a capable man. He was smart and good at making decisions. But he was mean. He tried his best to persecute those who would not submit to him. He changed all the rules of the Secretariat-Chancellery and replaced nearly all the officials with his trusted followers. Emperor Zhu Yuan Zhang saw that there were not enough officials in the Secretariat-Chancellery, so he appointed Wang Guang Yang as the right premier. The affairs of the Secretariat-Chancellery were decided by Yang Xian alone. Wang Guang Yang did his best to be obedient to Yang Xian, but still Yang Xian did not like him. Yang Xian instigated Liu Bing, the supervisor of the Legal Department, to accuse Wang Guang Yang of failing to be dutiful to his mother.

Emperor Zhu Yuan Zhang reprimanded Wang Guang Yang and sent him back to his home village. Yang Xian was not satisfied and again he pushed Liu Bing to ask Emperor Zhu Yuan Zhang to send Wang Guang Yang into exile in Hainan Island (now Hainan Province). This aroused Emperor Zhu Yuan Zhang's suspicion.

He suspected that Yang Xian was plotting a scheme. So he ordered his arrest along with that of Liu Bing and threw them into jail. Liu Bing confessed that he had been instigated by Yang Xian to do all this. Emperor Zhu Yuan Zhang was very angry and ordered soldiers to execute them both. Then he summoned Wang Guang Yang back to Nanjing.

In July 1373 Emperor Zhu Yuan Zhang appointed Hu Wei Yong as the left premier. Liu Ji felt very sad. He said to himself, "It would be a blessing for the people of the realm if what I said about Hu Wei Yong is inaccurate. But if what I said is accurate, the people will suffer a lot!" He was very worried.

In the border between Zhejiang Province and Fujiang Province, there was a place called Danyang. Outlaws and salt dealers gathered in this place doing all kinds of unlawful things. In 1371 when Liu Ji retired and went back to Qingtian (now in Zhejiang Province), his home, he learned of this problem. He submitted a memorandum to Emperor Zhu Yuan Zhang suggesting to establish an army station there so as to suppress these outlaws and salt dealers. Emperor Zhu Yuan Zhang accepted his suggestion and had some troops stationed there. The mischief-makers rebelled and occupied Danyang as their base. The local officials concealed these facts and did not report this to the court.

Liu Ji sent his elder son Liu Lian to Nanjing to report the facts to Emperor Zhu Yuan Zhang. This made Hu Wei Yong very angry because Liu Lian did not report to the Secretariat-Chancellery first. Hu Wei Yong hated Liu Ji for this. He instigated Wu Yun, the minister of the legal department, to lodge an accusation against Liu Ji. Wu Yun submitted a memorandum to the Zhu Yuan Zhang which read, "Liu Ji found that there was an air current for a king in Danyang and Liu

Ji intended to take this place for his grave. So he suggested to Your Majesty to establish an army station there so as to drive the people out of that place. The people there refused to give that place to Liu Ji. So they have rebelled." Having read the memorandum, Emperor Zhu Yuan Zhang asked the officials concerned to discuss this matter. Hu Wei Yong suggested to Emperor Zhu Yuan Zhang to inflict serious punishment on Liu Ji and put in jail. Emperor Zhu Yuan Zhang ignored Hu Wei Yong's suggestion. He just passed the suggestions of punishment to Liu Ji so as to give him a warning.

Then Liu Ji hurried back to Nanjing to have an audience with Emperor Zhu Yuan Zhang. He did not dare to defend himself before the Emperor. He just accepted all the blame. He did not dare to ask to be allowed to go back to Qingtian. By January 1375, Liu Ji was so worried and indignant that he fell ill.

Hu Wei Yong saw that Emperor Zhu Yuan Zhang did not care about Liu Ji very much. He pretended that he was concerned about Liu Ji's illness and went to visit him with a doctor. The doctor gave some medicine to Liu Ji. After Liu Ji had taken the medicine, he felt that there was a stone as big as a fist in his chest. He felt a severe pain. He sent somebody to inform Emperor Zhu Yuan Zhang about this. But Emperor Zhu Yuan Zhang did not take it seriously. In March 1375 Liu Ji's illness became much worse. Emperor Zhu Yuan Zhang sent an envoy to visit Liu Ji and learned that he was about to die; so he sent a party of officials to escort the man back to Qingtian. And soon Liu Ji passed away.

Since Yang Xian had been executed and Wang Guang Yang was dismissed, Hu Wei Yong held all the power of the Secretariat-Chancellery in his own hands. He could do anything he liked. He had the power to read all the memorandums submitted by the officials to Emperor Zhu Yuan Zhang. If any memorandum mentioned anything unfavorable to him, he would not pass it on. Many officials tried their best to curry favor with Hu Wei Yong.

Xu Da, Duke of the State of Wei, disliked Wu Wei Yong for his treacherous conduct. He once expressed view of Hu Wei Yong in front of Emperor Zhu Yuan Zhang; Hu Wei Yong found out, and he hated Xu Da for this.

Xu Da had a servant named Fu Shou. Hu Wei Yong secretly bought him over to work for him. But Fu Shou confessed this to Xu Da.

Hu Wei Yong was originally the Governor of Ningguo (now Ningguo, Anhui Province). At that time Li Shan Chang was in power. Hu Wei Yong presented two hundred ounces of gold to Li Shan Chang. Then Li Shang Chang promoted him to the position of a member of the Secretariat-Chancellery. From then on Hu Wei Yong and Li Shan Chang colluded with each other. Hu Wei Yong married his elder brother's daughter to Li You, Li Shan Chang's younger brother's son. In the position of the Left Premier he practiced graft and abused his power. He did anything he wanted.

One day a big bamboo shoot grew up from the bottom of the well in Hu Wei Yong's old house in Dingyuan. It grew as tall as a meter above the water in the well. His followers flattered him by saying that it was an auspicious sign for him. And it was said that at night there was a bright light shooting out to the sky from the grave of Hu Wei Yong's grandfather. All these signs made Hu Wei Yong believe that he would become emperor. He began to plot a conspiracy. It happened that a family member of Hu Wei Yong insulted the official who was guarding a pass when this family member was going through the pass on unlawful business. The official reported this to Emperor Zhu Yuan Zhang. Emperor Zhu Yuan Zhang was outraged and issued an order to kill Hu Wei Yong's relative. Hu Wei Yong apologized to Emperor Zhu Yuan Zhang on the excuse that he did not know what his relative was doing. Then, Emperor Zhu Yuan Zhang began to investigate the reason why Liu Ji had died. Hu Wei Yong was afraid that someone would reveal the truth to Emperor Zhu Yuan Zhang. Then he talked with his followers. He said, "Emperor Zhu Yuan Zhang does not care about those who have made great contributions to the good of the empire. How can he care about me? He will kill me any time. I'd better strike first so as to avoid being killed like a sitting duck."

At that time Lu Zhong Heng, the Marquis of Ji'an, and Fei Ju, the Marquis of Pingliang, often broke the law. Emperor Zhu Yuan Zhang blamed them many times. Lu Zhong Heng and Fei Ju were very afraid. Hu Wei Yong lured them by promise of gain. These two persons were brave but were simple minded. They saw that Hu Wei Yong was in power. So they colluded with Hu Wei Yong and became involved in Hu Wei Yong's conspiracy.

Hu Wei Yong recommended Chen Ning, who was originally the Governor of Suzhou (now in Zhejiang Province) to head up the

Administrative Supervision Department. Chen Ning was a cruel official who brutally abused and tortured people. Emperor Zhu Yuan Zhang criticized him for this cruelty, but Chen Ning did not care. His son Chen Meng Lin tried to persuade him to give up the cruel practices many times. Chen Ning was so angry that he beat his son to death. Emperor Zhu Yuan Zhang was irate. He said, "Chen Ning treated his own son this way. How will he treat his master?" When Chen Ning heard about that, he feared for his life, so he colluded with Hu Wei Yong more closely.

One day Hu Wei Yong and Chen Ning were sitting in the office of the Secretariat-Chancellery, studying the records of the army stations throughout the realm. He ordered Mao Xiang, a commander-in-chief of the army, to select from his soldiers and organize them into his own army. Hu Wei Yong sent Li Cun Yi, Li Shan Chang's younger brother, to persuade Li Shan Chang to take part in his conspiracy. At first Li Shan Chang refused. Later he became irresolute. At last he agreed to take part in Hu Wei Yong's conspiracy.

One day in November 1379, Hu Wei Yong's son was riding a horse in the busy marketplace and he bumped into a horse drawn cart; he was struck by the wheel and died. Hu Wei Yong had the cart driver killed. When Emperor Zhu Yuan Zhang heard about this, he was very angry with Hu Wei Yong. He ordered him to compensate the death of the cart driver. Then Hu Wei Yong speeded up his conspiracy.

At that time an envoy from the King of Japan secretly visited Hu Wei Yong. Hu Wei Yong asked him to invite the King of Japan to send one thousand soldiers to sail from Japan, pretending that they were escorting tribute to the Emperor. When the Japanese arrived in Nanjing, Hu Wei Yong would send his soldiers to join forces with them and launch a surprise attack on the palace and kill Emperor Zhu Yuan Zhang. If the surprise attack failed, he would loot the treasury houses and load all the wealth on the Japanese ships and sail to Japan. The envoy went back to Japan and told the king of this scheme. The King of Japan thought it was worth a try, and he sent soldiers on ships to support Hu Wei Yong. Hu Wei Yong also sent Feng Ji, originally an official of the Yuan Dynasty, to the desert as his envoy to ask the ruler of the Yuan Dynasty to send troops to assist him from outside.

On 6 January 1380 Hu Wei Yong told the people that sweet water was flowing out of the well in his residence. He invited Emperor Zhu

Yuan Zhang to visit and see this wonder. Emperor Zhu Yuan Zhang agreed. His carriage was driving out of the palace from Xihua Gate (the west gate of the wall of the palace) when suddenly Yun Qi, an officer of the Emperor's personal guards, rode up quickly on horseback and stopped the carriage. He was in such a hurry that he could not get his breath and could not speak. Emperor Zhu Yuan Zhang was very angry with him for his impoliteness. The guards struck him with their weapons. He was mortally wounded but before he died, he managed to raise his right arm and point at Hu Wei Yong's residence.

Emperor Zhu Yuan Zhang realized what he meant. He went up to the top of the palace wall and watched the residence. There were soldiers hiding in the yard. They were holding swords and spears. Emperor Zhu Yuan Zhang sent his royal guards to storm the residence. They arrested Hu Wei Yong and his followers. Under interrogation, Hu Wei Yong and his followers made their confession. Hu Wei Yong was executed in the marketplace. Chen Ning was also executed. About 15,000 men were involved in this case.

The officials suggested to the Emperor that Li Shan Chang and Lu Zhong Heng should also be killed. Emperor Zhu Yuan Zhang said, "When I took up arms, Li Shan Chang went to the gate of my army's camps and said, 'Now there is a sun in the sky!' At that time I was 27 years old. Li Shan Chang was already 41 years old. His suggestions were always to the point. So I put him in charge of the Secretariat. He made great contributions. So I made him a duke. I married my daughter to his son. Lu Zhong Heng joined me at the age of seventeen. He was an orphan. His father, mother, and brothers had all died. When I saw him, I said, 'Come and join me.' He joined me, and he fought very bravely and established a great military legacy. I made him a marquis. Li Shan Chang and Lu Zhong Heng joined me just as I was beginning my revolt. They became my trusted followers. I am not hard-hearted enough to punish them. You may just spare them."

On 11 January 1380 Emperor Zhu Yuan Zhang issued an imperial order to abolish the Secretariat-Chancellery. He distributed the power of the former Secretariat-Chancellery into the six ministries (the Ministry of Personnel, the Ministry of Revenue, the Ministry of Rites, the Ministry of War, the Ministry of Justice and the Ministry of Works). He decided to cancel the positions of premiers.

In December 1380 Song Lian, who had retired in Pujiang (now Pujiang, Zhejiang Province), was convicted because his son Song Shen had been involved in the Hu Wei Yong conspiracy. Song Lian was escorted back to Nanjing with a large wooden yoke fastened around his neck. Emperor Zhu Yuan Zhang wanted to put Song Lian to death. But Empress Ma said, "Ordinary people respect their teachers all their lives. Song Lian has been the teacher of the Crown Prince and your other sons. How can you be so hard-hearted as to kill him? Song Lian has been staying in his village for a long time. How could he know what was happening at your court?" Emperor Zhu Yuan Zhang considered what she said and changed his mind. He sent Song Lian into exile in Maozhou (now in Sichuan Province). That was sufficient, anyway: When Song Lian was escorted to Kuizhou (now Fengjie, Sichuan Province) on the way to Maozhou, he fell ill and died there.

Ten years later, in April 1390, convicts in the capital were being sent into exile in the border areas. Ding Bin, one of Li Shan Chang's relatives, had committed some crime and was to be sent among these convicts. Li Shan Chang interceded with the official concerned for Ding Bin. The Emperor heard about this and found it flagrantly inappropriate. He was in a rage. He issued an order to interrogate Ding Bin. Ding Bin once worked in Hu Wei Yong's house. He told the interrogator how Li Cun Yi, Li Shan Chang's younger brother, colluded with Hu Wei Yong. Emperor Zhu Yuan Zhang ordered to arrest Li Cun Yi and his son. After interrogation, Li Cun Yi made his confession. The interrogator wrote a report of the interrogation and sent it to Emperor Zhu Yuan Zhang. The report read, "When Hu Wei Yong was plotting his conspiracy, he sent Li Cun Yi to persuade Li Shan Chang to take part. When Li Shan Chang heard what Li Cun Yi had said, he was greatly surprised. He reprimanded Li Cun Yi loudly, 'What have you said? What you do will lead to the slaughter of our whole clan.'

"Not long later Hu Wei Yong sent Yang Wen Yu, one of Li Shan Chang's old friends, to talk Li Shan Chan into it, promising to make him king of the area to the west of the Huai River. Although Li Shan Chang still refused, it seemed that he was interested in the offer. So Hu Wei Yong went to persuade Li Shan Chang personally. But still Li Shan Chang did not promise. Soon after, Hu Wei Yong again sent Li

Cun Yi to talk to Li Shan Chang. Li Shan Chang said with a long sigh, 'I am already old. You should look out for yourself after I die.'"

At this time an official disclosed to Emperor Zhu Yuan Zhang that Li Shan Chang had covered up the report that General Lan Yu had captured Feng Ji, the envoy sent by Hu Wei Yong to the desert to ask the Yuan ruler to help him from outside. The officials of the Supervision Department presented letters to Emperor Zhu Yuan Zhang, asking him to charge Li Shan Chang. Lu Zhong Qian, a servant of Li Shan Chang, also reported that Li Shan Chang and Hu Wei Yong had colluded with each other. Then the final verdict was made. Li Shan Chang was found guilty of taking part in Hu Wei Yong's conspiracy. On 23 April 1390, under the order of Emperor Zhu Yan Zhang, Li Shan Chang killed himself by hanging. He died at the age of seventy-seven.

10. THE GREAT CONTRIBUTIONS MADE BY ZHU DI, KING OF THE STATE OF YAN

Zhu Di was the fourth son of Emperor Zhu Yuan Zhang. The Emperor had made him King of the State of Yan (the State of Yan was situated in the area of what is now the administrative district of Beijing) in April 1370 when he was ten years old. Ten years later, the young man went to Beiping (now Beijing) to take his seat as King. Zhu Di was a tall, strong, handsome man with a magnificent beard. He was both brave and intelligent.

At that time Yaozhu, the premier of the Yuan Dynasty, and Nai'erbuhua, the Minister of War of the Yuan Dynasty, commanded the Yuan troops to attack the northern border areas. Emperor Zhu Yuan Zhang decided to wipe out the Yuan armies under Yaozhu and Nai'erbuhua so as to pacify the border areas. He also intended to let those of his sons who had been made kings of the states adjacent to the Great Wall fortify the defense of the border areas and let them develop their abilities in commanding armies. So on 3 January 1390 Emperor Zhu Yuan Zhang ordered Zhu Di, King of the State of Yan, and Zhu Gang, King of the State of Jin (the State of Jin was situated in the area of what is now Taiyuan, Shanxi Province), to command armies to carry out a northern expedition against the Yuan armies under Yaozhu and Nai'erbuhua. At the same time Emperor Zhu Yuan Zhang put Fu You De, Duke of the State of Ying, commanding the troops stationed in Beiping, under the command of Zhu Di, King of the State of Yan. He put Wang Bi, Marquis of Dingyuan, commanding the troops stationed in Shanxi area (now Shanxi Province), under the command of Zhu Gang, King of the State of Jin.

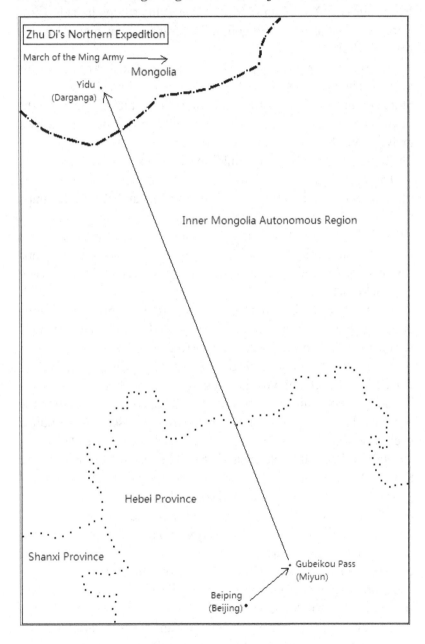

In March 1390 Zhu Di, King of the State of Yan, and Fu You De commanded the Ming armies to march out of the Great Wall through Gubeikou Pass (north of Miyun, Beijing). The Ming army scouts found out that Nai'erbuhua had stationed his troops in Yidu (now Darganga, Sukhbaatar, Mongolia). The Ming armies march quickly towards Yidu.

Just when the Ming troops were ready to attack, it started to snow heavily. The Generals of the Ming army asked Zhu Di, King of the State of Yan, to halt the action. But King of the State of Yan sad, "The Yuan generals and fighting men do not realize that our troops have arrived. We should go forward rapidly against the heavy snow." And on 30 March 1390, the Ming armies reached Yidu.

They got close to the camps of the Yuan army. There was only a piece of waste land between the Ming troops and the Yuan camps, but the Yuan troops did not notice that fast-approaching threat. The King of the State of Yan sent Commander Hetong, formerly a good friend of Nai'erbuhua, to the Yuan army camps. When Nai'erbuhua saw his good friend, he was joyful and sorrowful at the same time. They held each other and wept.

The Ming troops had crept up very close to the camps. Nai'erbuhua and his generals were in shock and feared for their lives. They planned to run away. Hetong advised them not to do it.

Then Hetong brought Nai'erbuhua before the King of the State of Yan and introduced him to the King. King of the State of Yan held a banquet to entertain Nai'erbuhua and assuaged his fears. After the banquet the King of Yan sent some soldiers to escort Nai'erbuhua back to his own camps. Nai'erbuhua was delighted. He called all his generals and men and told them that he intended to surrender to the King of Yan. The next day, Nai'erbuhua together with Yaozhu led their troops to the Ming army and surrendered.

When the report of the great victory in Yidu reached Nanjing, Emperor Zhu Yuan Zhang was overjoyed. He said, "Now the Yuan troops in the desert area have been wiped out. This is a great contribution made by King of the State of Yan." Afterwards, more and more Yuan men came to surrender. All the Yuan troops who had surrendered to the Ming army stationed in Beiping were put under the command of the King of the State of Yan. The Ming armies under the King of the State of Yan became very powerful.

11. The Death of the Crown Prince

When Zhu Biao was young, Zhu Yuan Zhang appointed Song Lian as his teacher. Under the teachings of Song Lian, Zhu Baio developed a very good understanding of Confusion classics, history and philosophy. When he was thirteen years old, Zhu Yuan Zhang ordered Zhu Biao to go back to his home to pay respects to his ancestors at their tombs so that he could get familiar with the ceremonies involved, get to know the hardships of the life of the ordinary people, and gain a realistic idea of the geography of the country. In 1368 Emperor Zhu Yuan Zhang named Zhu Biao the Crown Prince.

He appointed Li Shan Chang, the Left Premier, to serve concurrently as the Tutor of the Crown Prince; Xu Da, the Right Premier, to serve concurrently as the Protector of the Crown Prince, and Chang Yu Chun, the Manager of Governmental Affairs, to serve concurrently as the Guardian of the Crown Prince. In 1377 Emperor Zhu Yan Zhang ordered that all the reports about the governmental affairs should be handed first to the Crown Prince and be dealt with by the Crown Prince first, before being presented to the Emperor. The Crown Prince learned to handle governmental affairs quickly and correctly. He was a very kindhearted person, and especially he treated his younger brothers very well. When his younger brothers made any mistakes and were to be punished by Emperor Zhu Yuan Zhang, he would do his best to protect them.

In 1391 Hu Zi Qi, an official in the Ministry of Law, suggested to the Emperor to move the capital to Shaanxi (now Shaanxi Province), a region that was protected by mountains and rivers. Emperor Zhu Yuan Zhang thought it was a good idea and in August, he ordered the Crown Prince to make a tour of Shaanxi, to investigate the environment. Before the Crown Prince started out, Emperor Zhu Yuan Zhang said to him, "The area of Shaanxi is well protected by natural barriers; that much we know. You should go there to observe the customs of the people there and convey my best regards to the people there."

On 28 September 1391 the Crown Prince came back to Nanjing. He presented a map of Shaanxi to the Emperor. But not long later he fell ill. Still, he presented his suggestions about the establishment of the new capital to Emperor Zhu Yuan Zhang.

On 25 April 1392 Zhu Biao died at the age of thirty-seven. Emperor Zhu Yuan Zhang was very sad and wept bitterly. He wore a mourning robe for a full month to mourn for the Crown Prince.

Zhu Biao left behind five sons: Zhu Xiong Ying, the eldest; Zhu Yun Wen, the second; Zhu Yun Tong, the third, Zhu Yun Jian, the fourth, Zhu Yun Xi, the fifth. Zhu Yun Wen was a dutiful and devoted son. When his father Zhu Biao fell ill, he tended to his father day and night. After his father died, he was so sad that his own health suffered. Emperor Zhu Yuan Zhang patted him on his back and said, "You are really a very dutiful son. But you should think of me, your grandfather, and take good care of your health."

After Zhu Biao died, Emperor Zhu Yuan Zhang summoned all the officials to the court. While holding court, Emperor Zhu Yuan Zhang wept bitterly. Liu San Wu, a scholar of the Hanlin Academy, suggested to the Emperor, "Since the Crown Prince has died, his position as the crown prince should be succeeded by one of his sons, that is, a grandson of Your Majesty. This conforms to the ritual system." Then Emperor Zhu Yuan Zhang made up his mind to name one of Zhu Biao's sons, that is, his grandson, the Crown Prince, successor to the throne of the Ming Dynasty. On 12 September 1392 Emperor Zhu Yuan Zhang made Zhu Yun Wen the Crown Prince. At that time, Zhu Yun Wen was fourteen years old. Then Emperor Zhu Yuan Zhang let the youth take care of the general affairs of the court. Zhu Yun Wen proved himself a kind man, and all the officials of the court praised him as a magnanimous person.

12. Lan Yu's Conspiracy

Lan Yu, a man from Dingyuan (now in Anhui Province), was Chang Yu Chun's wife's younger brother. At first, he was under the command of Chang Yu Chun. He was a very brave man. He won many victories in battle against the armies of the Yuan Dynasty. Chang Yu Chun praised him in front of Zhu Yuan Zhang. Lan Yu was promoted from an army commander to the position of a leading officer in the Office of the Grand Military Governor because the great service he had rendered through his military exploits.

In 1371 Lan Yu took part in the expedition to conquer the area of Shu (now Sichuan Province) under the command of General Fu You De. Lan Yu commanded his troops to attack Mianzhou (now

Mianyang, Sichuan Province) and successfully took it. In 1372 he took part in the northern expedition under the command of Xu Da. The Ming armies marched out of Yanmen (now Yanmen Guan, Daixian, Shanxi Province). They attacked the Yuan troops in Luanshan Mountain (now in Huangyuan, Qinghai Province). Then the Ming armies marched northward and defeated the Yuan army by the side of Tula River in the mid-north part of Mongolia. In 1374 Lan Yu attacked Hezhou (in Liaoning Province) and successfully took it. The Ming troops captured fifty-nine senior officials of the Yuan Dynasty including Duke Tielinichi. In 1378 Lan Yu and Mu Ying commanded their troops to carry out an expedition against the Tibetans and won a great victory.

In 1379 Lan Yu led his troops back to Nanjing. Emperor Zhu Yuan Zhang made him Marquis of Yongchang (now in Gansu Province). In 1381 Lan Yu took part in the expedition to seize Yunnan (now Yunnan Province) commanded by General Fu You De. The Ming troops captured Dalima, one of the prime ministers of the Yuan Dynasty in Qujing (now in Yunnan Province). The King of Liang, under the Yuan Dynasty, in Yunnan, escaped but he died later. The whole area of Yunnan was conquered. Lan Yu made great contributions in conquering the Yunnan region.

In 1387 Emperor Zhu Yuan Zhang appointed Feng Sheng as the Grand General and Lan Yu as the Deputy Grand General of the army to carry out an expedition against Nahachu, the Minister of War of the Yuan Dynasty, who had stationed his great army of 200,000 men in Jinshan Mountain (situated to the north of Shuangliao, Jilin Province). The great army under Feng Sheng and Lan Yu reached Tongzhou (now Tongzhou District, Beijing) and was stationed there. Lan Yu learned that some Yuan troops were stationed in Qingzhou (now Barin Zuoqi, in the east part of the Inner Mongolia Autonomous Region, China), and he commanded his light cavalrymen to carry out a surprise attack. They won, and captured Nahachu.

At that time Tuogusi Temuer, the grandson of Emperor Shun of the Yuan Dynasty, succeeded to the throne of the Yuan Dynasty. He sent troops to attack the areas along the Great Wall. In March 1388, Emperor Zhu Yuan Zhang ordered Lan Yu to take an army of 150,000 men to carry out an expedition against the Ruler of the Yuan Dynasty. The great army marched out of Daning (now in Chifeng, Inner

Mongolia Autonomous Region, China) with Lan Yu in command. They headed to Qingzhou (now Barin Zuoqi, in the east part of the Inner Mongolia Autonomous Region, China). The Ming army's spies found out that the Ruler of the Yuan Dynasty was at Puyuerhai Lake (now Buir Lake, Inner Mongolia).

Lan Yu commanded his great army to march to Baiyanjing, a place twenty kilometers away from Puyuerhai Lake, via side roads, but he did not see any Yuan troops. He had a mind to turn back. But Wang Bi, a fellow general, mused aloud, "We have commanded more than 100,000 men to penetrate deep into the desert. If we turn back without any success, what shall we report to the Emperor?" Lan Yu said, "You are right." Then he ordered the soldiers to dig holes underground to cook their food so that no smoke would come out. At night the Ming troops marched in the dark to the south of the lake. The Yuan troops were camped to the northeast of the lake forty kilometers away.

Lan Yu ordered Wang Bi to lead some troops as a vanguard to go by horseback very quickly to carry out a surprise attack on the enemy camps. The Yuan generals thought that the Ming troops were short of food for the soldiers and grass for their horses and could not penetrate deep into the desert area. So they had not made any preparation against a potential attack.

It happened that there was a wind storm and the wind blew the sands up. This further prevented the Yuan troops from finding out how close the Ming troops had reached. The Ming cavalrymen fell upon the Yuan troops in a swoop. The Yuan soldiers were stunned, and very soon they were defeated. The Ming troops killed Manzi, the Minister of War of the Yuan Dynasty. Nearly all the Yuan soldiers surrendered. The Ruler of the Yuan Dynasty escaped with Tianbaonu, his eldest son and crown prince, and about thirty cavalrymen. Lan Yu sent cavalrymen to run after them but they could not catch up with them.

In this battle the Ming troops captured Dibaonu, the second son of the Ruler of the Yuan Dynasty, and the concubines and princesses of the Ruler of the Yuan Dynasty. And they captured 3,000 officials of the Yuan Dynasty including Duo'erzhi, King of Wu, Dalima, King of Dai, and some prime ministers. They seized enormous quantities of booty including jade seals, gold plates, gold seals and silver seals, and 150,000 horses, camels, cows and goats.

When the victory was reported to Emperor Zhu Yuan Zhang, he was greatly pleased. He issued an imperial order in praise of Lan Yu. He compared Lan Yu to General Wei Qing of the Han Dynasty, who defeated the strong Huns in the north, and General Li Jing of the Tang Dynasty who had conquered the strong Eastern Turkic Khanate in the north. When Lan Yu returned south, to Nanjing, with his great army, Emperor Zhu Yuan Zhang made him Duke of the State of Liang (Chinese: 涼國, now Wuwei, Gansu Province).

Lan Yu was a tall, strong, red-faced man. He was very courageous and had a good mind for strategy. He had the ability of a great general. After Chang Yu Chun, King of Kaiping, died in 1369, and Xu Da, King of Zhongshan, died in 1385, Lan Yu was appointed Commander-in-chief of the Ming army several times and made great military contributions. Emperor Zhu Yuan Zhang rewarded him richly. Eventually Lan Yu became very proud and did all kinds of things at his own will. He kept many servants and adopted sons in his home and on his farms. He became very perverse and violent.

He once seized the lands of the farmers in Dongchang (now Liaocheng, Shandong Province) by force. The Minister of Law carried out an investigation of this crime. Lan Yu was furious and drove the Minister of Law away. When Lan Yu returned from his northern expedition against the Ruler of the Yuan Dynasty, he reached Xifengguan Pass of the Great Wall (now Xifengkou, Hebei Province) at night. The officer defending the pass refused to let Lan Yu and his army go into the pass, according to the regulations. Lan Yu ordered his troops to attack the pass. His troops destroyed the gate and entered the narrow pass between the mountains.

When Emperor Zhu Yuan Zhang heard about this, he was very disappointed. In the battle by Puyuerhai Lake (Buir Lake), the Ming troops captured the concubine of the Ruler of the Yuan Dynasty. Lan Yu committed adultery with her. She felt so ashamed that she committed suicide. Emperor Zhu Yuan Zhang scolded Lan Yu seriously for this.

At first Emperor Zhu Yuan Zhang had intended to make Lan Yu Duke of the relatively prosperous State of Liang in Henan, in central China (梁國, now Shangqiu) in recognition of his great achievements in the northern expedition. But since Lan Yu had committed so many offences, the Emperor changed his mind and made him Duke of a different State of Liang (Chinese: 涼國, now Wuwei, Gansu Province) in the bleak and desolate northwest.

Emperor Zhu Yuan Zhang ordered the secretary of the court to keep a record of the offences Lan Yu had committed. But still Lan Yu did not reform himself. Once at a banquet held by the Emperor, Lan Yu talked to him very impolitely. In the army, Lan Yu arbitrarily removed senior officers from their positions without the permissions from the Emperor. Emperor Zhu Yuan Zhang scolded him for this several times. Later the Emperor appointed him as the Grand Tutor of the Crown Prince. Lan Yu was very unhappy with this position because it was below the position of the Grand Preceptor. He said, "Why can't I be the Grand Preceptor!" And Emperor Zhu Yuan Zhang did not follow Lan Yu's suggestions, because of his bad attitude. Lan Yu became resentful.

In February 1393, Jiang Xian, the Commander of the Royal Guards, filed an accusation against Lan Yu. He reported to the Emperor that Lan Yu was planning a rebellion. The Emperor issued an arrest warrant for Lan Yu and ordered the Minister of Law to carry out an investigation. A report was presented to Emperor Zhu Yuan Zhang which read, "Lan Yu conspired with Cao Zhen, Marquis of Jingchuan, Zhang Yi, Marquis of Heqing, Zhu Zhou, Marquis of Zhulu, He Rong, Count of Dongguan, Zhan Hui, the Minister of Personnel, and Fu You Wen, the Minister of Revenue, to hold a rebellion. They planned to carry out the rebellion when the Emperor goes out to the fields of the Royal Farm to personally till the land." (Yes, the Emperor actually participated in the annual labor to make sure he never forgot the hard life of the average peasant.)

Lan Yu and the others were found guilty. All of them and their family members were executed. Many marquises, counts and officials were involved and they were executed. Emperor Zhu Yuan Zhang issued an imperial order to publish all the names of the officials involved to the public. A book entitled "The List of Treacherous Officials" was compiled. This list includes one duke, thirteen marquises, two counts and many other officials and generals. In September 1393 Emperor Zhu Yuan Zhang issued an imperial order which read, "Lan Yu conspired to hold a rebellion. His conspiracy was discovered. Fifteen thousand people involved in this case have been executed. From now on, the rest of the people who were involved in the case of Hu Wei Yong

and the case of Lan Yu will be spared and will not be investigated."
By now, nearly all of the founding ministers and generals had been
executed.

13. Emperor Zhu Yuan Zhang Takes His Leave

On 8 May 1398 Emperor Zhu Yuan Zhang fell ill. But still he held
court and attended to state affairs as usual. On 5 the second May 1398
(1398 was an intercalary year which had two months of May), his
illness took a turn for the worse, and on 10 the second May, Emperor
Zhu Yuan Zhang passed away in the Western Palace at the age of
seventy-one.

Emperor Zhu Yuan Zhang left a posthumous edict which read, "I
have been entrusted by Heaven to rule the whole realm for thirty-
one years. I have had to prepare for unexpected crises and rack my
brain to think of ways to cope with every eventuality. I have worked
industriously every day to do good for the people. I came from
a very poor family. I did not have the broad knowledge which the
rulers in the past enjoyed. Heaven demands me to have the ability to
distinguish good from evil. I have done my best. But I am afraid that I
have not lived up to the requirements of Heaven. So I have gotten up
very early every day and worked till late at night. Still, I often worry
that I have not fulfilled the task Heaven has entrusted to me. Now I
have come to the end of my life as natural law requires. I do not have
the slightest thought of sadness. My grandson Zhu Yun Wen, the
Crown Prince, is a brilliant person. He is kind to the people, dutiful
to his father and mother and good to his brothers. He has won the
respect of the people of the whole realm. May he ascend the throne,
and may all the officials of the central government and local officials
assist him so as to bring a good life to the people. Don't use gold and
jade in my funeral ceremony. There is no need to carry out a large scale
engineering project in Xiaoling Mausoleum. My tomb may be simply
built in the present condition of the mountain. The officials and people
should just mourn for me for three days. After that, they should take
off their mourning garments and go on with their life as usual. The
kings should hold mourning ceremonies in their respective states and
should not come to the capital to attend my funeral ceremony."

On 16 the second May 1398 Zhu Yun Wen, the Crown Prince,
ascended the throne and became the Emperor of the Ming Dynasty.

On the same day the late Emperor was buried in Xiaoling Mausoleum. He was given the Posthumous Title of Emperor Gao (meaning the Supreme Emperor). His Temple Title was Taizu (meaning the Supreme Ancestor).

9. Model of the palace structure on Xiaoling Mausoleum

Emperor Zhu Yuan Zhang was endowed with civil and martial virtues. He was both brave and intelligent. He did more to make China great than all the emperors of the Han Dynasty, the Tang Dynasty and the Song Dynasty. When he rose up in arms, he was level-headed and observed the changes in the situation. He defeated the local warlords one by one with excellent strategic plans. He threw out corrupt governors and consolidated power in the hands of the emperor.

Emperor Zhu Yuan Zhang was a man of talent and bold vision. He had a great ability to size up his enemies, make a correct judgment and adopt the right strategies to conquer them. This is the reason why he could bring peace and order, and he came to rule the whole realm.

Historians highly praised Emperor Zhu Yuan Zhang for his wisdom and great martial ability. Since his goal was to save the people from the chaos, valiant men from all over willingly followed him. He fought for fifteen years and conquered the local warlords, and at last he established the Ming Dynasty.

10. "治隆唐宋" written by Emperor Kangxi of the Qing Dynasty

For a commoner to rise up and become ruler of the whole realm was a unique feat since the Western Han Dynasty. He knew that the reason why the Yuan Dynasty had fallen was that their rule was lax. In view of this, Emperor Zhu Yuan Zhang was more strict. He respected the learned Confusion scholars and enlisted the services of such talented people. He promoted education, the study of classics.

He required that all officials should be honest, upright and free from corruption. He seriously punished those who were corrupt. He ordered that all the officials in different departments of the central government should support each other and cooperate with each other.

He ordered the garrison troops to bring virgin land under cultivation and grow grain to ensure sufficient food supplies for his armies. Emperor Zhu Yuan Zhang commissioned water management projects to prevent flooding and drought. This boosted agricultural production. By eliminating rivalries between regional rulers, and improving the life of the nation, he brought the whole realm peace and tranquility. The Ming Dynasty he established is regarded as one of the greatest dynasties in Chinese history, and it lasted for more than two hundred and seventy years.

Emperor Kangxi (1654–1722) of the Qing Dynasty (1636–1912) wrote the following words of praise and had them carved on a stone plaque when he paid a visit to Xiaoling Mausoleum: 治隆唐宋, meaning: "The Ming Dynasty under the reign of Emperor Zhu Yuan Zhang was more prosperous than the Tang Dynasty and Song Dynasty."

CHAPTER FIVE: ZHU DI ASCENDS THE THRONE

1. EMPEROR ZHU YUN WEN'S PLAN TO ABOLISH THE STATES OF HIS UNCLES

So, the great man passed away in the second May. In June, Zhu Yun Wen as the new Emperor appointed Qi Tai to be Minister of War and Huang Zi Cheng to be the Official in charge of the Ceremonies to Worship the Ancestors of the Royal House and concurrently made him a scholar of the Hanlin Academy. Qi Tai and Huang Zi Cheng would participate in deciding state affairs.

Qi Tai was from Lishui County (now Lishui District, Nanjing). In 1395 he was promoted to a high position in the Ministry of War. Once, Emperor Zhu Yuan Zhang had asked him the names of the generals who were stationed in the border areas. Qi Tai was able to roll off all the names of the generals from memory. Then the Emperor had asked him about the maps of different places. Qi Tai produced a list from his pocket and presented it to the Emperor. Emperor Zhu Yuan Zhang praised him as a man of great ability. Thus, while Zhu Yun Wen was still the Crown Prince, he respected Qi Tai very highly.

Huang Zi Cheng was from Fenyi (now Fenyi, Jiangxi Province). During the reign of Emperor Zhu Yuan Zhang, he was a scholar of the Hanlin Academy. He had once been a tutor of Zhu Yun Wen, the Crown Prince. One day, while sitting by Dongjiaomen Gate (at the Palace of Nanjing), Zhu Yun Wen asked him, "The kings of the different states are my uncles.

They have powerful armies. Many of them do not observe the laws and do all kinds of things at their own will. How should I handle them?" Huang Zi Cheng replied, "The kings' guards are only sufficient to ensure the safety of the kings. If anyone intends to rebel, the court will send great armies to attack these states. Who can resist such great armies sent by the court? In the Han Dynasty, the seven states, such as the State of Wu and the State of Chu, were strong. But they were all destroyed. This is because the military power of the central government was much stronger than the power of the states. And the central government was carrying out the will of Heaven and the kings of the rebelling states were acting against the will of Heaven." Zhu Yun Wen accepted Huang Zi Cheng's view and was reassured.

After Emperor Zhu Yuan Zhang passed away, Zhu Di, King of the State of Yan, asked permission to come to the capital from Beiping to attend the funeral of the late Emperor. Emperor Zhu Yun Wen stopped him from coming with the instruction in the late Emperor's posthumous edict that "The Kings should hold mourning ceremonies in their respective states and should not come to the capital to attend my funeral ceremony." This made all the kings unhappy. They spread words of strong resentment and stirred up dissatisfaction. When Emperor Zhu Yun Wen heard about this, he asked Huang Zi Cheng, "Do you still remember what you said by Dongmenjiao Gate?" Huang Zi Cheng said, "I will never forget my words." Then Huang Zi Cheng and Qi Tai put forward their suggestion to abolish the states.

In July 1398 Qi Tai and Huang Zi Cheng came together to discuss a plan to abolish the states. The kings concerned were: Zhu Di, the fourth son of the late Emperor, who had been sent to Beiping (now Beijing) to take his seat of King of the State of Yan in 1378; Zhu Su, the fifth son of the late Emperor, who had gone to Kaifeng (now Kaifeng, Henan Province) to take his seat of King of the State of Zhou in 1381; Zhu Zhen, the sixth son of the late Emperor, who went to Wuchang (now in Wuhan, Hubei Province) to take his seat as King of the State of Chu in 1381; Zhu Bo, the late Emperor's seventh son, who went to Qingzhou (now in Shandong Province) to take his seat as King of the State of Qi in 1382; Zhu Zi, the eighth son, who had gone to Changsha (now in Hunan Province) to take his seat as King of the State of Tan in 1385; Zhu Tan, the tenth son, who had gone to Yanzhou (now in Shandong Province) to take his seat as King of the state of Lu in 1385;

Zhu Chun, the eleventh son, who went to Chengdu (now in Sichuan Province) to take his seat as King of the State of Shu in 1390; Zhu Bai, the twelfth, who went to Jingzhou (now in Hubei Province) as King of the State of Xiang in 1385; Zhu Gui, the thirteenth, who went to Datong (now in Shanxi Province) as King of the State of Dai in 1392; Zhu Pian, the eighteenth, who went to Minzhou (now Minxian, Gansu Province) as King of the State of Min in 1381.

Qi Tai intended to deal with Zhu Di, King of the State of Yan, first. He said, "The King of the State of Yan has a great army. He is ambitious. So the State of Yan should be abolished first." But Huang Zi Cheng said, "No, this is not right. The King of the State of Yan has been preparing for this for a long time. It will not be easy to knock him out quickly. The Kings of the State of Zhou, Qi, Xiang, Dai and Min, did many unlawful things during the reign of the late Emperor. We have sufficient reasons to abolish their states. Now that we are going to punish the kings of different states according to the crimes they have committed, it would be better to start with King of the State of Zhou. He and the King of the State of Yan were both sons of Empress Ma. They are full brothers. If we abolish the State of Zhou, it will be a heavy blow to King of the State of Yan."

Then it happened that Zhu You Dong, Zhu Su's second son, lodged an accusation with the government against his father Zhu Su, King of the State of Zhou, informing Emperor Zhu Yun Wen that his father was planning a conspiracy. The accusation implicated the Kings of the State of Yan, Qi and Xiang. In July 1398, Emperor Zhu Yun Wen ordered Li Jing Long, Duke of the State of Cao, to lead some troops on a fast sortie to Kaifeng to arrest Zhu Su, King of the State of Zhou. Very soon Zhu Su was arrested and escorted to Nanjing, the capital.

By August 1398 Emperor Zhu Yun Wen was inclining to release the King of the State of Zhou and let him go back to his state. But Qi Tai and Huang Zi Cheng insisted that he continue to be held. The matter was pending for a long time. At last Qi Tai and Huang Zi Cheng succeeded in persuading Emperor Zhu Yun Wen to punish the King of the State of Zhou. Emperor Zhu Yun Wen deprived Zhu Su the title of King and demoted him to the status of a common person and sent him into exile in Menghua (now Weishan, Yunnan Province). Zhu Su's sons were sent away to other places.

In November 1398 some officials in the State of Yan and the State of Qi reported to Emperor Zhu Yun Wen that their respective kings were plotting a rebellion. Emperor Zhu Yun Wen asked Huang Zi Cheng, "Which one should I deal first?" He answered, "The King of the State of Yan has been pretending to be ill. But actually he is training his soldiers every day. And he has many strategic planners around him. Now that his secret plan has been revealed, we must deal with him as soon as possible." Then Emperor Zhu Yun Wen summoned Qi Tai into the palace and asked him, "Now I intend to deal with the King of the State Yan. But he is good at strategic planning and his soldiers are good fighters. What shall I do?" Qi Tai answered, "The Yuan troops are attacking the northern borders. We may make use of this and send generals with great armies to Kaiping and station their troops there. And we can order the troops of the State of Yan to go out beyond the Great Wall to resist the Yuan attacks. In this way the defensive force of Beiping will be greatly reduced. Then we can deal with King of the State of Yan." Emperor Zhu Yun Wen was impressed.

Accordingly, he appointed Zhang Bing, a senior official in the Ministry of Works, as the Governor of Beiping, and appointed Xie Gui as the Commander-in-chief of the army in Beiping. Both of them had the task to keep close watch on the movements of the King of the State of Yan. Emperor Zhu Yun Wen appointed Xu Zu Hui, Duke of the State of Wei, and Li Jing Long to command the armies of the whole realm and make preparations to attack the State of Yan.

In February 1399 King of the State of Yan came to the capital to have an audience with Emperor Zhu Yun Wen. He entered the palace through the special road for the Emperor. When he arrived before Emperor Zhu Yun Wen, he did not bow down and pay his respects. Zeng Feng Shao, the Minister of Supervision, accused Zhu Di of failing to respect the Emperor. But Emperor Zhu Yun Wen said, "The King of the State of Yan is my closest relative. Don't mention this anymore."

Zhuo Jing, a senior official of the Ministry of Revenue, presented a secret memorandum to the Emperor which read, "The King of the State of Yan is an extremely wise man. He is a man of talent and bold vision. He bears a strong resemblance to the late Emperor. Beiping is a geographically favorable place. It has been the capital for the Jin Dynasty and Yuan Dynasty. The soldiers in Beiping are all very good fighters. Now, we must remove Zhu Di from the State of Yan and remake him King of Nanchang. In this way we can easily put him under control in case he starts a rebellion. A person may plan to rebel without yet putting the plan into action, because he is waiting for the chance to come. When he thinks that he is powerful enough, he will put his plan into action. We must have sharp eyes to find out what his plans are and use greater power to destroy his power." When the memorandum was delivered to the palace, Emperor Zhu Yun Wen summoned Zhuo Jing into the palace the next day.

The Emperor asked the official, "The King of the State of Yan is my uncle. How can you come to this conclusion?" Zhuo Jing knelt down, touched his head to the ground and said, "What I have said in the memorandum is the best plan to deal with the present situation. I hope Your Majesty will understand this and adopt my plan."

But Emperor Zhu Yun Wen did not give any answer. In March 1399 the King of the State of Yan retuned to Beiping. In this month Emperor Zhu Yun Wen sent General Song Zhong to station 30,000 troops in Kaiping (now Zhenglan Qi, Inner Mongolia Autonomous Region). He also ordered that the elite troops of the Guards of the office of King of the State of Yan be sent to Kaiping to join the army under General Song Zhong. He sent General Geng Xian to station an army in Shanhaiguan Pass (situated fifteen kilometers northeast of Qinhuangdao, Hebei Province). He ordered General Xu Kai to station an army in Linqing (now Linqing, in the northwest part of Shandong Province).

In April 1399, Zhu Pian, King of the State of Min, was accused of breaking the law. Emperor Zhu Yun Wen ordered that Zhu Pian be deprived of the title of King of the State of Min and demoted him to a commoner. Zhu Bo, King of the State of Xiang, was accused of having produced counterfeit money and having killed people at his own will. Emperor Zhu Yun Wen sent an order to convict him and sent officials to arrest him. Zhu Bo said, "I have heard that during the reign of Emperor Gao, high ranking officials who had committed crimes were ordered to kill themselves. I am a son of Emperor Gao. I am a king. How can I endure the insults of officials and beg them to spare me?" So he set fire to his palace and burned himself and his family members to death.

Zhu Bo, King of the State of Qi, was accused of having carried out a conspiracy. Emperor Zhu Yun Wen ordered his arrest and had him escorted to Nanjing. Zhu Bo was deprived the title of King and demoted to the status of a common person, and he was thrown into jail. Zhu Gui, King of the State of Dai, was made a commoner and he was imprisoned in Datong (now in Shanxi Province).

All these events put the King of Yan in a state of consternation.

2. Zhu Di, King of Yan, Fights Back

In March 1399 Zhu Di, King of the State of Yan, went back from Nanjing to Beiping. He knew that he was under suspicion of rebellion, so he feigned a severe illness. In April 1399 a memorial service was held for the late Emperor in Nanjing. The King of the State of Yan sent Zhu Gao Chi, his eldest son and successor, along with his next two sons, to Nanjing to attend to the ceremony. One of his subordinates pointed out that it might not be wise to send all his sons to the capital. But he responded, "I am sending all of my sons to make the Emperor believe that I have no ill intent."

When his three sons arrived in the capital, Qi Tai suggested that Emperor Zhu Yun Wen detain all of them. But Huang Zi Cheng said, "No, that is not the right way. It would be better for us to let them go back so the King will understand that Your Majesty does not suspect that he would rebel. In this way we can carry out a surprise attack and catch him." Emperor Zhu Yun Wen accepted Huang Zi Cheng's suggestion and let Zhu Di's three sons go back to Beiping after the ceremony. When the three sons arrived home, the King of the State of Yan was very happy and said, "It is a blessing sent by Heaven that we father and sons can meet again!"

In June 1399, Ni Liang, an officer of the Guards of King of the State of Yan, sent a report to the court asserting that Yu Liang and Zhou Duo, two high ranking officers under King of the State of Yan, were conspiring to rebel. The two were arrested, escorted to the capital and executed.

Emperor Zhu Yun Wen sent an imperial edict to condemn King of the State of Yan. The King pretended that he had gone mad. He ran along the streets in Beiping and shouted like a lunatic. He ran into eateries to grab wine and food from the customers. He spit out all kinds of insane words. Sometimes he slept on the earth outside for a whole day. Zhang Bing and Xie Gui went into the residence of King of the State of Yan to see how ill he was. The King was sitting beside a hot charcoal stove in the hot summer. Even so, he was trembling. He said, "I still feel very cold." He walked around with a cane.

Zhang Bing and Xie Gui reported what they had seen at the court. Emperor Zhu Yun Wen and the court officials believed that the King of Yan had really gone mad. But Ge Cheng, a leading official in the Office of King of Yan, secretly told the two, "The King of the State of Yan is not at all ill. You should be on guard against him." It happened that Deng Yong, an officer of the King's Guards, was sent to the capital to report to the court. Qi Tai, under permission of Emperor Zhu Yun Wen, arrested Deng Yong and interrogated him. Deng Yong told Qi Tai that King of the State of Yan had made preparations to rise up in arms.

Qi Tai immediately sent envoys to arrest the officials of the Office of King. And he secretly ordered Zhang Bing and Xie Gui to deal with King of the State of Yan himself. He sent a secret order to Zhang Xin, the Commander-in-chief of the Beiping troops — once a trusted officer of King of Yan — to arrest him. When Zhang Xin received the order, he was so worried that his mother asked him what was wrong. Zhang Xin told her that he'd been ordered to arrest the King of the State of Yan. She advised him, saying, "No, You should not do that. I hear that King of the State of Yan will come to rule over the whole realm. An Emperor will not die. You will not be able to arrest him." So Zhang Xin hesitated. Then Qi Tai sent an envoy to urge him to go ahead.

Zhang Xin made up his mind to tell everything to the King of the State Yan. He went to his residence three times but King would not receive him. Then he took the cart designated for women working in the residence and came to the gate and insisted that he should see King of the State of Yan. At that, the King of the State of Yan summoned him in. Zhang Xin knelt down beside the King's bed and told him everything.

But King of the State of Yan still pretended that he was so ill that he could not speak. Zhang Xin said, "I hope Your Highness will not pretend to be ill anymore. I have an order to arrest Your Highness. If you have no intention of launching a rebellion, Your Highness should allow yourself to be arrested and go to the capital with me. If Your Highness has such an intention, Your Highness should tell me the truth."

The King saw that Zhang Xin was very sincere. He got out of bed, made a bow to him and said, "It is you who have saved my whole family." Then the King of the State of Yan summoned Yao Guang Xiao, his strategic adviser, to his residence. Yao Guang Xiao was a monk. He was the abbot of Qingshou Temple in Beiping. After Yao Guang Xiao had arrived, they began to discuss the rebellion plans. Suddenly a rainstorm came up, accompanied by a strong wind. Some of the roof tiles fell down to the ground. This made the King very unhappy. But Yao Guang Xiao said that it was a good omen. The King of the State of Yan inquired why. Yao Guang Xiao said, "Has Your Highness not heard? When a dragon is flying in the sky, rain and wind will accompany the dragon. The tiles have fallen. It means the residence of Your Highness will be replaced by a palace with yellow tiles." Then they went on with their planning. The King of the State of Yan heard that the court was going to take action against him, so he ordered Zhang Yu and Zhu Neng to send eight hundred guards to his residence.

In July 1399 Emperor Zhu Yun Wen issued an order to arrest some officials under King of the State of Yan. Then Zhang Bing and Xie Gui had troops surround the residence of the King and demanded that he turn in the officials on the Emperor's list. The soldiers shot arrows into the residence. What to do, what to do? Yao Guang Xiao told the King, "The court has sent envoys to arrest the officials serving under Your Highness. Your Highness may arrest all the officials on the list and then ask Zhang Bing and Xie Gui to come in to take them. When they come in, Your Highness may order your guards to take hold of them."

On 4 July 1399 King of the State of Yan ordered some guards to hide behind the gates of the hall. He sent an official out of the residence to inform Zhang Bing and Xie Gui that the officials on the list had been arrested and asked Zhang Bing and Xie Gui to go into the residence to get them. When Zhang Bing and Xie Gui went in, they were captured by the guards. When the soldiers surrounding the residence learned that Zhang Bing and Xie Gui had been seized by the King of the State of Yan, they all ran away. That night, the King of the State of Yan ordered Zhang Yu and Zhu Neng to command soldiers to take control of the nine gates of the city wall of Beiping. They successfully completed their task. Then the whole city of Beiping was under the control of King of the State of Yan.

On 5 July 1399, the King of the State of Yan sent a memorandum to Emperor Zhu Yun Wen which read, "Emperor Gao made his sons kings of different states so as to protect the Emperor. Qi Tai and Huang Zi Cheng are treacherous court officials. They cherish ill intentions. In a few years Qi Tai and Huang Zi Cheng have deprived Zhu Su, Zhu Bo, Zhu Bai, Zhu Gui and Zhu Pian of their titles. Zhu Bai is the most pitiful. He and all his family members were burned to death in his palace. I know that Your Majesty does not have the intention to abolish the states of your uncles. This has been done by treacherous court officials. Now the treacherous court officials are trying to harm me. Your father and I were the sons of Emperor Gao and Empress Ma. We were the closest brothers. Now the treacherous court officials are in power. Your Majesty is isolated. The whole realm is in great danger. Emperor Gao left the following instruction, 'If there are treacherous officials in the court, the kings of the states may lead against them on behalf of the emperor.' I am now waiting for Your Majesty's order to act."

On 6 July 1399, the King's troops took Tongzhou (now Tongzhou District, Beijing). On 8 July 1399 they took Jizhou (now Jixian, Tianjin). The defenders of Zunhua (now in Hebei Province) and Miyun (now part of Beijing) surrendered. At that time, General Yu Zhen was defending Juyongguan Pass (twenty kilometers north of Changping, Beijing) and General Song Zhong was defending Huailai (now in Hebei Province). On 11 July 1399 the King's troops took control of Juyongguan Pass. General Yu Zhen went away to Huailai to join Song Zhong. On 16 July 1399, the King's troops attacked Huailai and took it. Zhu Zhong and Yu Zhen were captured. They would not surrender, so they were killed. On 18 July 1399 the King's troops conquered Luanhe (now in Hebei Province).

When the King's memorandum denouncing the treacherous court officials reached the court, Qi Tai suggested that Emperor Zhu Yun Wen deprive Zhu Di the title of King of the State of Yan and send a great army against him. Emperor Zhu Yun Wen agreed and appointed Ge Bing Wen as the Grand General, Li Jian as the Left Deputy Grand General and Ning Zhong as the Right Deputy Grand General to command a great army to carry out the northern expedition. Emperor Zhu Yun Wen also ordered Wu Jie, Marquis of Anlu, Wu Gao, Marquis of Jiangyin, and many generals to take their troops north. Before the generals started their march, Emperor Zhu Yun Wen said to them, "It is inauspicious to raise an army against my uncle. Now, you are going to fight against King of the State of Yan, but you should not kill him and don't make me guilty of killing my uncle."

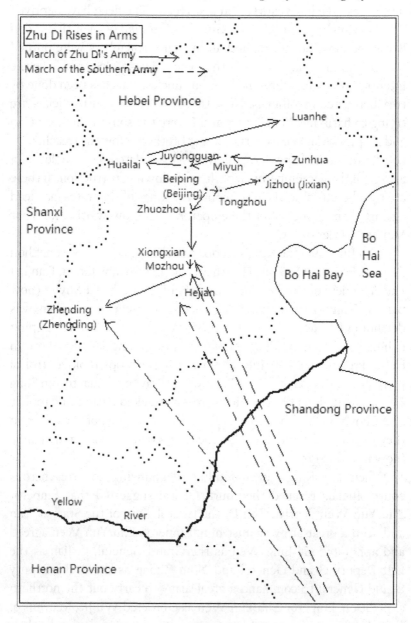

On 12 August 1399 Geng Bing Wen took 300,000 men to Zhending (now Zhengding, Hebei Province). Xu Kai stationed his 100,000 men in Hejian (now Hejian, Hebei Province). Pan Zhong stationed his troops in Mozhou (now in Hebei Province). Yang Song commanded his 9,000 men to Xiongxian (in Hebei Province).

The King of the State of Yan sent Zhang Yu to gather intelligence about Geng Bing Wen's camps. Zhang Yu came back and reported, "Geng Bing Wen is old. His troops are not disciplined. Pan Zhong and Yang Song are brave but they are not resourceful. I suggest that we should make a surprise attack on Pan Zhong and Yang Song, and catch them." The King agreed.

Then he personally commanded his troops to Zhuozhou (now in Hebei Province). On 15 August 1399 the troops of the State of Yan were stationed in Lousang, a village in Zhuozhou. The King treated his soldiers with good food. At about sunset, the troops crossed Baigou River (a river flowing through the north of Xiongxian). The King told his generals, "It is the Moon Festival tonight. Our enemy soldiers will be drinking wine to celebrate this festival. They are not on the alert. We will surely defeat them." At midnight the Yan troops reached Xiongxian, and they began a surprise attack on the city. General Yang Song and all his 9,000 men were killed.

The King of the State of Yan judged that Pan Zhong, who was in Mozhou, still did not know that Xiongxian had been conquered and felt he would surely command his troops to come to reinforce the city. So he ordered Commander Tan Yuan to lead one thousand soldiers to hide in the water under a bridge south of Xiongxian. When Pan Zhong and his troops duly came along, they passed the bridge and marched towards the city of Xiongxian. Then all the soldiers in the water came out and occupied the bridge. At the same time the King of the State of Yan had his troops rush out of the city to attack Pan Zhong's troops. Pan Zhong was attacked from the front and from the rear. Pan Zhong himself was captured. Most of his soldiers were killed or drowned, and on 17 August the troops of the State of Yan took Mozhou.

The King of the State of Yan asked his generals where they should attack next. Zhang Yu said, "We should march to Zhending directly. Although Geng Bing Wen has many soldiers in his army, most of them are new recruits. Our troops may carry the momentum of our victory and destroy Geng Bing Wen." The King of the State of Yan said, "Good idea!"

Meanwhile Zhang Bao, a general under Geng Bing Wen, happened to come in to surrender. Zhang Bao said to the King of the State of Yan, "Geng Bing Wen has an army of 300,000 men. Now, 130,000 soldiers have arrived. Half of them are stationed on the northern bank of Hutuohe River and the other half are stationed on the southern bank." The King of the State of Yan highly praised him for his act of changing sides.

Then he sent Zhang Bao back. He let Zhang Bao pretend that he had been captured in battle and had seized an opportunity to escape. He had Zhang Bao tell Geng Bing Wen how thoroughly the troops under Yang Song and Pan Zhong had been defeated in Xiongxian and Mozhou, and he told Geng Bing Wen that the troops of the State of Yan would come soon to attack Zhending. His purpose was to induce Geng Bing Wen to move his troops to the northern bank, so that he could wipe them all out in one battle. When Zhang Bao went back, he told Geng Bing Wen that the Yan troops would be coming very soon. Geng Bing Wen moved his troops from the southern bank to the northern bank.

On 25 August 1399, the King of the State of Yan personally commanded light cavalrymen to ride to the southwest of Zhending and they destroyed two of Geng Bing Wen's camps. Geng Bing Wen came out of the city to fight. Zhang Yu, Tan Yuan and Zhu Neng commanded the Yan troops to attack. The King of the State of Yan commanded some troops to ride along the city wall to attack Geng Bing Wen's army from the rear. Geng Bing Wen was disastrously defeated and withdrew into the city.

Geng Bing Wen still had over 30,000 men, so he arranged his troops in battle formation. Zhu Neng commanded thirty dare-to-die cavalrymen to attack the battle formation with loud shouts. The soldiers under Geng Bing Wen were unable to withstand the onslaught; they were routed and dispersed. About 3,000 of them surrendered. Geng Bing Wen ran into the city of Zhending and shut the gates. On 28 August 1399 the King of the State of Yan attacked the city. His troops attacked for three days but could not take it. So the King of the State of Yan withdrew his troops back to Beiping.

When Emperor Zhu Yun Wen heard that Geng Bing Wen had been defeated in Zhending, he was fuming. "How could such an experienced, clever old general be brought down? What shall I do?" Huang Zi Cheng said, "Victory and defeat are both common in battle. There is nothing to worry about. If we gather all the soldiers in the realm, we may have over 500,000 men. We can attack Beiping with these 500,000 men. We will surely catch the King of the State of Yan." Emperor Zhu Yun Wen asked, "Who will be capable of commanding such a great army?" Huang Zi Cheng replied, "Li Jing Long." So Emperor Zhu Yun Wen sent Li Jing Long to replace Geng Bing Wen as the Grand General.

On 1 September 1399 Wu Gao — the Marquis of Jiangyin, General Yang Wen, and General Geng Xian marched their troops from Liaodong (now in Liaoning Province) to attack Yongping (now Lulong, Hebei Province).

Li Jing Long reached Dezhou (in Shandong Province) and gathered the runaway soldiers originally under Geng Bing Wen. He ordered that all the troops sent from different places should concentrate in Dezhou, and he gathered a great army of 500,000 men. On 11 September 1399 Li Jing Long marched them to Hejian (now Hejian, Hebei Province).

News of this reached the King of the State of Yan and he said to his generals, "Li Jing Long is only a good for nothing young man from a wealthy family. He has never commanded troops in battle. He is ferocious in appearance but feeble in essence. He is proud but he is not resourceful. The court has put these 500,000 men in the hands of this greenhorn. His incompetence will surely ruin the great army. If I stay in Beiping, he will not dare to come. Now I will go to rescue Yongping. When he hears that I have gone out, he will surely come to attack Beiping. Then I will bring my troops back to attack him. In this way he will surely be defeated."

The generals worried that he was not leaving enough troops in Beiping to defend the city. The King of the State of Yan said, "The troops remaining in Beiping are really not sufficient to go out of the city to fight against the enemy. But they are sufficient to defend the city. My purpose in leaving Beiping is to lure Li Jing Long to come on the attack. When I have defeated Wu Gao and relieved Yongping, I will bring my army back to Beiping and defeat Li Jing Long."

He ordered Zhu Gao Chi, his eldest son and successor, to remain in Beiping to defend the city, and he ordered Yao Guang Xiao to assist him. The generals suggested that they should send troops to defend Lugou Bridge, fifteen kilometers southwest of Beiping. But the King said, "My purpose is to lure Li Jing Long to come to Beiping and make him stay at the foot of the city wall. It is not necessary to send troops to Lugou Bridge to stop him from coming to this strongly defended city."

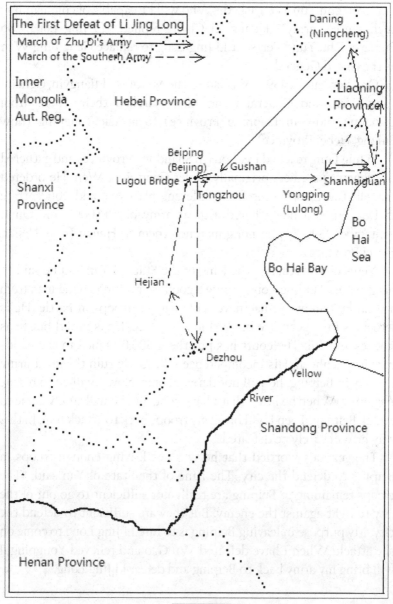

On 19 September 1399 the King of the State of Yan personally commanded his troops to rescue the city of Yongping. His troops reached Yongping on 25 September. Wu Gao withdrew his troops to Shanhaiguan Pass (situated in today's Qinhuangdao, Hebei Province). Zhu Di's troops gave hot pursuit and killed many enemy soldiers. Wu Gao fled back to Liaodong. In October 1399, the King of the State of Yan commanded his troops to march towards Daning (now Ningcheng, Inner Mongolia Autonomous Region).

Zhu Quan, the late Emperor Zhu Yuan Zhang's seventeenth son, had been made King of the State of Ning there. He had many Mongolian cavalrymen in his army. When the troops of the State of Yan marched along side roads to Daning and conquered the city, the King of the State of Yan went into Daning to see his younger brother Zhu Quan, King of the State of Ning. They talked with each other very happily. Several days later the King of the State of Yan told the King of the State of Ning that he was leaving. The King of Ning escorted him to the city gate. Suddenly the conquering soldiers rushed up and forced him to go along with them. The King of the State of Yan took all the Mongolian cavalrymen south with him. So the army of the State of Yan became much stronger.

In October 1399 when Li Jing Long learned that King of the State of Yan had attacked Daning, he commanded his great army to march to Beiping. When he crossed Lugou Bridge, he said with a laugh, "Zhu Di has not sent any troops to defend this bridge. From this alone, I can see that he is not a capable man." Then he commanded his great army to press on, to the foot of the city wall of Beiping. He ordered his soldiers to build strongholds in front of each of the nine gates of the city wall. Then he ordered his troops to attack Lizheng Gate (the central southern gate). The southern troops almost destroyed it. The Yan soldiers fought bravely to resist the attack. In this critical moment, the women in the city went up to the top of the city wall and threw rubble down on the men below. The southern troops had to retreat. Li Jing Long sent some troops to take Tongzhou (in the east of Beijing). He had them pitch nine camps in Zhengcunba (ten kilometers east of Beijing). Then Zhu Gao Chi selected some brave soldiers to go down the city wall by ropes and baskets at night and they started surprise attacks on the enemy camps.

On 4 November 1399 the King of the State of Yan and his troops reached Gushan (east of Tongzhou). At night the water in the Canal was frozen. King of the State of Yan and his troops crossed the Canal on foot. On 5 Li Jing Long's army and the King of Yan's army fought in Zhengcunba. The troops of the State of Yan destroyed seven of Li Jing Long's camps. Zhang Yu and other generals pressed ahead to the Beiping city wall. The troops of the State of Yan within the city came out, with drums beating and loud shouts. Li Jing Long was attacked from the rear and from the front. His army was disastrously defeated.

Li Jing Long fled south when evening fell. The next day, his soldiers in the nine strongholds were still fighting tenaciously. The troops of the State of Yan took four of the strongholds. When the remaining southern troops heard that Li Jing Long had run away, they gave up their weapons and food supplies and ran away to the south as well. Li Jing Long and his troops regrouped in Dezhou.

On 1 April 1400 Li Jing Long took his army back north from Dezhou. Guo Ying — the Marquis of Wuding, Wu Jie — Marquis of Anlu, and other generals, marched from Zhending (now Zhengding, Hebei Province). The two armies would meet by Baigou River (flowing through the north of Xiongxian, Hebei Province). On 18 April 1400, Li Jing Long's army reached Hejian (now in Hebei Province). The King of the State of Yan marched forth from Beiping and reached Gu'an (in Hebei Province). Zhang Yu and his troops marched ahead to Baigou. On 24 April 1400 the army under Guo Ying and Wu Jie joined forces with Li Jing Long's army by Baigou River. Now there were 600,000 men in Li Jing Long's army.

Li Jing Long arranged his great army in battle formations along the river. On that day the King of the State of Yan commanded his troops to cross to the south bank to fight Li Jing Long. But many of his soldiers were killed by explosions as Li Jing Long had planted mines. The King of the State of Yan suffered a great setback and had to withdraw his troops back across to the northern bank. That night he appointed General Zhang Yu to command the central army, General Zhu Neng to command the left army, General Chen Heng to command the right army as the vanguards, and General Qiu Fu to command the cavalrymen to follow the vanguards. There were about 100,000 men in this army of the State of Yan.

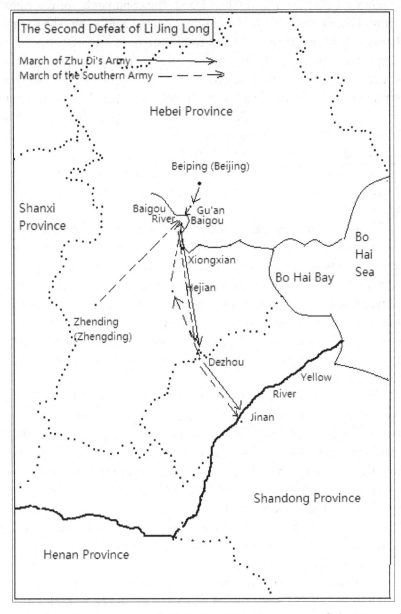

The Second Defeat of Li Jing Long

March of Zhu Di's Army ⎯⎯→
March of the Southern Army ⎯ ⎯ ⎯→

Hebei Province

Beiping (Beijing)

Shanxi Province

Baigou River
Gu'an
Baigou

Xiongxian

Hejian

Bo Hai Bay

Bo Hai Sea

Zhending (Zhengding)

Dezhou

Yellow River

Jinan

Shandong Province

Henan Province

In the early morning of 25 April 1400, the troops of the State of Yan crossed Baigou River and the battle began. Ping An, a general of the southern army, attacked the Yan battle formation under General Fang Kuan and destroyed them. The situation was not favorable for King of the State of Yan.

General Ping An killed Chen Heng, the commander of the right army of the State of Yan, and wounded General Xu Zhong. The King's horse was hit by arrows; he had to change horses three times. The battle went on heatedly. In the late afternoon Li Jing Long's army started a fierce attack on the troops of the State of Yan. Suddenly a strong whirlwind rose and broke the pole of Li Jing Long's pennant denoting him as a Grand General. This caused great disorder in his battle formations. The King of the State of Yan took this moment to command the cavalrymen to ride to the rear of Li Jing Long's army and set fire to the southern army. The strong wind blew the fire to the battle grouping. Many generals and men of the southern army were killed.

The southern army was routed and thrown into utter confusion. Li Jing Long fled back to Dezhou. On 27 April 1400 the King of the State of Yan commanded his army to attack Dezhou. On 7 May Li Jing Long retreated from Dezhou to Jinan (now in Shandong Province). On 9 May, the King of the State of Yan entered Dezhou. Tie Xuan, who was in charge of escorting food supplies to the army under Li Jing Long, retreated to Jinan with Li Jing Long. Sheng Yong, the Commander-in-chief of the army in Shandong, was in Jinan. He was determined to defend the city.

On 16 April the army of the State of Yan attacked Jinan. There were still over 130,000 soldiers there. Li Jing Long sent his troops out of the city and commanded them to array themselves in battle formations. The King of the State of Yan sent his cavalrymen to ride into the southern army before their battle formations were completed. The southern army was defeated and Li Jing Long ran away to the south. The King of the State of Yan laid siege to the city of Jinan. Tie Xuan and Sheng Yong commanded their troops to defend the city resolutely. The army of the State of Yan attacked Jinan for three months but could not take it.

Yao Guang Xiao, the strategic adviser of King of the State of Yan, told him, "Our soldiers are very tired now. It would be better for us to withdraw our troops back to Beiping. We may wait for the chance to take Jinan later." The King of the State Yan took his advice and turned back. Then Sheng Yong and Tie Xuan commanded their troops to pursue the army of the State of Yan. They successfully recovered Dezhou. On 10 September 1400, Emperor Zhu Yun Wen promoted Tie

Xuan to Governor of Shandong Province and appointed Sheng Yong Grand General to replace Li Jing Long. Li Jing Long was summoned back to Nanjing. Emperor Zhu Yun Wen granted him a pardon and did not punish him for his defeat.

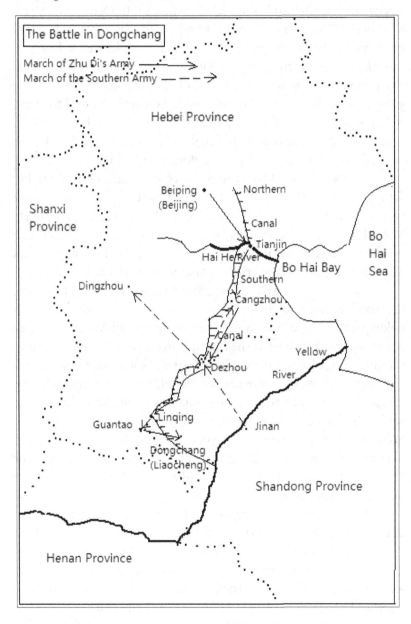

On 1 September 1400, Emperor Zhu Yun Wen ordered Sheng Yong, the Grand General, to head up a northern expedition. Wu Jie, the Deputy Grand General, sent his troops to Dingzhou (now in Hebei Province). Xu Kai, the Commander-in-chief, commanded his troops to Cangzhou (also in Hebei Province). In October 1400, the King of the State of Yan intended to take Cangzhou. But he marched his army to the north, proclaiming that he would attack Liaodong (now Liaoning Province). When Xu Kai heard that, he failed to make any preparation for resisting an attack. He sent his soldiers out to get wooden poles to repair the city wall. When the King of the State of Yan reached Tianjin, he ordered his troops to take boats and sail southward along the Southern Canal (which still flows from Tainjin through Cangzhou to Linqing, Shandong Province).

On 27 September 1400, the army of the State of Yan reached Cangzhou. They attacked the city fiercely, and on 29 September they took it — and they captured Xu Kai. On 4 November the army of the State of Yan passed Dezhou, and eight days later they reached Linqing (in the northwest part of Shandong Province). On 14 November the Army of the State of Yan reached Guantao (in Hebei Province). On 25 December they arrived at Dongchang (now Liaocheng, Shandong Province). Sheng Yong arranged his troops in battle formation. Those holding firearms and bows were positioned out front. When the troops of the State of Yan started their attack, many of them were killed by the guns and poisoned arrows. The King had some cavalrymen attack the left wing but they were not successful. Then he commanded the cavalrymen to attack the central formation. Sheng Yong ordered his soldiers in the central formation to move aside and let the King and his cavalrymen in. When the King of the State of Yan was in the midst of the battle formation, Sheng Yong ordered his troops to surround him in many rings. The King fought like a monster but he could not make a breakthrough.

Zhu Neng and Zhou Chang commanded the Mongolian cavalrymen to attack the northeast corner of the enemy battle formation. Sheng Yong sent the troops on the southwest corner to reinforce the northwest corner. So the forces attacking the King of the State of Yan were weakened. Zhu Neng took the chance to fight with renewed vigor and successfully protected the King of the State of Yan as he broke out of the enemy encirclement. Zhang Yu did not know that

King of the State of Yan had made his escape. He broke into the enemy battle formation to save the King. But he was killed.

In this battle, more than 10,000 soldiers of the State of Yan were killed. The army of the State of Yan was seriously defeated and most fled to the north. The troops under Sheng Yong went out in hot pursuit and more soldiers of the State of Yan were killed. Zhu Gao Xu, King of the State of Yan's second son, commanded an army to head out and they arrived in time to defeat the pursuing army. The King of the State of Yan was very pleased with Zhu Gao Xu.

When he found out that Zhang Yu had been killed in the battle, he wept bitterly. When the King of the State of Yan and his army made it back to Beiping, he held a mourning ceremony for Zhang Yu and those generals and men who were killed in the battle of Dongchang. He made Zhang Yu Duke of Rongguo and King of Hejian posthumously.

On 16 February 1401, the King of the State of Yan again commanded his army to march southward. On 20 February the army of the State of Yan reached Baoding (now Baoding, Hebei Province). At that time, Sheng Yong stationed his army of 200,000 men in Dezhou. Wu Jie and Ping An stationed their troops in Zhending (now Zhengding, Hebei Province). On 12 March 1401 Sheng Yong marched his army to Jiahe (now in Hebei Province). On 20 March the King of the State of Yan marched his army from Baoding to Jiahe. His army was twenty kilometers away from Sheng Yong.

On 22 March the army under Sheng Yong and the army of the State of Yan fought in Jiahe. General Tan Yuan of the State of Yan commanded his troops to attack. But General Tan Yuan was killed. The King of Yan and General Zhu Neng and General Zhang Wu commanded some cavalrymen to ride to the rear of the enemy battle formation and killed several generals.

On 23 March the two armies fought again. Sheng Yong arranged his army in battle formations in the southwest. The King of Yan arranged his army in battle formations in the northeast. The battle was fought from nine o'clock in the morning to three o'clock in the afternoon. Suddenly a strong northwest wind rose. It blew dust high into the sky and it blew directly to the southern army. The troops of the State of Yan took the chance to start a fierce attack. The army under Sheng Yong was disastrously defeated and ran away. Sheng Yong withdrew back to Dezhou.

On 4 the second March 1401, Emperor Zhu Yun Wen dismissed Qi Tai and Huang Zi Cheng from office and sent them out of the capital. Actually, the Emperor sent them to other places to recruit new soldiers.

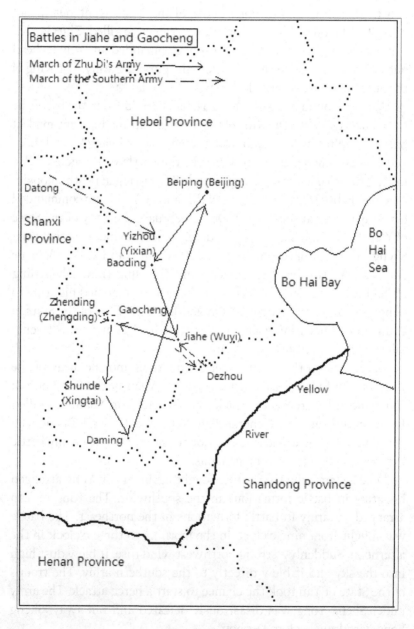

On 7 the second March, Wu Jie and Ping An took their troops from Zhending to Gaocheng (in Hebei Province). The King of the State of Yan took his troops from Jiahe to Gaocheng to fight them. On 9 the second March, the armies clashed. The State of Yan suffered a great loss. Many of their soldiers were killed by firearms and arrows.

On 10 the second March, the two armies fought again. Suddenly a strong wind kicked up. It destroyed the roofs of the houses and pulled trees out of the ground. The army of the State of Yan took the opportunity to start a fierce attack and they defeated Wu Jie and Ping An.

Wu Jie and Ping An withdrew their troops back to Zhending. On 20 the second March, the army of the State of Yan took Shunde (now Xingtai, Hebei Province). On 24 the second March, they took Daming (in the south part of Hebei Province).

When the King of the State of Yan found out that Qi Tai and Huang Zi Cheng had been dismissed and sent out of the capital, he wrote a memorandum to Emperor Zhu Yun Wen which read, "Recently I hear that treacherous court officials have been driven out of the court. I will withdraw my army back to Beiping. But the armies under Wu Jie, Ping An and Sheng Yong are still concentrated around Beiping. It is very clear that although your treacherous officials have been dismissed, their policy is still being carried out. I dare not carry out Your Majesty's order to relieve my military power."

When Emperor Zhu Yun Wen got the memorandum, he discussed it with Fang Xiao Ru, a scholar of the Hanlin Academy and adviser to the Emperor. Fang Xiao Ru said, "The troops of the State of Yan have stayed in Daming for a long time. Recently the weather in Daming has been rainy and hot. The soldiers are very tired in such weather. Your Majesty should order the generals in Liaodong to command their troops into Shanhaiguan Pass. They should attack Yongping. The generals in Zhending should march their troops across Lugou Bridge and attack Beiping. Then the King of the State of Yan will surely turn back to rescue Beiping. Then we may send a great army to march behind his army. In this way we will surely catch him. We shall write a reply to him. It will take many days to deliver the reply letter to him. Then his soldiers will become slack. During this period we can dispatch our troops according to our plan."

Emperor Zhu Yun Wen took his advice and asked him to draft a reply letter. Then Emperor Zhu Yun Wen sent a senior official as his envoy to deliver the letter to the King of the State of Yan. When the envoy saw him, the King asked, "What did the Emperor say?" The envoy said, "The Emperor said that if Your Highness disbands your army in the morning, His Majesty will order his army to withdraw in the evening." The King responded, "He is telling a lie. Even a child would not fall for that."

In May the army of the State of Yan was stationed in Daming. Sheng Yong, Wu Jie and Ping An sent some troops to cut off their food supply line. The King of the State of Yan was irate. He sent General Li Yuan with some troops to penetrate deep into Peixian (in Jiangsu Province) and burn all the food supplies for Sheng Yong's army in Dezhou. On 15 July 1401 Sheng Yong ordered Fang Zhao, the general defending Datong (in Shanxi Province) to attack the counties around Baoding. The troops under Fang Zhao took Yizhou (now Yixian, Hebei Province) and were ready to attack Beiping. When King of the State of Yan got this information, he withdrew his troops back to the north. On 24 October the army of the State of Yan returned to Beiping.

In November 1401 some of the eunuchs who had committed crimes ran away from the palace in Nanjing to Beiping to avoid being punished by Emperor Zhu Yun Wen. They told the King of the State of Yan that the defense of Nanjing was very weak and the city of Nanjing could be easily taken. He exclaimed, "War has been going on for years. When will it come to an end? If I can have a chance to have a decisive battle by the Yangtze River, I will not come back no matter whether I win or lose." Yao Guang Xiao said to the King, "Your Highness does not need to occupy any cities. Your army should march as quickly as possible to the capital. This is the best plan to destroy our enemy."

On 12 December 1401, the King went southward with his army. They stationed themselves in Lixian (in Hebei Province). On 1 January 1402 General Li Yuan of the State of Yan commanded his troops to Gaocheng (in Hebei Province) and defeated the southern army under General Guo Jin. On 5 January General Zhu Neng of the State of Yan defeated the southern army in Hengshui. Then the King of the State of Yan commanded his army to Guantao. On 12 January the army of the

State of Yan took Dong'e (now in Shandong Province) and Dongping (in Shandong Province).

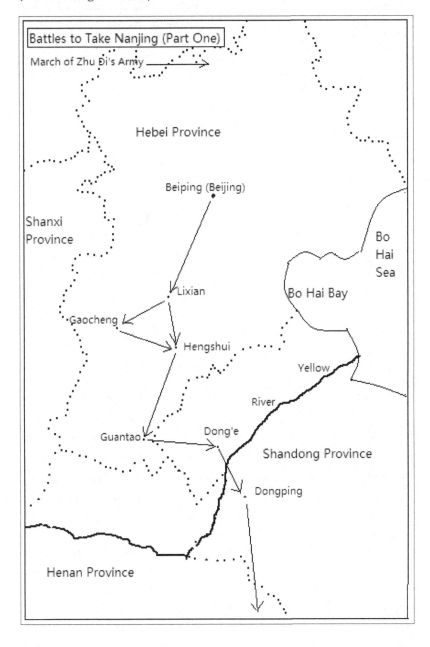

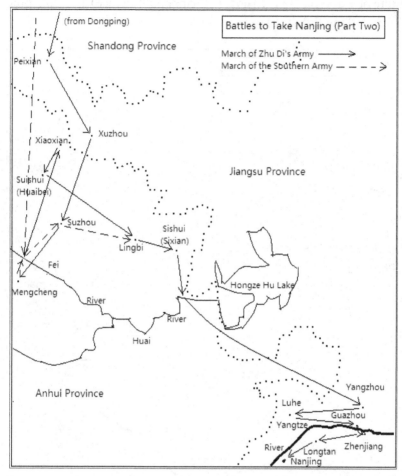

On 27 January the Yan army took Peixian (in Jiangsu Province). On 30 January they reached Xuzhou (in Jiangsu Province). They attacked Xuzhou on 21 February but could not take it. The King of the State of Yan gave up on Xuzhou and commanded his army to march southward. On 1 March they reached Suzhou (in Anhui Province). On 9 March the army of the State of Yan reached Mengcheng (in Anhui Province). On 14 March Ping An commanded 40,000 soldiers to follow the army of the State of Yan. King of the State of Yan set a trap in the underbrush by the side of Fei River. The King sent some troops to lure the southern army into the ambush and defeated them. Ping An withdrew his troops to Suzhou. In this month the army of the State of Yan took Xiaoxian (now Xiaoxian, in the north part of

Anhui Province). On 2 April 1402 the army of the State of Yan reached Suishui (in the west of Huaibei, Anhui Province). On 25 April Ping An and He Fu stationed their troops in Lingbi (in Anhui Province). On 27 April the army of the State of Yan fought with the troops under Ping An and He Fu. The southern army was defeated. On 29 April the army of the State of Yan attacked the strongholds of the southern army in Lingbi. He Fu ran away. Ping An was captured.

The King of the State of Yan saw that Ping An was a capable general and spared him. He sent soldiers to escort Ping An back to Beiping. On 7 May 1402 the army of the State of Yan took Sizhou (now Sixian, Anhui Province). Then the army of the State of Yan marched to the north bank of Huai River (which flows through Henan Province, Anhui Province and Jiangsu Province). Sheng Yong had already commanded over 30,000 men on the south bank of the river. On 9 May King of the State of Yan sent Qiu Fu and Zhu Neng to command several hundred soldiers to go ten kilometers to the west. They took small boats to cross Huai River to the south bank. They started a surprise attack on Sheng Yong. His troops were so scared that they scattered. Sheng Yong escaped by a small boat.

On 11 May the army of the State of Yan was very active in what is now Jiangsu Province. They marched to Yangzhou and on 18 May they took the city. On 19 May they reached Luhe. On 3 June they crossed the Yangtze River from Guazhou and on 6 June they took Zhenjiang. On 8 June the army reached Longtan. The officials in Nanjing were shocked and many of them fled.

Emperor Zhu Yun Wen was at a total loss. Fang Xiao Ru said, "We still have 200,000 troops in the capital. They can resist the attack until reinforcement comes. At the same time we can have peace talks with the King of the State of Yan so as to delay his attack." Emperor Zhu Yun Wen sent some envoys to see him and promised to cede the areas to the north of the Yangtze River to the King of Yan if he would make peace. But the King resolutely refused.

Emperor Zhu Yun Wen sent many officers out of the capital to different places to ask for relief troops. But all of them were captured by enemy patrols.

On 13 the army of the State of Yan marched towards Nanjing and pressed ahead to the Jinchuan Gate (the north gate of the city wall of Nanjing). At that time Zhu Hui, King of the State of Gu, and Li Jing

Long were defending Jinchuan Gate. They opened the city gate to let the army of the State of Yan into the city.

Emperor Zhu Yun Wen shut Empress Ma and all his concubines in the palace and set fire to it. All the women were burned to death. It is said that Emperor Zhu Yun Wen and about forty followers escaped through a tunnel. When the King of the State of Yan entered Nanjing, he could not find the Emperor. The palace maids pointed at the dead body of Empress Ma and said that it was the corpse of the Emperor. He ordered the eunuchs to carry the body out from the palace and buried it with the funeral ceremony for an emperor. He issued orders to search for and arrest Qi Tai, Huang Zi Cheng, Fang Xiao Ru and other officials, twenty-nine of them in all. Most of them were found and executed.

3. Zhu Di Ascends the Throne of the Ming Dynasty

On 14 June 1402 the court officials presented a memorandum to the King of the State of Yan suggesting that he should ascend the throne of the Ming Dynasty. Yang Rong, a scholar, asked the King of Yan, "Will your Highness hold a memorial ceremony for Emperor Gao in Xiaoling Mausoleum first, or ascend the throne first?"

The King realized that he should hold a memorial ceremony for Emperor Gao first. Then the kings and the officials awaited him by the roadside. They had prepared an imperial carriage. When the King arrived, they presented him the jade seal of the Emperor and invited him to ascend the imperial carriage. Then they all shouted, "Long live the Emperor!" He ascended the imperial carriage and he was carried to Fengtian Hall of the palace. All the officials expressed their congratulations. There Zhu Di ascended the throne of the Ming Dynasty. He decided that the title of his reign would be Yongle (meaning Forever Happy). On 4 April 1404 Emperor Zhu Di made his eldest son Zhu Gao Chi Crown Prince.

Emperor Zhu Di sat on the throne for 22 years (from June 1402 to July 1424). He achieved many great deeds. In March 1406 Li Cang, the King of Annan, held a rebellion in Annan (now Vietnam). Emperor Zhu Di sent an army to pacify the rebellion and captured Li Cang and his son Li Rui. He changed the name of Annan into Jiaozhi. Jiaozhi was divided into fifteen prefectures and became a part of the territory of China.

11. Portrait of Zhu Di, Emperor Chengzu of the Ming Dynasty

In March 1408 Alutai, the Premier of the fallen Yuan Dynasty, made Buniyashili, a descendant of the emperors of the Yuan Dynasty, Khan of the Yuan Dynasty. In January 1410 Emperor Zhu Di personally commanded a northern expedition. When Alutai and Buniyashili got news that Emperor Zhu Di was coming, Alutai ran away to the east and Buniyashili ran away to the west. On 13 May Emperor Zhu Di and his great army crossed the vast Gobi Desert. His army caught up with

Buniyashili by Orhon River (which flows from south to north through the central part of Mongolia) and defeated his army. Buniyashili ran away westward with seven cavalrymen. In the later years Emperor Zhu Di carried out several northern expeditions to the desert to wipe out the remnants of the fallen Yuan Dynasty.

At that time prefectures of Suzhou (in Jiangsu Province), Songjiang (now part of Shanghai), Jiaxing (in the northeast part of Zhejiang Province), and Huzhou (in Zhejiang Province) suffered from floods. In April 1403 Emperor Zhu Di appointed Xia Yuan Ji to take charge of the water management projects in these prefectures. More than 100,000 able bodied men were mobilized to carry out these projects. Xia Yuan Ji worked very hard. He led the laborers to dig canals and dredge rivers to lead the floods to the sea. When the projects were completed, they did a lot of good to the farmlands in these prefectures.

In China, there were many books about Confucian classics, history, philosophy, literature, various schools of thought, astronomy, geography, medical science and doctrines both Buddhist and Taoist. In 1403 Emperor Zhu Di ordered the scholars to put all the books together and compile one whole set of books. The scholars worked very hard for several years. In winter 1408, they finally completed compiling the great set of books. Emperor Zhu Di named it Yongle Dadian (the Yongle Great Encyclopedia, in Chinese: 永樂大典). This great encyclopedia contained 22,933 sections bound into 11,095 books with 370 million Chinese characters.

In June 1405 Emperor Zhu Di sent Zheng He, a eunuch, to command 37,000 soldiers on 62 big sea ships on a mission to the countries in the west. From 1405 to 1435, Zheng He made seven such voyages. He had been to the territories of what are now over thirty countries including Cambodia, Thailand, Malacca, Malaysia, Indonesia, Bangladesh, India, Sri Lanka, Maldives, Iran, Saudi Arabia, and Kenya. He established good relationships with these countries. Many of these countries sent envoys to China to present tribute to Emperor Zhu Di.

In January 1403 Emperor Zhu Di issued an imperial order to change the name of Beiping to Beijing (northern capital). In July 1406 Emperor Zhu Di decided to make Beijing the capital of the Ming Dynasty. He sent some high ranking officials to take charge of building the palaces. On 22 September 1420 Emperor Zhu Di issued an imperial order which read, "From January next year, the original capital is changed into Nanjing. Beijing will become the capital." On 1 January 1421 a grand ceremony was held in the Ancestral Temple in Beijing to put the memorial tablets of the ancestors of the royal family of the Ming Dynasty in the Ancestral Temple. Then Emperor Zhu Di sat on the throne in Fengtian Hall of the palace to receive the congratulations expressed by the court officials.

On 4 April 1424 Emperor Zhu Di personally commanded a northern expedition against Alutai, the Premier of the fallen Yuan Dynasty. The army of the Ming Dynasty reached a place in the northwest part of what is now South Hangay of Mongolia. But they could not find Alutai. Then Emperor Zhu Di decided to turn back. On 16 July 1424 he fell ill. On 17 July the army of the Ming Dynasty was stationed in Yumuchuan (situated in the north part of Inner Mongolia Autonomous Region, China). The next day, Emperor Zhu Di passed away at the age of sixty-five.

On 10 August the carriage carrying Emperor Zhu Di's body reached Beijing. He was buried in Changling Mausoleum in the Imperial Mausoleums of the Ming Dynasty (situated in Changping, Beijing). He was given the posthumous title of Emperor Wen (meaning Emperor of Culture). His temple title was Taizong (meaning Supreme Ancestor). Ten years later, his grandson Emperor Zhu Zhan Ji changed his temple title into Chengzu (meaning Ancestor with great achievements).

Historians highly praised Emperor Zhu Di. They said, "Emperor Wen got used to military life when he was young. He was made king in Beiping area which had favorable and majestic geographical conditions. He took the whole realm of the Ming Dynasty when the rule of Emperor Zhu Yun Wen was weak. After he had ascended the throne, he practiced thrift. He paid close attention to water control projects so as to relieve the people from the disasters of floods. He put the right people on the right positions. He was a man of great talent and vision, similar to Emperor Zhu Yuan Zhang. He carried out several northern expeditions across the Gobi Desert to put down the remnants of the fallen Yuan Dynasty. In his late years his mighty reputation was heard far and wide. Over thirty countries sent envoys to present tribute to him. Under his rule, the territory of China grew to be larger than it had been during the Han Dynasty and the Tang Dynasty. He made great accomplishments benefiting the nation and people of China. Under his reign, China became powerful and prosperous."